THE HOUSE IS FULL

Will Hodgkinson grew up in a larger-than-life family. His father, Neville, was an award-winning science writer until he received a calling from the Brahma Kumaris in 1983. He currently lives with them on a retreat in Oxfordshire. His mother, Liz, continues to write for the *Daily Mail*. His brother, Tom, created the *Idler*. As well as working as the rock and pop critic for *The Times*, Will decided it was high-time to record his family's colourful story.

'[Hodgkinson] has a lovely, light style . . . his set pieces are very funny . . . He is attentive to the minute social divisions that define the British middle classes . . . it's a relief to read a memoir that is so affectionate, so moan-free, so reluctant to apportion blame'   Rachel Cooke, *New Statesman*

'An utterly charming, funny and touching memoir'
               Sathnam Sanghera, author of *Marriage Material*

'A rip-roaringly funny read'   Viv Groskop, *Red Magazine*

'Thoughtful, heartfelt and so well drawn . . . [It] deserves to become as well loved as *My Family and Other Animals*'
               Travis Elborough, author of *London Bridge in America*

'I laughed until I levitated'   Jarvis Cocker

THE HOUSE IS FULL OF YOGIS

WILL
HODGKINSON

THE BOROUGH PRESS

The Borough Press
an imprint of HarperCollins*Publishers*
1 London Bridge Street,
London SE1 9GF

www.harpercollins.co.uk

This paperback edition 2015
1
First published in Great Britain by Blue Door 2014

A catalogue record for this book is
available from the British Library

ISBN: 978-0-00-751464-9

Printed and bound in the United States of American by
RR Donnelley

For Nev, Mum and Tom

Some names have been changed.

(But most have stayed the same.)

1

The First Party

'I don't believe it,' said Mum.

She was scratching at two cables of ancient wire sticking out of a dusty hole in the brickwork next to the peeling green paint of the front door, after the Volvo had wobbled over the rubble-strewn drive and come to a shaky halt. 'They've even taken the bloody doorbell.'

A year before our father had his Damascene moment, we moved into our first big home.

99, Queens Road was a semi-detached, four-bedroom house on the edge of Richmond, Surrey, which our parents bought for £30,000 from an older couple called the Philpotts. There was no central heating in 99, Queens Road, nor was there a kitchen to speak of; just a Baby Belling cooker, a rattling old fridge and a twin-tub washing machine stranded in the centre of the room like a maiden aunt who had turned up two decades earlier and never left. There was a milk hatch cut into the outside wall that had come free of its hinges.

The Philpotts, who called their 42-year-old son's room

The Nursery and who claimed to speak Ancient Greek on Sundays, had ripped out pretty much everything but the bricks. The carpets had gone. There were no light bulbs. If you opened cupboards you found only empty spaces, suggesting the Philpotts had even filched the shelves.

'Come on Sturch,' said my father Nev, using a nickname with a derivation long forgotten. It might have had something to do with Lurch, the monstrously ugly butler from The Addams Family. 'Let's go and explore upstairs.'

In our old house, my brother Tom and I shared a bedroom, which was less than ideal because of our very different approaches to being children. One Christmas Eve, I came upstairs after kissing our parents goodnight, fully intending to obey Nev's gentle command to go to sleep and wait until the morning to see what Santa Claus had brought, knowing I would wake up at three and feel around in the dark for the happy weight of a stocking at the end of my bed. Tom was in there already, constructing an elaborate arrangement of strings and levers. When I asked him what he was doing he told me not to question things I wouldn't understand.

All was revealed around midnight. When Nev walked in, stockings laden with toys, a hammer hit the light switch, pulling a network of strings running up the wall and activating a camera next to Tom's bed. Nev's hair turned into a wild frizz at the shock of it. Satisfied with having disproven the existence of Santa Claus once and for all, Tom dozed off until eight o'clock. He was nine years old.

That was four years ago. 'Out of the way, Scum,' said Tom, pushing me aside as he hunched up the stairs of the new house. He looked at the bedroom facing the street, lay down on the single bed the removal men had put in there half an hour earlier, pulled out of his pocket a copy of George Orwell's *1984*, and said without looking up, 'Oh, do get out of my room.'

There is a photograph in our family album of Tom, an insouciant four-year-old, kicking back in a rusty toy car while I, only two and already so outraged at life's unfairness that my nappy is exploding out of my shorts, try in vain to push him along. It says it all, really.

Nev and I went to explore the room at the back of the house, which Nev suggested could be my bedroom.

'Look at this place!' I said, clomping across squeaking, uneven floorboards. 'It's got a window and everything.' I tried to open it but it just made a juddering sound. 'And wow, a cupboard with double doors.' At first they appeared to be jammed, but after giving them a good yank they came open – and flew off their hinges. 'Oh well. Now the room is even bigger.'

I looked out of the window. The garden was long and thin, with a scrappy strip of lawn, a collapsing shed on the left and a vegetable patch along the right. There was a hole in the ground near the end of the garden, which was surrounded by rotting apples. (The Philpotts had taken the apple tree with them.) There was also a late-middle-aged woman with a helmet of frosted hair, bent over and hurriedly collecting something into a plastic bag.

'Isn't that Mrs Philpott?' I said.

Nev came over and peered through the dirty glass. 'I believe it is. What on earth is she doing here?'

Mum rushed out of the back door. Mrs Philpott stood up and, arching her eyebrows, said: 'I'm collecting jasmine.'

Mum took root before her, hands on hips. 'You do realize that we own this house now.'

Mrs Philpott stared at the younger woman and tilted her head forward, smiled slightly as if dealing with a simpleton, and explained: 'It costs two pounds at the garden centre.'

Mum smiled back. 'That may be so. But now you have sold this house to us, so you're going to have to find somewhere else to snip it.'

Mrs Philpott looked at our mother imperiously. She marched down the garden with her cuttings of jasmine, sensible shoes clipping along the cracked paving stones of the garden path and out of our lives forever. So began life at 99, Queens Road.

Tom and I had baked beans on toast that night, eating sitting on the tea chests that filled the kitchen while our parents had an Indian takeaway from silver foil containers. After he finished, Tom poked a finger deep into a nostril, stared at what he found up there, rolled it into a ball, and flicked it at me.

'Tom just threw a bogey at my face.'

'Is this true?' said Nev.

'Guess so.'

'Right, Tom. I'm going to fine you 50p. Until you learn to treat people with a bit more respect I'm going to have to hit you where it hurts – the wallet.'

Tom dug around in his pocket, pulled out a 50p coin, and flicked it at Nev. He grabbed wildly for it, missed, and the coin clattered off before coming to a halt somewhere underneath one of the boxes.

'Butterfingers,' said Tom, with a yawn.

In a few days' time, Tom would start at Westminster School. He had won a scholarship, leaving me to fester at a private boys' school our parents had moved me to a year earlier. That was around the time the serious money for Mum's tabloid articles with titles like *How to Turn Your Tubby Hubby into a Slim Jim* began to kick in. I protested that I had been perfectly happy at the local primary school, but this change, along with getting rid of a beautiful car called a Morgan that had the minor disadvantage of breaking down on most journeys, was an inevitability of our new, prosperous, aspirant life. Once the house was cleared of any remaining Philpottian traces and transformed into a temple of soft furnishings and comfort befitting a young modern family on the up, our new life was to unfold here.

'I want the front room for my study,' announced Mum. 'You're going to have to put shelves up in there, Nev. And I can't live with this kitchen a minute longer. What we need is a high-end, top-quality fitted kitchen from John Lewis, with a nice cooker.'

'But you never do any cooking,' said Tom.

'That's not the point,' said Mum. As she turned her Cleopatra-like nose towards the mouldy ceiling she added, 'I shall also need a microwave.'

For the next few months, the house underwent its metamorphosis. Beige carpets ran up and down the stairs and hallways. Florid Edwardian Coca-Cola posters and reproductions of Pre-Raphaelite scenes of medieval romance filled freshly painted walls. Nev replaced the doors of my cupboard. We had a drawing room – I didn't even know there was such a thing as a drawing room before then – complete with chaise longue, real fake fire and a three-piece suite upholstered in green linen by GP & J Baker. At least the Philpotts had left the built-in bookcase that ran along two walls of the drawing room, which meant *Your Erroneous Zones*, *Fear of Flying*, *Our Bodies, Ourselves* and the complete works of Jackie Collins now took up spaces once filled with dusty books on Greek history and Latin grammar. We also had a TV room with beanbags, an Atari games console and a pinball machine, which was a present to Nev from Mum from around the time I was born. An oak dresser found space between the microwave and the new fridge-freezer and gave the kitchen a hint of rusticity. A sweet tin with scenes from ancient Chinese life on its four sides took up occupancy too, on a shelf alongside boxes of Shreddies, Corn Flakes and, in a nod towards healthy eating, Alpen.

Nev worked long hours at the *Daily Mail*, which, from the way he described it, sounded like a cross between a newspaper office, a prison and a lunatic asylum. There was a woman who was paid to *not* write anything, a man called Barry with a severe and very public flatulence problem, rats in the basement, a section editor who pinned journalists up against the wall and printers who threatened strike action if anyone so much as suggested they stop at two pints at lunchtime. Despite all this, Nev seemed to be doing well. As the medical correspondent he was breaking big stories: he had the scoop on the first test-tube baby a few years earlier, and now he was one of the first British journalists to cover DNA sequencing and stem cell research. One evening he came back home and announced that an exposé he had written about American petro-chemical companies illegally dumping waste into city water supplies had earned him an award from the San Francisco sewage department.

'That's what you get for writing a load of shit,' said Mum.

Whatever he achieved, however, never seemed to be enough. The more his star rose, the worse his mood grew. We became used to Nev getting the splash – the front page – and the good cheer that briefly followed, which could result in anything from being allowed to stay up and watch an episode of *Hammer House of Horror* (and creep up the stairs in sickening terror afterwards), to going on what he called a Magical Mystery Tour, which was a trip to the fun fair on Putney Heath. But it didn't last. A day or so after Nev broke a major story on a campaign against fluoride in drinking water, or even after winning an award from the San Francisco Sewage Department, he would come back home late, sink into a chair, and scan the day's papers with a mounting air of defeat.

'Well,' he said one evening, 'there go my plans for a feature on Prince Charles's new interest in alternative medicine.'

'How do you think *I* feel?' said Mum, clearing our plates a few minutes after putting them on the table. 'Eve Pollard beat me on the interview with the world's first man-to-woman-and-back-to-man-again sex change. And she can't write to save her life!'

Nev and Mum sat at our round pine table, eating takeaway and talking about work. Sweat beads gathered on Nev's furrowed brow as he bent over a tin foil carton of pilau rice and went through the stack of newspapers that were delivered to our house each morning. One evening, two weeks after we moved into 99, Queens Road, he had just taken off his crumpled beige mackintosh as we sat down for dinner. The phone went. Mum told him it was the office. He rubbed his head as he said, 'Yes . . . OK . . . Is there really nobody else available?', and when he put the phone down, his shoulders dropped, his head shook, his eyes clenched, and he screamed, '*Fuck*!' He stood up and shrugged on his mackintosh.

'I've got to go back to the office.'

'Oh, Nev, you can't,' said Mum, with the wounded look of a loving wife and mother seeing all her efforts go to waste. 'I've just put the frozen pizzas in the microwave.'

Another night, I got Nev to help me with my mathematics homework. It involved fractions. Maths seemed at best a pointless abstraction and at worst a cold-blooded form of mental torture, particularly as my maths teacher was an eagle-like man with a beaky nose and talons for fingers who smelt of stale alcohol. 'On the morrow we shall attempt t'other question, which shall be fiendishly difficult,' he told us, before dozing off in the corner.

Nev understood mathematics. His parents had wanted him to be an accountant. Tom was a mathematics genius, but asking him anything only got snorts of derision. Mum's inability to understand even the simplest sums rendered her close to disabled. Nev was the one with the magic combination of patience and skill. That night, though, my ineptitude got the better of him. The entire concept of algebra appeared nonsensical, particularly as the numbers and letters kept jumping about on the page. Eventually, after I had frozen entirely at the prospect of a minus number times a minus number somehow equaling twenty, Nev screamed 'The answer's right there in front of you!' and hammered his finger down on a page of my homework until it left an angry grey blur. His face looked like a balloon about to pop. He wiped his brow, muttered something about being too tired to think straight, and walked out, clutching his head.

The following morning before assembly, I managed to filch all the answers for the maths homework from a boy in the class in exchange for a fun-size Mars Bar. I assumed that would be the last of it but unfortunately the boy, a normally reliable Iranian called Bobby Sultanpur, had just found out that his father had been named by the Ayatollah Khomeini as an enemy of the people, hence his including the words 'Please let us see a return to glorious Persia in our lifetime' as part of the answer to an algebraic formula. And I had copied everything out so diligently, too.

'Hodgkinson!' growled our teacher, his fetid, whiskery breath a few inches from my face, 'Your sudden concern for the plight of the Persian aristocracy strikes me as devilishly suspicious. You shall be detained at the conclusion of the school day when fresh horrors, in the form of a combination of long division and trigonometry, shall await you.'

The next Sunday, Tom had some of his new Westminster friends over. They silently trooped up the stairs and into his room like angle-poise lamps on a production line. I followed them. Tom slammed the door before I could get in. Some sort of strange new music, definitely different to *Teaser and the Firecat* by Cat Stevens, our favourite family album, which Nev described as 'deep', seeped underneath the door. I knocked. A boy I had never seen before answered.

'It's, uh, your little brother,' said the boy, arching his head over to Tom, who was sitting with two other boys by a small table, dealing cards. He was wearing a baseball cap and chewing gum in an open-mouthed way, like a ruminating cow.

'Tell him to get lost,' he said. 'No, wait. Gambling is thirsty work. Scum, be a good kid and get us some Coca-Cola, will you?'

'Fold. Man, I'm out. I'm on a one-way ticket to the poorhouse,' said a boy, who I discovered later had a father who owned around half of Fitzrovia.

'I'm folding too,' said another one. 'These high stakes give you the sweats.'

I looked down at the table. The boys were gambling away their setsquares, compasses, protractors and rubbers.

'What are you playing?' I asked Tom. 'Can I have a go?'

'Sort out the brewskis and I'll think about it.'

Mum was in the TV room, singing along to *Songs of Praise* in a high-pitched falsetto. Nev was at the kitchen table, hunched over a stack of papers, muttering. I crept past both of them with a bottle of Coca-Cola from the fridge. Neither noticed.

'I've got the drinks,' I said to Tom. 'Now can I play?'

Shuffling the cards, Tom said, 'Shall we deal him in?'

'Does that mean we have to explain the rules?' said someone.

Tom sighed and nodded. Then he looked at me and said: 'The thing is, we haven't really got time to "'hang "out".' He made the inverted commas sign. 'We're kind of in the middle of a serious situation here. Haven't you got any of your own friends to annoy?'

As it happened, I did have a friend. A small, sandy-haired child. Will Lee was terrified of water, had a teddy bear called Tipper-Topper, and lived a few streets away in a house as old and as tasteful as ours was new and brash. We had met as four-year-olds at the house of two sisters called the Webbers, during The Lone Ranger of

10

Knickertown. To put the labyrinthine complexity of this role-playing game in simple terms it involved The Lone Ranger (me) and Tonto (Will Lee) riding into a forsaken place called Knickertown (Becky and Elaine Webber's bedroom) where the piratical inhabitants (the girls) robbed us of all our clothes before casting us naked into the desert (the landing) at the mercy of unspeakable dangers (Mrs Webber). It proved a bonding experience. Becky and Elaine are lost to memory but Will and I have remained inseparable ever since.

I rang the doorbell to Will Lee's tall, terraced house. A hundred-year-old wisteria clung to the Victorian brickwork and the car, a crumbling estate, rarely washed, gave evidence of the highborn provenance of its owners. Will's father answered. Hugh Lee was a tall, bald man in his sixties with narrowed eyes and pointed ears. He wore tweeds. He peered down.

'Hm.'

He turned his head upwards and bellowed 'Willerrrgh', before shuffling off to his studio underneath the stairs.

I bounded upstairs, past the three-dimensional paintings of muted, abstract shapes the house was filled with, and which Hugh Lee had been working on every day but never putting on sale since he retired from the Civil Service two years earlier. Will was in his room. I rattled on the glass-framed door and heard a startled yelp come from within.

'Oh. It's you. I was reclassifying my fossils.'

Will's room was not like mine. There were no cheap plastic toys or stacks of comics. There were microscopes, atlases, posters of star formations and glass trays containing the stones Will had collected on the shores of Dorset.

'Look at this,' he said, holding up a grey pebble with a few indistinct lines along its smooth surface. 'What do you think of that?'

'It's a pebble. What am I meant to think about it?'

Will closed his eyes. 'It's a trilobite. It's 300 million years old.'

'Let's go up to the attic.'

The attic was the best room in the house. Hugh Lee had only semi-converted it, putting in windows and laying down a hessian carpet but leaving the spindly retractable staircase and sloping roof, turning it into a den-like space which Will's much older half brothers and half sister, now all living elsewhere, had used throughout their teenage years. Next to a record player and a stack of records was a book with a plain brown cover and the words *Les Demoiselles D'Hamilton* etched in gold down the spine.

'You have to see this,' said Will, sitting cross-legged and opening the book on his lap with slow reverence. 'This guy has an amazing ability to convince women to take their clothes off.'

I looked through the sepia-tinted, dreamy photographs of young women in French country houses, stepping out of tin bathtubs, riding bicycles through the woods in flowing white dresses, and admiring each other's semi-nude bodies, breasts falling out of thin white blouses. Years later I discovered that the photographer, David Hamilton, had used nymph-like teens as his models, but to me, an eleven-year-old, they seemed sophisticated, fully grown, untouchable. The pictures reminded me of a holiday in the South of France where the women on the beach had gone topless and there was a photographer's studio in the local town with nudes, posed and artful, in the windows.

'He's a lover of the human form,' said our father, awkwardly, as we passed the studio, before pushing us away from the window and towards the nearest ice-cream stand. Even then, Nev appeared to view the body like other men might view an affair: guilt inducing.

I looked at a David Hamilton image of two girls, their hair in loose, messy buns, sitting on a bed and admiring themselves and each other in an oval mirror. The girls wore dresses, but one of them had pulled the dress up to her waist. She was kneeling. You could see the tan line around her pale white bottom. The photographs were as confusing as they were fascinating. I was used to the sight of breasts because we got the *Sun* and Mum had told me not to expect all girls to look like Page Three girls, but this was something else entirely: exotic and romantic, otherworldly.

'I wonder where you meet women like this,' I said.

'France,' Will replied, authoritatively.

I wasn't sure whether looking at David Hamilton's girls, and what we called the FF (Faint Feeling) it inspired, should make me feel guilty or not. A few years earlier, Nev had suggested there was nothing wrong with sex. When I asked him about the basics of reproduction he explained that a man put his willy inside something a woman had called a vagina. 'It sounds horrible,' I said, but he told me people liked it. On his rather more official talk on the subject two weeks after we moved into 99, Queens Road he sat me down at the kitchen table, took out a textbook, sweated even more than usual, and, as he pointed shakily to an anatomical drawing of the male reproductive system said, in a faltering voice, 'And here we have the *vas deferens.*' The talk was high on technical detail but it left me none the wiser about what you were actually meant to do when the time came.

School wasn't helping matters. Mine was boys only, which meant girls were less a different sex and more a whole different race. I might have got to meet a few local examples of their kind on weekends had not our parents enrolled me in Saturday Club, a school-run activities service featuring judo, chess, photography and other off-curriculum subjects. There was a way of avoiding the lot of them, however. All you had to do was accompany a certain teacher to the store cupboard and allow him to whack you on the bottom with an exercise book every now and then. Three or four of us sat in there each week, wedged into the narrow space between the metal shelves and the wall. If you hit him back he would say, 'Ooh, you devil you!' and pinch your cheek excitedly, but he asked for nothing more. That's why I felt it was unfair when this teacher was hounded out of the school by an angry mob of outraged parents. Some idiot had told his mother about the store cupboard scene, thereby ruining a perfectly good way of bunking off Saturday Club. From then on I only ever saw the teacher in the changing rooms at the local swimming pool.

The official sex education talk came from Mr Mott, our Rhodesian science teacher with tiny red eyes and a sandy white beard who threatened to whack us with his 'paddle stick' should we do so much as snigger at the mention of a spermatozoa. The science room, a poky basement that stank of ammonia and chlorine, was always hot, and he decided to give us the lesson on an unseasonably close autumn morning.

'Your bodies will be goin' through many changes,' he

14

shouted, marching up and down the room and intermittently bashing a pre-adolescent head with the paddle stick. 'You will be gittin' pubic hair. You will find your pinnis goin' hard at inappropriate moments. You will develop fillings for a gil, or, in some cases, a led.'

'Yeah, Sultanpur,' said Christopher Tobias.

Mr Mott allowed himself a little smile. 'Settle down, you bunch of jissies. Right then. We will now be looking it the female initomy.'

It was so hot, and it had been such a long time since I had had anything to drink, that I began to feel faint. I dared not ask Mr Mott to be excused; that would be asking for trouble. Instead, I tried to concentrate on the matter at hand. 'Look at this vigina,' Mr Mott barked, tapping the diagram projected above his head with his paddle stick. Hodgkinson, you little creep, git up here and blerry well locate the clitoris.'

My head was swimming with the heat, but to ignore an order from Mr Mott was to sign your schoolboy death warrant. I stood up quickly. And that's when the blackout must have happened. The next thing I knew I was lying on the floor while the school nurse, a young blonde woman with large lips and a concerned but accommodating manner, fanned me with a copy of *It's OK to Say No*.

It was left to the adult world, the world of parents, to provide clues about what went on between men and women, and the real evidence came at our first party at 99, Queens Road. It was on Bonfire Night, a tradition that brought out the best in Nev because of his deep and profound love for blowing things up, fireworks, fire, destruction and chaos in general. And he really outdid himself that year. Alongside getting a huge box of Chinese

15

fireworks with deceptively delicate names like 'Lotus Blossom in Spring' and 'Floating Stars in the Night Sky', he took us to Hamley's to find something special. He found it. The Flying Pigeon was an enormous construction that looked like five sticks of strung-together dynamite. It came with a long rope on which it zipped backwards and forwards.

Nev scratched his chin as he studied the Flying Pigeon. 'This does look pretty good. But it's very expensive, and it does say that it's designed for major displays only and definitely not garden parties . . .'

'But Nev. Imagine seeing that thing in action.'

A mischievous grin coursed over Nev's face. The battle for the Flying Pigeon was over. He was powerless in the face of pyrotechnic mayhem.

The party would be a chance to see our parents' friends again. Among our favourites were Anne and Pete, an actress and a globetrotting businessman who had been our next-door neighbours in the old house until moving to a run-down vicarage in Faversham in Kent. Despite Anne and Pete not having kids, their home had its own games room complete with table football, a fruit machine from the 1940s and all manner of mechanical automata. Every time Pete came back from a work trip to the States he returned with unusual and unavailable toys, for us and for himself.

'He was always larger than life,' Mum said of Pete, as she put trays of baked potatoes into the oven. 'He had an MG when he was at university, while the rest of us were trying to scrape enough to get a bicycle. He's one of those working class Yorkshiremen that just know how to make money. He was chasing after me for a while. Not that I was interested. Nev may have his faults, but at least he's got long legs.'

Guests filtered in. Tom and I were on drinks duties. Tom, wearing a black velvet jacket and a clip-on bowtie, took to the job with a lot more enthusiasm than I did, possibly because it gave him a chance to harangue every new person who came along with his latest thoughts on literary theory, advancements in physics and all-round egghead boffin theorizing.

'Yes, yes . . . our mother struggles with the great writers,' he said to one woman in a silver tiara and a plunge-neck ball gown, as he offered her a prawn cocktail. 'She can manage Jane Austen and the like, but forget about Proust. Beyond her.'

The house filled up. There always seemed to be a woman with a hand on Nev's shoulder, leaning forward and laughing with him about something. I carried trays of champagne into the drawing room, and all the glasses got whisked away in a flash. Some adults, usually men, took a glass without bothering to look at me; others, usually women, seemed charmed by the idea of an 11-year-old waiter and thanked me effusively and called me a darling child. With typical flamboyance, Pete brought a crate of champagne and a trade-sized jar of pink and white marsh-mallow sweets called Flumps. I poured half of the Flumps into a bowl and offered them around, along with the champagne. The Flumps did not prove appealing to adults so I decided to eat a lot of them myself, just so they didn't feel unpopular.

Sandy and John Chubb arrived. John Chubb was some sort of a lord and Sandy, although a working-class girl who had left school at fifteen, had the plummiest voice

17

of anyone I knew: rich, low and gracious. They lived in a huge house in Oxford with two toddlers, where John Chubb spent his weekends windsurfing and Sandy taught yoga in high security prisons, which always struck me as a dangerous career choice for this most glamorous of women. Sandy, looking regal with her thick black hair tied into a bun and a diamond necklace dazzling at her long swanlike neck, came up to Tom and me with presents, even though it wasn't our birthdays: an album each. She got Tom *Transformer* by Lou Reed and me *Scary Monsters (and Super Creeps)* by David Bowie. We stared at the cover photographs of these bizarre men, transfixed.

Sandy sat down with us by the record player and put on the Lou Reed album. On the back was a photograph of a butch man and a sexy woman. 'Which one is Lou Reed?' I asked her, through a mouthful of Flumps.

Sandy looked at me meaningfully. 'They both are, Will dear. It's all about transvestites, and hustlers, and other exotic people from the New York Underworld.'

'But what are they doing there in the first place?' I asked her, wondering where on earth the short, muscular, strutting man and the pouting, slender woman would fit in employment-wise to the New York Underworld, which I assumed was America's equivalent of the London Underground. I certainly couldn't imagine them in the ticket office.

'It's a very different scene over there. Anyway, have a listen to this.'

A song called 'Vicious' came on, to roars of approval from the guests. Annie started shimmying with a bearded man, Sandy got up and tried to make a reluctant-but-amused John Chubb dance, Mum was saying something about everyone being so bloody conventional and Pete was cornered by a curvaceous woman who was pressing her considerable cleavage up against him, causing his eyebrows to raise in tandem with the glass of beer in his hand.

I continued to fulfill my role as champagne and Flumps waiter until the Flumps ran out, which was strange because nobody had actually wanted one. Apart from a single Flump that Tom had picked up, stared at, and attempted to jam up my nose, I had, I realized, eaten the lot of them.

Nev appeared, charcoal marks on his sports jacket. 'OK everybody, let's go outside. I've lit the bonfire.'

It was a huge, bright red pyramid, stacked high with dried branches, planks, an old wooden chair and a punk-themed Guy Fawkes effigy at the top (punks being déclassé in 1981). Nev, Tom and I had been building it for days, adding anything that would burn, and now it was a mighty inferno. Mum brought out the tray of baked potatoes while Nev tied the rope for the Flying Pigeon between the apple tree and a pole holding up the washing line, and I, regretting having stuffed myself with Flumps for the last hour, sat down on the grass and leaned against the large wooden box containing all the fireworks and clutched my stomach.

This was the kind of party I liked, even if I was beginning to wish Flumps had never been invented. There was nothing better than Nev having fun because he spread it in our direction. He liked the same things as us: building dens in the woods, making fires, playing board games and going on Magical Mystery Tours to the local fun fair. He was clearly good adult company too, because all these interesting, lively people wanted to be with him. Mum didn't like any child-related activities and she probably never had, but she enjoyed a party, while Tom relished having a bunch of adults around on whom to test out his maturity. I was overhearing him declaiming to a silent listener about the life of Dr Johnson, and Mum telling someone about her latest article on why she would rather be interviewing a top celebrity in a fancy cocktail bar than being bored at home looking after her children, when Nev appeared.

'Sturchos,' he said, grinning down at me excitedly, 'I'm going to get it all going with the Flying Pigeon. Want to come over here with me to get a good view?'

'You go ahead,' I moaned, waving him away. 'I think I've eaten something that disagrees with me. I'll just stay here for a bit.'

Nev bounded off, telling everyone to clear the line of fire. If only I didn't feel like I was going to send a hundred half-digested Flumps hurtling towards the ground I would have been up there with him, as Nev's passion for anything involving fire and the destruction it wrought was matched only by my own. It was terrible to think that I wouldn't be close to the mayhem – Nev was much more fun than most fathers because health and safety had never been at the top of his priorities – but my conviction was that if I just sat still for a couple of minutes I could recover from this unfortunate situation in time to enjoy the rest of the party, not to mention the rest of the fireworks in the box behind me.

'OK everyone,' said Nev, sparking the wick of the Flying Pigeon with a disposable lighter. 'Here we go . . .'

The wick fizzed and sparked. People cheered. There was a high-pitched squeal, like it really was a pigeon whose tail had just been set on fire. A shower of sparks burst out. The pigeon took flight, zipping along the rope, spinning around and sending multicoloured rays of exploding gunpowder out into the night sky . . . and then it stopped. It fizzled out. Only one of the sticks of gunpowder had been used up.

Nev went to examine his prize item, poking around it to discover that the connection between the first stick and the rest had been broken. 'Well, I'm not going to see that go to waste,' he said, and before anyone could tell him not to he ripped the Flying Pigeon off the rope and chucked it onto the bonfire.

It sat there for a few seconds, before blasting into the air in a flash of colour. Then it turned and headed down, straight towards me. There were screams. Nev was running towards it, pipe-cleaner legs leaping forward. It looked like it was going to come down right on top of me – and then it was gone. But I could still hear it fizzing away. Where did it go? It all happened so quickly that I didn't have time to get up and run before I realized.

From the open-mouthed faces of the people all staring at me, it looked like they had realized too. It was in the box of fireworks.

'Will, get out of the way!' shouted Nev. He almost made it over, but it was too late: the chaos began. A rocket screamed its way out of the box and headed straight towards Pete's admirer, who displayed a nimbleness her curves belied and leapt into a rhododendron bush. A Catherine Wheel span wildly and helicoptered along the ground towards John Chubb's titled ankles. A psychedelic Mount Vesuvius of dynamite exploded everywhere. I put my hands over my head and crouched as World War III

21

broke out on a suburban lawn. Every time I peeked through my fingers, another firework had escaped. People were running, shouting useless warnings to each other and generally dissolving into panic. There was a red roar behind me for what seemed like ages (actually about a minute). Then it stopped.

I poked my head out. John Chubb and Pete were standing alert and looking up as if defending the party from an airborne invasion. People emerged from behind trees. There were groans but no injuries. I didn't appear to be hurt.

There was one more explosion, followed by a whizzing sound and the sight of a single white light, floating silently in the night sky, mingling with the stars. It was a parachute firework. I looked up, and then looked at Nev, who was staring at this peaceful, brilliant light in contemplative wonder. He wore an expression I hadn't seen before: transported and spiritual. He was motionless.

Then he shook himself into action and ran and picked me up from the ground.

'Sturch! Are you all right?'

'All right? That was the best fireworks display ever!'

What a dad. Who else could cause a grown-up party to descend into such anarchy? Unfortunately other guests, particularly the women, did not share my enthusiasm. They rounded on Nev as one, screaming at him for almost committing them to a lifetime of blindness and singed hair. And why was his poor son lying there next to an arsenal of lethal fireworks? To see Nev, perspiration clouding up his metal-framed glasses, twitching at his tank top as an army of harridans led by his wife accused him of something approaching child murder was far more disturbing than anything that had happened before.

'For Christ's sake,' shrieked Mum, the ferocity of her coal-black eyes made a little less scary by the fragment of Roman Candle jutting from her bouffant, 'Will could have been killed.'

'But I'm fine,' I shouted.

'You keep out of this,' she shouted back. 'Honestly, Nev, sometimes I think you must have gone round the bend.'

Mum and Pete's wife Annie went back into the house, arms linked, shooting Nev freezing glances over their shoulders. Pete and John Chubb told Nev not to worry, that nobody was hurt, and that women were mad anyway. Tom stood up, brushed down his velvet jacket, and walked towards the house with his hands clasped behind his back, kicking up dust with his shoes as he resumed his soliloquy on Dr Johnson.

'Don't listen to them, Nev,' I said, as we stood next to each other by the bonfire and watched the flames dance. 'You did them all a favour. That's going to be the fireworks night everyone remembers for the rest of their life.'

He smiled. 'The Flying Pigeon certainly livened things up, didn't it?'

'It's the best thing that has ever happened to me.'

And it was. It was even better than the time Nev got us stuck on a cliff on the Cornish coast. We had to be rescued by helicopter, which dropped us down onto a golf course while Mum watched the whole thing from a sun lounger by the pool of the hotel. In my school essay on the subject I added that there was a terrible storm and several people died.

The guests seemed to forgive Nev for his reckless

behaviour quite quickly, as it was only an hour or so later that everyone piled into our drawing room with glasses of red wine or champagne and chatted, laughed and made flirtatious gestures towards one another. I used the opportunity to discard the evidence of my Flumps-related gluttony and chuck the empty jar in the dustbin. Nev looked a little flustered as not one but two women purred around him, while Mum held court as she regaled tales of constant harassment by the men of Fleet Street to a group of men who appeared to have somehow found it within their power to not harass her. I had learned that on these occasions it was easy to stay up late if you amused the adults, so I decided the time was right to try out a few of my favourite jokes on them. Before long I was sitting on the lap of the woman with the large cleavage, who kept calling me a gorgeous lad while intermittently pressing me to her bosom and glugging from a glass of champagne.

'Here's another one,' I said, once I had the attention of most of the people in the room. 'There was an old lady who bought a very large house. It was such a nice house that she felt she should give it a name, so, after thinking about it for at least a minute, she decided to call it Hairy Bum.'

I had them laughing and I hadn't even got to the punch line.

'After living in Hairy Bum for a year she started to feel rather lonely in that big house all by herself, so she got a little dog. She called the dog Willy. Willy and the old lady were very happy until one day Willy went missing. The old lady was terribly worried. She searched everywhere but she couldn't find him. Eventually she went to the police station and she told them . . .'

24

I had to stifle a few giggles here.

"'I've looked all over my Hairy Bum, but I can't find my Willy!'"

They roared. The woman with the cleavage bounced me up and down. Somebody decided I deserved to taste champagne for the first time. Tom might impress them with his erudition and his little velvet jackets and bow ties, but I was knocking them dead with my ribald gags. Sandy sashayed towards the record player and put the David Bowie album on. I think the quarter of a glass of champagne I was allowed to drink may have gone to my head in a not unpleasant manner because I definitely felt a little unsteady as I went to the toilet. The other children who had been there for the fireworks had long gone, but they were a glum lot anyway and talking to strange kids was never easy. Adults could be very entertaining with a few drinks inside them.

Eventually, Mum told me I really should be getting to bed. It must have been around midnight. The Flumps-induced stomach ache returning might have been why, at an hour when I imagine the party was winding down, I was still lying awake, listening to the sound of a man and a woman entering the room next door. I couldn't hear their voices but after a series of bumps and bangs I heard the woman groaning, and the bed squeaking, and with my limited understanding of what Mr Mott had taught us I came to a simple but most likely accurate conclusion: they were having sex.

Then something else occurred to me. That was our parents' room.

It couldn't be them, could it? After all, they had two children already. Perhaps the madness of the night was causing the natural order of things to be upturned. And as gruesome as the sound was, it was reassuring too. It indicated a sense of stability.

I never heard it again. But I did get a Scalextric for Christmas.

2

The Boat Holiday

Why our father thought it was a good idea to take the family on a boating holiday on the River Thames is one of those mysteries destined to remain unsolved. I invited Will Lee, who couldn't swim. Tom brought along a French exchange student, a blond boy with a brightly coloured rucksack called Dominic, who thought he was coming to London to see Madame Tussauds. Our mother was entering into her feminist phase, which had previously been confined to buying ready meals and denigrating Nev but which was to reach a whole new level before the holiday was over.

With the benefit of hindsight, Nev should have done what had worked for holidays past: go to the travel agent on the high street, find a Mediterranean package deal, and lie on a beach for a week in ill-fitting swimming trunks while Tom was chained to the hotel room with a bout of diarrhoea and an Aldous Huxley novel, I went snorkelling and got stung by jellyfish, and Mum sat by the pool with a Danielle Steel, a glass of wine and a packet of Player's

No. 6. That way everyone got to do what he or she enjoyed. Instead, Nev set in motion a chain of events that culminated in near death, nervous breakdown, divorce and a devotion to meditation, spiritual study, communal living and the attainment of world peace through soul consciousness that continues to this day.

Before the holiday actually began it did sound quite pleasant. Judging by the photographs of joyous families in the pages of the riverboat hire brochure, it would be a summery adventure in the English countryside that involved drifting down the Thames, waving cheerily to the anglers on the banks and jumping off the side for a swim as the sun sank into the rippling water while Will Lee watched from the deck. Dominic came over a day earlier from the suburbs of Paris armed with a guide to London, a pair of Ray-Bans and a shaky grip of the English language. Will Lee's mother Penny had, with the kind of everlasting hope only a mother can have, packed her son's swimming trunks and inflatable water wings.

Our boat, the *Kingston Cavalier III*, looked impressive when we reached the boatyard: strong and proud against the weeping willows along the bank of the Thames. A large white motorboat with three levels, it had two tiny bedrooms, one with two berths and one with four, a flat roof and an outdoor deck at the back. Dominic went into the boat, came out again, and burst into tears. Tom pointed at the top bunk, said, 'That's mine,' and hurled himself up onto it with a paperback of Bertrand Russell's *Why I Am Not A Christian* and a yawn.

While Will Lee and I loaded on the suitcases and a large hamper filled with fun-size Mars Bars, cocktail sausages and bottles of wine, Mum changed into her nautical outfit of white three-quarter-length trousers, espadrilles with heels, black-and-white T-shirt and a white captain's hat. Nev spent an hour with the manager of the boat hire company, going through the boat's workings, the laws of the river, and what to do when you needed to moor, anchor and guide the boat through a lock, nodding intently throughout. We were each in our own way prepared.

It started off well. Nev steered the *Kingston Cavalier III* out of the boatyard with calm, Nev-like diligence. When Tom told Dominic that we were heading in the direction of London he perked up, said, 'Madame Tussauds, c'est la?' and pointed down the river. Tom gave him a thumbs-up and went back to Russell. At first, Mum seemed content to sit in a folding chair on the deck with a glass of wine and a copy of *Patriarchal Attitudes* by Eva Figes, and make less than generous comments about the size of the bottoms of the women who hailed us from boats going in the other direction. Will and I climbed onto the roof and stayed there. The lapping lulls of the water and the singing of the birds, even the unchanging hum of the engine, were as restful and as reassuring as the sight of an old friend or a cup of hot chocolate before bedtime. Sunlight streaked through the willows and bathed the river in a golden glow. Cows in the fields beyond the banks bowed their gentle heads to the ground. Crickets chirped. The warmth of the sun soaked the land and brewed a woozy kind of contentment.

Then it began.

'I hope you don't think for a minute that you're the captain of this ship just because you're a man,' Mum squawked, like a peacock whose tail had been yanked. 'I can do a much better job than you. I can play tennis better than you, I can earn more money than you, and I can damn well steer a boat down the river better than you. I'm no longer going to be the woman you wish me to be, or fear me to be.' Her captain's hat wiggled with indignant satisfaction at that particular line.

Nev pushed up the bridge of his glasses. 'What on earth are you talking about?'

'You've had your turn. Now it's mine.' Whether she was talking about driving the boat or life in general she didn't specify, but as we were going along a wide, quiet stretch of the river with no lock, island or pleasure cruiser in the way, Nev gave a light smile and said, 'Of course you can drive the boat, although I can hardly see how you'll be able to do a better job than me. Do you want me to explain the basics to you?'

'Stop patronizing me, you male chauvinist pig,' she said, jerking him out of the way by the scruff of his v-necked tank top and grabbing the wheel.

Mum cranked the boat up a gear and sped off down the river. This caused the wind to catch her hat and for it to fly off her head. It only fell down onto the deck below, where Dominic was listening to 'Ça Plane Pour Moi' on a Sony Walkman, but Mum twisted round to see where it went – and forgot to take her hands off the wheel. The boat swerved violently towards port, or, as she kept insisting on calling it, starboard.

'What are you doing?' yelped Nev, who had made the elemental mistake of trusting Mum enough to steer the ship while he went to the toilet. He leapt up the narrow steps, but it was too late. She launched the boat straight towards the bank.

'Stop panicking,' she shouted, in a panicked voice. 'I know what I'm doing.'

What nobody had explained to Mum was that going near the bank on a river doesn't just run the danger of hitting it with the side of the boat; you can also run aground. Her deep hatred of mud, water and nature in general meant she had never explored rivers, and didn't realize that they start off shallow and get deeper in the middle. The boat slowed down, made an angry grunt, and came to a halt.

'What's going on?' she said, hair billowing about in the wind. 'There seems to be something wrong with this vessel. Did you get ripped off again?'

'We've run aground.'

'Don't be stupid. The boat is still in the water. We're surrounded by the bloody stuff.'

'The bottom of the boat is stuck in the mud.'

'Mud! I'll soon get us out of it,' she said, slapping her hands together as if preparing to defeat an old foe. Dominic handed her back the captain's hat. She adjusted it to a jaunty angle, and then she turned the engine on. Before Nev could stop her she did the one thing you mustn't do if you run aground: rev up and attempt to move forward. This only serves to push the boat deeper into the riverbed.

'Stop it!' Nev shouted over the roar, trying to wrestle her away from the wheel. 'Turn the bloody engine off.'

'All right, keep your hair on,' she said, bumping him out of the way. Then she did the second thing you mustn't do: put the boat into reverse. The mud sucked up into the propellers. Nev switched the engine off.

There was a brief moment of silence, save for the moo of a cow.

'If you had been listening when I was getting instruction on how to drive this thing,' said Nev, gasping, his chin remaining unmoving with stoic solemnity as beads of sweat collected in the lines of his forehead, 'you would have known better than to do that.'

'If you're so smart why don't you get us out of this mess you've caused, Mr Smarty Pants?'

The river brings out the best in people, or at least in some people, because a boat of a similar size stopped to help. A middle-aged couple – small, round and in matching blue shorts and tight blue vests, like Tweedle Dee and Tweedle Dum, only married – told us to check in the hull for any leaks caused by damage to the bottom of the boat. It seemed to be all right. They said we mustn't turn on the engine. They moored their boat against ours and told us boys and Mum to step onto it. Mum kept her nose upwards and her gaze in the opposite direction as the man stuck out a short, wide arm to help her across. The couple tied a rope to the front of our boat and pulled us out like a knife through melting butter. They looked at one another and nodded in satisfaction.

Once we were all back on the boat, and Mum was persuaded that it was a good idea to let Nev drive for a while, it settled down.

'What kind people,' said Nev, as the boat moved steadily along the centre of the river and resumed its calm mechanical hum, 'they really saved us back then.'

'They were so fat though, weren't they?' Mum replied, back on her folding chair with a glass of wine. 'Why do fat people insist on wearing clothes that are too small for them? Do they simply not look at themselves, or can't they see what the rest of us have the misfortune to see? There's a term for it, you know. Body dysmorphia.'

Nev shook his head and looked to the river before us, rather than his wife, who was applying lipstick, as she added, 'Surely these boats come equipped with mirrors.'

Will and I stayed on the roof of the boat, forcing wood-lice and spiders into gladiatorial battles, making them form a tag-team against a caterpillar or simply throwing them overboard to face their watery deaths.

By the evening, it looked like Mum had given up trying to be captain of the ship. Nev dropped anchor next to a small island in the middle of the Thames at sunset. Dominic was the first to explore it: he pushed through tangleweed and bracken before disappearing out of view. He ran back, screaming, chased by an angry goose. The water was shallow enough for even Will to venture into the river, up to his waist in the murky green as rays of light flashed across the tiny ripples. A swan glided past, followed by a line of fluffy grey cygnets, horizontal question marks aligned by nature's symmetry. Tom, never the most physical of boys, stuck his foot in the water from the side of the boat, decreed, 'cold,' and scrabbled about in the hamper for a biscuit. Dominic and I pushed off and swam into deeper water as Nev and Mum watched from the boat, sitting next to each other, smiling. I have no idea what they were talking about, but in that brief moment it seemed like they were pleased that they had children, pleased at how life had panned out, pleased to be with each other and to laugh at the world together.

Sitting on a blanket under the canopy of a willow tree, wrapped in towels, we ate cold sausages in bread rolls with tomato ketchup. Mum brought her folding chair onto the island and sank into it while Nev poured Coca-Cola from a two-litre bottle into plastic cups.

'It's wonderful to see the boys so happy,' said Mum. 'It's like a scene from *Swallows and Amazons*. I used to love that book. I remember getting it as a present for passing the eleven-plus and going to grammar school. My brother failed, of course. He went to the secondary modern and look at him now.'

We had heard the story about her glittering education and her brother's miserable one a hundred times before. I was waiting to hear her compare Uncle Richard to their alcoholic father, who had a minor accident during a brief stint as a lorry driver and used it as an excuse to never work again, but it didn't come. Instead she said that she was lucky to have such lovely children, and she liked seeing us with our friends, and it was getting late and we needed to get into our pyjamas and clean our teeth.

Mum's brand of second-wave feminism was in keeping with the 1980s: individualistic and money-based. She argued, inarguably, that there was no reason why her earnings shouldn't match that of a man doing a similar job, and that girls had not only a right but also a duty to get the best education they could. Given that she entered Fleet Street at a time in the 1970s when it was entirely male-dominated save for the fashion and food pages, you can see why she became so strident. Until recently a woman could not buy anything on hire purchase without a male signatory; an unmarried woman could not get a mortgage; it was not possible to rent a flat with a man unless she was married. On our boat trip Mum was bridling at the choices she had made when she was too young to know better: changing her name, getting

34

married, having children, becoming secondary, in the eyes of the law at least, to a man.

Now she had got to the point in her career where, because Nev was working at the *Daily Mail* and she was doing big celebrity interviews and lifestyle features for the then more populist *Sunday People*, she was earning a lot more money than him. Fleet Street was at the height of its powers, with over ten million people reading the *Sunday People* and the *Daily Mirror*. Mirror Group's all-powerful printers' union demanded high pay to keep the presses rolling and journalists' wages fell in line accordingly. Cushioned and given confidence by a very good salary, Mum felt that certain inequalities needed to be addressed.

Margaret Thatcher was a role model as far as she was concerned: a working-class woman who had got ahead through her own will and intelligence and put the emphasis on material improvement and self-reliance. Mum also took anything associated with the traditional role of the mother as a sign of weakness. Cooking was subjugation, which is why we lived on a diet of frozen pizzas. Getting involved in our schools – beyond screeching at me when I got a D in maths – was for less intelligent, more mundane women, which meant that she acted with outrage when the PTA asked her to bake a cake for the school fête (after calming down, she offered to buy them one from Marks & Spencer's). And when she stayed out in the evening and matched the men in her office drink for drink and cutting barb for cutting barb, she was doing it for the cause.

One of the most confusing aspects of Mum's declarations of feminism was that it was other women who were the most frequent source of her wrath. They were the agents of their own misfortune, apparently. Nev, Uncle Richard, her own father and most other men may not have been up to much, but as Mum told it even they were less pitiable than the old school-friend of hers who had been the cleverest girl in the class, only to get married at eighteen to a man in wire-framed glasses who made the family say grace before every meal and clothed his terri-fied daughters in matching dresses buttoned up to the neck. As for higher profile feminists, Germaine Greer was only bearable if you agreed with everything she said and Andrea Dworkin was a brilliant and brave pioneer, but wrong in one fatal regard: she equated feminism with hairy armpits. Any sensible modern woman knew that taking care of your appearance with fashionable clothes, matching colour schemes and high-end beauty products does not suggest sexual availability but self-worth. A decent wage and a trip to the salon whenever you felt like it: those were the rightful spoils of the women's liberation movement.

Will and I tortured no more insects that evening. Dominic didn't mention Madame Tussauds. Tom stopped reading, even. It was dark by the time we were back on the boat, and we took it in turns to clean our teeth in the tiny washbasin before Mum and Nev said goodnight and closed the door of their cabin. We heard the sound of things crashing and breaking, followed by shrieks of laughter, followed by snoring.

Will and I climbed up onto the roof of the boat and lay on our backs, and listened to the grasshoppers harmo-nize under the stars. For a while there, it did seem like we were a reasonably functioning family.

36

It turned out to be a brief glimpse of Eden in what proved otherwise to be a descent into Hell. The following morning, Mum stomped off into whatever town we were near to buy the papers while Nev moored the boat and cooked sausages on a camping stove. She came back holding up a copy of the *Sunday People*, crumpling in the wind and turned to a page with her article on it. Its headline was: *How to Fight the Flab and Look Totally Fab*. It had a picture of our mother in a purple velour tracksuit, attempting to jump in the air and smile at the same time. Nev also had a much smaller piece in the *Daily Mail*. It was about a pioneering, morally complex and potentially revolutionary research programme of isolating embryonic stem cells. It didn't come with a photo byline.

We continued our pointless journey down the river. When she eventually tired of reading her own article, Mum, back in her folding chair, shouted at Nev, 'I hope you don't expect me to play the Little Lady, doing all the ironing and cleaning and cooking. You're bloody lucky I'm here at all. I should be out writing a feature. Do you know how in demand I am?'

Nev, who was steering the boat, replied: 'Why don't you go off and write your feature then? You could even fight the flab if you walked the thirty miles or so back to London.'

'Don't be silly. Do you think that just because you're a man you've got a right to tell me what to do?' She grabbed her captain's hat and stomped towards the steering wheel. 'Get off. It's my turn.'

After a brief tussle, Nev shrugged and handed it over. 'Just try not to run aground this time.'

We came up to a lock. There was a shriek. 'Nev! What do I do?'

'Take your foot off the power,' he shouted, and she did – but not in time. We hit the brick wall of the lock with a loud crunch.

'Tell your wife to put the boat into neutral,' shouted the lock keeper as the boat whined and juddered helplessly against the side of the lock, and Will and I helped Nev tie the ropes. Mum raised her nose in a westerly direction. Nev took over once more and told Mum to get away from the wheel and stay out of harm's way.

'That was your fault,' she yelped. 'You didn't tell me how to stop it.'

'Oh, shut up, you hideous bat. There can only be one captain of this ship and that's me. Once we get through this lock I'm going to have to assess the damage.'

While we waited for the lock to fill up, Mum decided to tell Dominic and Will why they shouldn't mistake her for the kind of mum who helps her children with their homework or cheers them on at the school sports day. 'You're more likely to find me in a glamorous bar, interviewing a famous celebrity,' she said, pushing up her hat and leaning against the side of the lock. 'My career is far more important for me to do all those things silly women do. *Anyone* can bake a cake. *I'm* part of an exclusive club which holds the media power in London.'

'Tower of London?' said Dominic, hopefully.

'It's a miracle we're not mentally deranged,' said Tom, lackadaisically. He was sitting on the bank, reading. 'I'm going to have to spend a significant portion of the money left to me in your will on psychiatric fees.'

'I just don't see the point in pretending to be something I'm not.'

Despite this, she did then pretend to be something she

wasn't: a bridge. Once through the lock, we all climbed back on the boat. Mum was the last one on. She pushed the boat off from the side, but being in the middle of a tirade about why on earth working-class people had to walk around with so few clothes on the moment the sun came out, she failed to notice that her feet were going in one direction and her hands, which were raised against a pillar, were going in the other.

'Oh no!' she screamed. 'Help!'

Nev turned round to see his wife forming an arch over the water, her behind raised high above her hands and feet, but he was steering the boat and too far away from her to help. Dominic had escaped downstairs to look at photographs of London landmarks, Will and I were on the roof with our dead, dying and wounded insects and Tom was back on the deck, making the most of Mum's folding chair while he could.

Theoretically, Tom could have saved her. He was only a few feet away. But he looked at her, raised his eyes, and said, 'Try not to make too much of a splash.' Will and I sat and watched, frozen. I looked over at Nev. He had his hand over his mouth. 'Somebody help me!' she pleaded, before plopping into the water.

We looked down. For a few seconds all you could see was the captain's hat, floating between the boat and the wall of the lock. Then Mum appeared, her bouffant flattened, mascara running down her cheeks, spluttering.

'Quick!' she shrieked. 'Throw me something! Throw me something to hold onto!'

Tom looked around, stood up, stretched, and chucked the folding chair at her. It landed with a splash a few inches away from her head before sinking out of view.

'Oh,' said Tom, peering over the boat and scratching his head. 'That didn't work.'

I threw her a rope and pulled her up to the side of the boat until she reached the ladder that ran along its side. With her waterlogged trousers, black-lined face and dripping black hair hanging in clumps from the side of her head, she looked like a deranged rock star trawled up from the riverbed.

When she dried off, after Nev made her a cup of tea and I got her a dry towel to wrap around herself, she dissolved into self-pity.

'It was awful,' she said, shivering. 'I've never been so scared in all my life . . . I had a moment of blind panic. And I *hate* getting my hair wet. Why didn't anyone help me?'

I shrugged. 'Couldn't really make it in time.'

'And I couldn't leave the wheel,' said Nev. 'If I had, the boat might have crushed you when you fell in the water.'

'I was reading,' said Tom, picking his nose.

'This whole holiday was your stupid idea,' Mum snapped at Nev. 'You know I hate larking about on rivers. I *don't* like the countryside, I *don't* like mud, I *don't* like water and I *don't* like being stuck on a boat with four horrible boys and a useless man.'

Given her track record, you might think that now would have been a good time for Mum to sit out the rest of the holiday and stay in a place where she could cause as little damage as possible, like below deck. And at first, deprived of her folding chair, she did indeed disappear into her cabin and indulge in a much-needed (for us) bout of splendid isolation. But she went back to her old ways the very next day.

It was somewhere around Teddington that she decided to take over once more. Initially, Nev refused to let her. He pointed out that her attempts to drive the boat had not been entirely successful.

'Would you have me chained to the kitchen, cooking and cleaning?' she wailed, sweeping her arms in the air. 'Who paid for our house by scribbling away? Whose brains got Tom a scholarship to Westminster? And yet here you are, trying to be the big man. I must say, I find your attitude highly offensive. I suppose you also think that unmarried women are useless nuisances, spare mouths? I wonder how the sisterhood would respond to this, should I write an article about it.'

'Why don't you do us all a favour and put a sock in it?' Nev snapped, which was quite a strong reaction for him. 'I've never patronized you, and given your horrible cooking, the kitchen is the last place I'd want to keep you.'

'Give me that steering wheel, you. I'll show you.'

Mum no longer had on the captain's hat, but she did her best to look authoritative nonetheless as she stood at the prow of the boat. She kept both hands on the wheel and looked ahead. A pleasure cruiser passed and people on it waved; she ignored them. A bunch of kids on a boat similar to ours pointed at her and shouted, 'Look, it's Cher.'

We needed to refuel. We came up to a river marina, but getting into it required a degree of skill. A jetty ran around it and it was, of course, filled with boats. Nev, who had been at the back, taking a series of deep breaths with his eyes closed, attempted to take over for this key bit of manoeuvring.

'I'm perfectly capable of controlling my craft,' she

41

announced, pushing him away, 'even if it does hurt your phallic pride too much to let me.'

'Liz, you're going in too fast,' he said, as calmly as he could manage. 'Take it out of gear.'

Rather than do as she was told, she decided to try and pull the boat round. We thudded up against the jetty. The harbourmaster came running forward. 'Turn off your engine!'

Boats surrounded us, but by a stroke of incredible good fortune Mum had managed not to ram into any of them. 'Do you know what you're doing, darling?' said the harbourmaster, a youngish man who swaggered up with the proprietary air of someone used to getting people who didn't know what they were doing out of trouble. 'Don't you think you should let your husband take over?'

Mum lowered her eyebrows, gritted her teeth, and snorted. If steam could have puffed out of her ears, it would have done. 'I'm going to park the boat by that petrol tank up there,' she said, pointing at the filling station fifty metres or so in front of us. Then she slammed the engine on – and put the boat into reverse.

Mum's hands flew up in shock. We shot backwards, straight into three boats. Various people stared at us in horror. 'What on *earth* are you doing?' asked one silver-haired woman, peering at Mum with narrowed eyes. The woman was wearing a perfectly aligned, pristine white captain's hat, which matched her fitted blazer. Mum, who with her unkempt bouffant and extended nails now resembled the terrifying children's character Struwwelpeter, appeared to think the best thing to do was to escape from the scene of the crime as quickly as possible. She slammed the boat into forward. But it didn't work.

The boat strained, and groaned, and cried, and whined, and bleated like a big metal baby, and moved only a few inches. Nev turned the engine off.

He stared at her.

She looked at him with big, wide, apologetic eyes. Her chin wobbled. Then she began to cry.

After assessing the damage, the harbourmaster told Nev that Mum had most likely got the propeller caught up in the ropes of the other boats. The only way to deal with the problem was to dive down and untangle them. Meanwhile, the man on the boat that Mum hit first came out to apply wood glue to our splintered hull. His wife offered to make everyone a cup of tea. The silver-haired lady watched from a safe distance and smoked a cigarette in a holder and turned her head slowly from side to side in a disapproving but satisfied way.

Nev, in his oversized red swimming trunks, lowered himself into the water. He dived underneath the boat and blindly did his best to untangle the mass of knots that Mum had wrapped around our propeller and, it turned out, the rudder. He would come up for air, gasping and spluttering, spit out a jet of oily green water, and head back down again.

It took two hours.

By the time the last stretch of rope was removed from the propeller, Nev was shivering uncontrollably.

Mum dared to reappear, to hand him a towel. 'Oh, well done Nev,' she said, breathily. 'Good work.'

'Go away,' he said. For the first time, it really did look like Mum had broken him. But then he disappeared below deck, came back a few minutes later fully clothed, and said: 'Right'.

He filled up the boat with petrol and, after thanking the couple that had helped us, glided it out of the marina just before the marina closed. That evening we moored near Hampton Court, where Henry VIII had chopped off the head of Anne Boleyn in order to make way for the significantly more docile Jane Seymour, and ate fish and chips on the bank of the river, Mum sitting a little apart from the rest of us. She stayed by the boat while Nev, Tom, Dominic, Will and me went walking along the Thames. We found a rope, attached to a high bough of a tree, hanging down at the point where the raised bank met the river. Nev swung out on it, manoeuvring his middle-aged but slender body onto the seat of the rope and taking off over the water. Dominic made French-sounding whoops. Will Lee, being small, shot out across the river as if catapulted. Tom somehow managed to step on and off the rope with the same air of indifference he might have had catching the bus on his way to school.

'Suppose we'd better get back,' said Nev with a sigh, after an hour of rope swinging and peace.

As Tom, Dominic, Will and I played a game of Monopoly that night, we could hear Nev and Mum talking in the cabin next door. This time, however, it was Nev doing most of the talking. 'Look at the woman who made me a cup of tea, after I almost caught hypothermia untangling the mess you made,' he said. 'That's the kind of woman I respect. Rather than interfering and criticizing the whole time, she was supportive and helpful. What good have you done on this holiday? You've gone out of your way to be as silly as possible; to try and do things you can't do just to prove a point. And it all went wrong.'

'I have to stand up for feminism.'

'Where were your feminist credentials when it was time to dive under the boat? Or are you going to tell me that's a man's job? Why didn't you prove the equality of the sexes when I almost froze to death untangling the ropes and drinking gallons of river water? It's got nothing to do with feminism. It's all about your ego and your silly, childish pride and your need to show everyone that you're the boss, even when you don't have a . . . a ruddy clue about what you're meant to be doing. You don't stand for anything. You just can't bear it when the attention is on someone else.'

We sat in the uneasy silence that followed.

'The main reason I wanted to get a scholarship to Westminster,' said Tom, as he bought the first hotel of the game, 'is so I can become a boarder and get away from these people. I was born into this family by mistake.'

'My muzzer,' said Dominic, 'she was to make sex with all of London in the time of the 'ippy.'

For the rest of the trip, our parents communicated with each other through a series of grunts. Torturing insects lost its appeal for Will and me while Dominic cried for most of the following night, tormented by homesickness. 'Imagine your family is just like ours, but a tiny bit worse,' Tom recommended. 'Then being here will become a whole lot more bearable.'

Nev let all of us boys drive the boat on the last three days of our water-bound adventure. Mum sat at the back, still with her nose in the air but now, if not exactly contemplative, then at least quiet. We never made it to the London of Dominic's dreams, turning back before we got to Richmond, but his guidebook did feature Windsor Castle, and we were heading straight for it.

'Regardez,' said Tom to Dominic, as the castle came into view. 'La Reine habite ici.'

'And now at the last time,' said Dominic excitedly, 'I am getting to see ze real England. Ze England of terrible wars and battles for ze power of ze throne.'

Tom looked at him and said: 'What do you think you've been getting for the last week?'

It was a bright day. Nev managed to moor the boat without causing any further damage. Dominic led the way towards the castle. A large boy in shorts walked past holding two Mr Whippy ice creams, which he took it in turns to lap at: Mum watched him go by, opened her mouth as if about to pass comment, and appeared to think better of it. An elderly couple in grey anoraks sat on a bench by the towpath, a foot away from each other, silently watching the river. Two boys played Frisbee with their father. A couple, younger than our parents, lay on the lawn outside the castle, throwing a gurgling, smiling baby into the air.

Dominic, at least, was happy. We were there for the Changing of the Guard, we went up the Round Tower that was built in the reign of Henry II, and we managed to get quite close to Queen Mary's dolls' house. A blue-rinsed authority figure shouted at me after I rapped on the breastplate of a suit of armour once worn by Prince Hal. Will Lee found a spider amidst the gilded splendour of the State Apartments. He picked it up by a leg and hurtled it towards a Van Dyck. Nev bought Dominic a guidebook. Tom informed the woman at the information desk that the guidebook contained an aberrant apostrophe.

Mum had a coffee and a cigarette in the café. She had taken up smoking again.

We arrived back at the boat harbour that evening. The man looked over the *Kingston Cavalier III* and kept saying 'Oh dear oh dear oh dear', shaking his head as he itemized the damages with Nev. He told Nev that the bill for repairs was likely to be around two thousand pounds. Nev raised a hand to his furrowed forehead and nodded. He looked at Mum, clenched his fist, and let it fall limply open.

As the man went into a small office to write an invoice we stood in a row, next to a poster on a shellacked fence that read: Luxury Leisure Boats . . . For the Ride of your LIFE!!

Will Lee tugged Nev on the shirtsleeve and said, 'This hasn't been an entirely successful holiday, has it, Nev?'

Nev wiped his brow, looked at Will Lee, and said: 'What makes you say that?'

3

The Wrong Chicken

'The Lees have invited us to a dinner party,' said Mum, who was attempting to decipher Hugh Lee's scratchy handwriting, written in fountain pen on the back of a self-portrait by Duncan Grant. 'It's in two Saturdays' time. I think.'

'Bugger,' puffed Nev from underneath the kitchen countertop, where he was trying to plug in a new dishwasher. As a gush of water poured out of the wall and onto the floor, Mum continued, 'Hugh Lee may be irascible, but at least he's fun, unlike most old men. What happens to men when they reach sixty? It's like they are wiped clean of what little personality they once had.'

'I wouldn't say that about your father,' said Nev, emerging from the recesses of the kitchen with soaked beige trousers and a spanner.

'In his case it could only be an improvement.'

Since returning from the boat holiday, the arguments between the parents had died down. Now they treated each other with cold civility. Nev got a promotion and

Mum moved to the *Sun*. She cooked a little – she had learned how to put lamb chops in the oven – and they sat around the table and talked about work, colleagues, politics, newspapers, religion . . . anything as long as it didn't reveal how they felt about each other. It took me years to realize most families only talked about the weather. Meanwhile, Tom held forth on his new privileged life at Westminster School.

'The head boy has the right to drive a flock of sheep across Westminster Bridge,' he said, bouncing his fork off a rubbery lamb chop. 'And we have a massive pancake fight called The Greaze. The cook throws the pancake up in the air and we scramble for a piece of it. The person who gets the most wins a gold sovereign and we all get a half-day, and if the cook fails to throw the pancake up high enough we're allowed to throw our Latin books at him.'

'What's the point in learning Latin?' I asked. 'It's not like you're ever going to go to Greece.'

Meanwhile, I was concerned that the topic of that lunch break's conversation at school had been the various animals my classmates had. Everyone apart from me seemed to have a faithful dog, an entertaining guinea pig or, in the case of Christopher Tobias, a parrot that could say 'bollocks' every time it saw an elderly person. There was a tabby cat who padded about in our kitchen every now and then, but that was it. I was feeling particularly miserable after scoring one out of ten in a mathematics test, so the lack of an animal in the house contributed to a wave of melancholy I believed it was the duty of the parents to do something about.

'I've been thinking,' I said, thumping the bottom of a

bottle of tomato ketchup until a tiny globule landed on my chop, 'can we get a pet?'

'No!' screeched Mum. 'What a horrible thought. What has an animal ever done for me?'

'Provided you with a lamb chop,' offered Tom.

'Pets are a suburban indulgence. It's not for the animal's sake that you have it, is it?'

'What about the smallest pet going, like a hamster, or a gerbil?'

'Not even an ant.'

The following weekend we visited Nev's parents. Min and Pop, as Nev called them, lived in Minehead in Somerset, in a 1930s house along a street so quiet you felt conspicuous walking along it. Before that they had lived in a similar house in Tadworth in Surrey. They moved to Minehead, on Granny's insistence and against the wishes of Grandpa, after he retired as a tax inspector. He had stayed in the same job, in the same office, in the same chair, for forty years. He would have stayed in the same house too, had he been allowed.

'Say what you want about Pop,' said Nev, as we drove down to Minehead, 'at least he sticks to his guns.'

Grandpa wasn't one for change. He only ate two things: bananas and baked beans on toast. He only liked one piece of music (the Hallelujah Chorus). His chief reason for wanting to stay in Tadworth, beyond his conviction that change of any kind could only ever be for the worse, was that he liked his garden. Granny, however, was resolute, pointing out that the house in Minehead still had a garden big enough to grow all the fruit and vegetables he wanted. Not that he ate them. Neither did Granny. She only trusted food if it came out of a tin. A few years later she found a house with a smaller garden. Then she made him move into a first-floor flat. Then he died.

On that trip, however, he was still going strong. He pressed 50p coins into my and Tom's palms, with the sense of occasion with which he had been doing it since we were four and six.

'Thanks,' said Tom, tossing the coin in the air. 'I'll open a Swiss bank account.'

'Good idea,' said Grandpa, tapping his nose with his index finger. 'Look after the pennies and the pounds will look after themselves.'

Sunday lunch consisted of cold meats and tinned vegetables in the pathologically neat dining room, among paintings of horses and scenes of rustic splendour, which was the closest Granny and Grandpa got to seeing the countryside; they didn't actually appear to like it despite living in it. If they did go for a rural outing it involved driving to a National Trust car park, sitting in the car, eating sandwiches from a Tupperware box, and driving home again. Mum mentioned we were thinking of going abroad for our next holiday.

'Wouldn't if I were you,' said Grandpa, cutting up his beans on toast into neat little squares.

'Why not?'

He stopped cutting his toast for a moment and looked up. 'Went to France once. Won't be doing that again.'

I decided to attempt to alleviate the mood with a joke. The one about the hairy bum had got a big laugh at the fireworks party.

'So she said . . .' and I held out my arms for the killer line, '". . . I've looked all over my Hairy Bum but I can't find my Willy."'

51

Granny made an indistinct humming noise. Grandpa poked bleakly at a tinned carrot. Tom shook his head. Eventually Granny held up a plate and said to nobody in particular: 'More Spam?'

For the rest of the afternoon we sat in front of the television, as Granny chewed on an endless stream of toffees from a bowl on a side table and Grandpa dozed off in an armchair. Eventually I asked Granny if I could have one of her toffees. She turned to Mum and said: '*May* he, Mummy?'

They watched football. Granny complained about the way the players all hugged each other when they scored a goal. They watched *Coronation Street*, and Granny wondered why television always had to be accompanied by such awful pop music. (I think she was talking about the theme tune.) Mum got her talking about newspapers for a while. Granny told us she didn't approve of the way men in the news wore their hair so long, but then journalism was not a place that attracted the right sort of people. Nev would have been much better off sticking to accountancy.

It was the night of the dinner party at the Lees' house. Hugh Lee answered the door in a cravat and jumbo cords, clutching a dusty bottle of wine, while Penny could be spotted in the kitchen, briskly moving from oven to hob. As Mum and Nev, looking young and garish against the muted colours and matured sensibilities of Hugh and Penny Lee, drank wine downstairs and talked loudly about how awful their parents were, Will and I disappeared into the attic. I looked through the stack of records leaning against the record player. Most of them were jazz and classical but there were a few interesting ones in there too, not least *Electric Ladyland* by The Jimi Hendrix Experience.

'Wow. They're a bit rough,' said Will, staring at the dank and gloomy cover of the album, with its photograph of naked women apparently made to look as bad as possible, as I took the scratched and dusty vinyl out of the inner sleeve and put it onto the record player.

'That's what I thought,' I said. 'Where did he get them from?'

'He shagged them all. You could do that in those days.'

The Sixties was another world, a world of terrifying, beautiful women in multicoloured clothes and dark, visionary men on cosmic journeys. It certainly wasn't much like the worlds I knew: of Granny and Grandpa's unspoken resentments; or the interiors' magazines-inspired colour schemes of 99, Queens Road; or even the discreetly wealthy good taste of the Lees. As the searing-knife guitar of 'Gypsy Eyes' was replaced with 'Burning of the Midnight Lamp's musical shrug detailing the end of a love affair, with Jimi Hendrix making heartbreak sound so very cool by the smiling way he says 'loneliness is such a drag', we sat on beanbags opposite one another, the record player between us, staring at the album spinning round and taking it in turns to hold the sleeve.

'He died, you know,' I said to Will. 'I heard a radio programme about it. Apparently he was killed by The Man.'

'Who is The Man?'

'Generally it's the government,' I said with a sigh, hands behind my head as I sunk deeper into the beanbag. 'In Jimi Hendrix's case it was the record company. They wanted to wall him in. Imprison his spirit. You can't tame a free bird like Jimi.'

'The 'suits', said Will, philosophically.

We nodded, solemnly and knowingly. We heard the sound of footsteps on the metal ladder.

'Is that The Man?'

It was Penny Lee. 'Hello, you two,' said Will's mother, with a bright smile. 'I thought I'd bring you some supper.' Somehow she had managed to carry up the ladder with her a tray with plates of baked beans on toast, glasses of apple juice, two bananas and a stack of Bourbons. And she had a dinner party to host. 'What *is* that bizarre music?'

'Jimi Hendrix,' I said. 'Do you remember him from when you were young, back in the olden times?'

'Oh, I was never one for the hit parade,' she replied with a brisk shake of the head. 'Do remember to clean your teeth, Will dear. They were rather green the last time I looked.'

For the next hour, from eating supper to listening to Jimi Hendrix to making a compare-and-contrast study of the women on the cover of *Electric Ladyland* with the ones in David Hamilton's photographs, we were entirely unaware of the disaster unfolding twenty feet below. It was only when I broke a ruler by whacking it on Will's head, after which Will told me it was the lucky ruler his elder sister had used to pass her A-levels and I had to go downstairs and confess to my crime, did we discover anything was amiss.

We saw Penny first. She was in the hallway on the telephone, eyebrows resolute as she gave the address of the house to the person on the other end of the line. From within the dining room, we could hear only groans.

'Mummy, Will's broken Catherine's special ruler,' said

Will, poking her in the stomach with one of its jagged edges.

'Not now, dear,' she said, in a tone that was, for her, perhaps a little brusque. 'We have a serious situation to deal with, I'm afraid.'

We went into the dining room. The guests, the women in Monsoon dresses and Liberty scarves and the men in tweed and corduroy jackets and tank tops, were leaning deep into old oak chairs, clutching their stomachs. Nev was laid out on the sofa, prostrate and sweating. At first I thought they had simply drunk too much red wine, as I had seen my parents and their friends do countless times before, but soon I realized this was different. Penny was rushing about making arrangements, and Mum was sitting cross-legged in a chair with a cigarette, but everyone else was in the throes of agony.

'It was the chicken risotto,' announced Mum. 'It's floored them all.'

'You seem to be all right,' I said.

'It takes more than a chicken to take me down.'

It was only years later that I discovered what had actually happened. Penny had two chickens in the freezer, one for the dinner party and one for Christmas. She had taken them both out, put one back, and momentarily put the thawed chicken where the frozen one had been. The results were much worse than the upset stomach food poisoning usually causes. It was salmonella. Everyone apart from Mum (whose fussy eating habits meant she hadn't actually had any chicken risotto) and Penny (who was too selfless to fall ill) was affected. Hugh roared and groaned and disappeared into the upstairs bathroom with a bottle of Châteauneuf-du-Pape. One woman went blind for a week.

55

Another became delusional and thought John Inman was sexually abusing her. It was a good thing Mum resisted the urge to write about the whole thing. Penny was a top-ranking civil servant in the Department of Health at the time.

I leaned over the sofa and looked at Nev, his glasses steamed up and his tight, dry lips taking on a worrying blue tint. 'Are you all right, Nev?' I asked, but he merely reached a thin hand out towards mine and made a rumbling noise.

'Honestly, trust Nev to get it worse than the rest of them,' said Mum, as I leaned over my father and wondered if this would be the last time I would see him alive. She touched up her lipstick before standing in the middle of the room and announcing, 'He'll do anything for attention.'

An ambulance pulled up outside silently, its ominous flashing lights heralding the seriousness of the situation. Nev, unmoving, was raised onto a stretcher, and a utili-tarian red blanket was pulled tightly and neatly over him. He looked like an Action Man in trouble. Mum told me she was going to travel with Nev to the hospital but that there was no need for me to go too. Ambulances came for two more guests, and the rest crawled off in various directions. With Hugh locked up in the bathroom, Penny was left on her own.

'Oh dear,' she said, still with a nervous smile, stacking up plates and putting them in neat piles next to the sink. 'Dear me.'

'It wasn't your fault, Mummy,' said Will, fiddling with a wine glass until he dropped it onto the floor with a yelp.

'I rather think it was,' said Penny, magicking a dustpan

and brush and sweeping away the shattered glass. 'It was frightfully silly of me to take the two chickens out of the freezer in the first place. I don't know what I was thinking.'

'I wouldn't worry,' I said, rifling through a box of After Eights on the table until I found one of the little paper sleeves still containing a chocolate mint. 'Nev will be fine. It'll be like the time we were in Richmond Park and he fell out of a tree and landed on his bum. He couldn't sit down for a week, but after that he was right as rain. I very much doubt it will have any lasting effects.'

Nev almost died. He was so severely ill that he slept for eighteen hours a day, and the act of getting up and going to the toilet exhausted him so much that he had to go straight back to bed again. That night, as he lay feverish in a hospital bed, Will and I played a game of peashooter tennis, listened to Jimi Hendrix do his fifteen-minute version of *Voodoo Chile*, and went to sleep.

Nev returned home a week later. It was Tom who broke the news, one afternoon when he came in from school. 'Nev's back,' he said, after opening the fridge and glugging orange juice from the carton. 'And he doesn't look good.'

Mum was out that afternoon, interviewing a celebrity, so I crept up to our parents' bedroom. Nev was lying in bed, motionless. He was extremely thin, and without his glasses his face took on an incomplete, mole-like aspect. The room was hot and airless. On the dressing table were three aluminium tubes with little labels on them.

'What are these?' I said to Nev, holding up one of the tubes.

In a barely perceptible whisper he said what sounded like 'I oo'.

'You what?'

He tried again. 'My poo.'

'Yuck!' I dropped the tube, and for a horrible moment I thought the top was going to come off and send Nev's diseased stool all over the new beige carpet. (I later saw the same aluminium tubes in the Lees' kitchen, where Penny had repurposed them as spice containers.) The effort of talking was too much for Nev. He looked worse for it. It was terrible to see my father like this. The man who built dens with us in the woods, who climbed trees with us, who slipped me £500 notes when I was losing at Monopoly, was wasting away. Too ill to talk, too ill to move, he was inching ever closer to death. This might be the last time I would ever see my beloved father. These might be the last words I ever spoke to him.

'Can I have a gerbil?'

I think he made some sort of a grunt of affirmation. Or it might have been the bed squeaking. It was hard to tell.

'Only I've been thinking about what Mum said about not being allowed a pet, and I've decided it would actually be a really good way for me to have some responsibility. And I noticed that there's some cash in the top drawer of your cupboard, and gerbils only cost about four pounds, so if you have no objections I'll just take a twenty and go and get one from the pet shop now. But it's totally your decision. If you don't think it's a good idea, say something.'

He didn't say anything.

The gerbil I chose was a tiny rat-like creature with a twitching nose and a nervous disposition. I knew when I saw him that he was the one: he was away from his little brothers and sisters in the cage, alone, clawing at the glass.

He needed me. I called him Kevin. With the notes I took from Nev's drawer I also bought a little cage with a wheel. Then, with the money left over, I bought *Smash Hits* by Jimi Hendrix. It was educational. Nev would have wanted it that way.

Kevin didn't appreciate his new surroundings. My bedroom was large, and my now semi-permanent Scalextric track looked like a raceway that had fallen on hard times: a grandstand only half painted, racing cars in the pit stop desperately in need of repair, and spectators missing limbs, although the last detail was a punishment from Tom in retaliation for stealing and losing then lying about stealing and losing his Sony Walkman. I had imagined Kevin would feel powerful in this miniature society in decline, but to my disappointment he scrambled under the bed the moment I released him from his cardboard box. Even the exciting sight and sound of cars going around the track wouldn't entice him out of his shadowy hiding place.

With Kevin unavailable, I made the most of my second purchase of the day. I put the two speakers of my little stack stereo system on the carpet, facing each other, and my head between them. The music was incredible. From the heavy rock of 'Purple Haze' to the tenderness of 'The Wind Cries Mary', it offered transports into distant lands. I closed my eyes and let the magic carpet ride of Jimi Hendrix take me on a journey.

'What is this shit?'

Tom was standing over me, the sleeve in his hand. His mouth turned down into a grimace as he held his head back. 'Good God, not Jimi Hendrix. This is the kind of hippy vomit the idiots at school listen to. I can almost smell the patchouli oil. Crap.'

'That's a matter of opinion.'

'No. Fact.'

'By the way, what's happened to your hair?'

Tom had undergone a radical transformation. Earlier that day, he had a floppy fringe befitting a public school boy who liked to walk around the grounds of Westminster School in his gown, spouting Ovid. Now the back and sides of his head were shaved and he had a big sprout of orange hair puffing out of the top, like a prize mushroom. He was dressed differently too. An oversized black jumper, black drainpipe jeans and brothel creepers had replaced the velvet jacket and bowtie he usually wore.

'What?' he said, glowering.

I stared at Tom for a while. I made sure he noticed my eyes going from the top of his head to the bottom of his feet. Then I put my head back between the speakers and, after a little chuckle, said, 'Nothing.'

'What, you little shit?'

'It's 'Hey Joe'. My favourite song.'

Tom attacked me. He knocked the record and the stylus made a horrible scratching sound. 'You idiot!' I screamed, in a much higher-pitched tone than I would have liked. 'If you've damaged it you're buying a new one.'

Tom got off me and turned his head in confusion. 'What was that?'

'What?'

'I just saw some sort of animal run out of the room.'

'Oh no. Kevin!'

As my terrible luck would have it, he ran into Mum and Dad's room. At least Nev would be too severely ill to notice him, and perhaps even me catching him, so I crept in. Mum was in there, alongside a man who was taking Nev's temperature and looking serious.

'The problem is that it has reached his blood stream,' said the doctor. 'It's rare to get it this badly. Has he been run down recently?'

'He's always had to watch his vitamin levels. He's got a weak constitution.' Mum crossed her arms and nodded, as if this diagnosis brought some sort of finality to the situation. 'Everyone else recovered ages ago. He's been overworked . . . By the way, this is my son Will. What is it, darling?'

I could see Kevin, twitching his nose underneath a small round table in the corner of the room. All I needed to do was encourage him to run back out again. Then I could grab him and put him in his cage.

As I moved towards the little table, slowly and sideways, like a drugged crab, I said: 'I . . . I just had to see Nev. I've been worrying about him so much.'

'Liar,' came Tom's voice from the other side of the door.

'Will, if this is one of your pranks . . .'

This required extra effort. 'It's not,' I cried, wobbling my voice and wishing for tears, although they never came. 'I don't want to lose him.' I turned my head away. Kevin was no longer under the table. I had no idea where he was. I sat down on the side of the bed and hid my head in my hands while secretly staring at the floor, watching out for a gerbil.

The doctor gave a deep, low sigh. 'This is a difficult time for your family. But I'd like to emphasize how in most cases like this the patient does pull through. The best course of action is to let your husband get as much rest as he can.'

Kevin was right next to the bed. It should have been achievable to just lean down and grab him, but I didn't want Mum and the doctor to see so I lay face down on the side of the bed and sobbed while stretching my arm out and inching it ever closer to the gerbil.

'Will, I know it's upsetting,' said Mum, 'but we really need to leave Nev to get as much peace and quiet as possible.'

Then she screamed.

'A rat!' She jumped onto the bed.

Nev groaned. I managed to get hold of Kevin, who bit me. I put him in my shirt and dropped him into his cage. Mum had to wait for the doctor to leave before she had the chance to come in and start yelling.

My twelfth birthday came while Nev was still in bed, woefully thin and exhausted by trips to the bathroom but no longer on the verge of death. He and Mum got me a BMX bike, which I had long dreamed of owning. Tom bought me a record. He hadn't bothered to wrap it up and it was second-hand; the album sleeve was ripped and over the price sticker in the top right hand corner he had scribbled 'Happy Birthday Scum'. It was *The Byrds' Greatest Hits*.

'Who are The Byrds?'

'Presumably you have heard of The Beatles? They're the American version, ergo, better suited to your limited intellectual capacity.'

Reader, I hit him.

With Nev out of action and Mum working late whenever she got the opportunity, we relied increasingly on a local girl called Judy to look after us. One afternoon when

Tom was out, an afternoon Will Lee and I had intended to occupy by building Kevin his very own adventure park out of Mum's new Salvatore Ferragamo leather boots and a few toilet rolls, Judy turned up with three other teenage girls and a Ouija Board.

'What's a Ouija board?' I asked.

'It's a way of contacting the spirits of the dead,' said Judy. 'You normally speak to people who used to live in the house you're in, but you never know who you'll find. We got the ghost of Jim Morrison once. Turns out he had a thing for teenage girls from Richmond.'

Will and I studied the board. It had ornate and slightly scary Edwardian etchings of a smiling sun, a frowning moon and some ghostly silhouettes. The letters of the alphabet were spelled out, and there were also the words 'yes', 'no' and 'goodbye', for the spirits to use when in a hurry.

I looked at this group of teenagers. Four girls, at a guess aged around seventeen, in pixie boots and legwarmers. They set up the board and argued about which one of them Jim Morrison's ghost had been talking about when he said she was 'well hot'. Will Lee and I hovered around them, poked our heads over their shoulders, and generally tried to get their attention.

'Leave us alone,' said one of the girls, after they turned the lights off and put a single candle in the middle of the kitchen table. 'We need to concentrate for our séance to work.'

As we left them to it, they put all of their hands together on the plastic heart-shaped object designed to move around the board.

'Voices from the Other Side, talk to us.'

'It's moving,' one of them shrieked.

On the other side of the door, meanwhile, we did our best to listen in. They could hear us sniggering.

'Go away.'

We stuck our heads round the door. 'What's happening? Found any dead people?'

'We've contacted a Victorian man called Bartholomew,' our babysitter replied. 'He had two wives and six children, although three of them died in childbirth and one grew up to become a whore in Islington.'

'What's a whore?' asked Will.

The girls refused to tell us, and for that reason we decided to play a trick on them. Nobody had got round to fixing the milk hatch that had broken off its hinges, so its little wooden door was simply jammed into position on the outside wall of the kitchen but not actually held on by anything. This would allow us our revenge. We went round to the side of the house and tried to listen to the girls' conversation with Bartholomew. It was impossible; only when they giggled could we hear them. So we waited until they weren't giggling. That would mean they were absorbed in a tense moment of Ouija board mysticism.

'OK,' I whispered to Will, 'one, two, three.'

We pushed the door of the milk hatch as hard as we could. We heard chilling, terrified screams. We ran round to see what had happened. The milk hatch had landed right in the centre of the Ouija board, smashing the plastic heart. The girls were standing up, away from the table, with widened eyes and their hands over their mouths. Pasty-faced suburban girls, they were even paler than usual.

'I'm never doing it again.'

'We're dealing with forces we don't understand.'

'We just asked Bartholomew a question,' said Judy, 'and that *thing* flew onto the table.'

'What was the question?' said Will.

The girls shuddered in unison. '"How did you die?"'

Without Nev to help me with homework, school became one form of torture after another. If it wasn't games – freezing on the brittle mud of a football field as a defender after being picked last, apart from Bobby Sultanpur who had one leg shorter than the other – it was science, with Mr Mott threatening to whack us with his paddle stick if we did so much as set fire to the annoying kid's blazer with a Bunsen burner. Music lessons were a waste of time altogether. Our teacher, Mr Stuckey, had a vague connection with Andrew Lloyd Webber, which meant that our school provided the boys for the choir in the West End production of *Evita*. About half of my class was in the choir. They got five pounds a night, they went up to Soho on a coach once or twice a week, and they had Mr Stuckey's full attention. He sat around a piano and trained the chosen ones while the *Evita* rejects had to sit in a cold, grey back room and amuse themselves in whatever ways unsupervised twelve-year-old boys could.

Art was appalling, but not because of the art teacher. He was a man with red hair and a beard in a fisherman's jumper who told us that Mrs Oates, our English teacher, who put on white lacy gloves before handling a piece of chalk and got emotional as she told us the word gay had been ruined forever, slept in the same bed as a cannon. It was years before we discovered her husband was Canon Oates, a high-ranking member of the clergy. Art was appalling because I couldn't draw or paint. The concept of perspective eluded me. You had to have *something* in school to be good at, even if you were diabolical at everything else. I might have scraped through English with a bit of dignity if it hadn't been for Mrs Oates and her horrific taste in literature. She considered *A Wizard of Earthsea* by Ursula K. Le Guin a masterpiece and dismissed *The Secret Diary of Adrian Mole*, which I had read over an afternoon of uncontrollable laughter, as vulgar. And sooner or later it always came back to the Bible, surely the most boring book ever written. The only lesson that was vaguely bearable was French, and that was because Mr Gaff had a fascination with combustion engines which meant that once you got him on the subject he would spend the entire lesson talking about them rather than the clauses and declensions he was meant to be concentrating on. It felt like a minor victory.

Worst of all was the comment I got when another ink-blot-stained exam paper came back scrawled in angry red marker pen. 'After your brother, you're a bit of a disappointment. Aren't you, Hodgkinson?'

If only those teachers could see the torments Tom put the rest of the family through. While Nev was still a silent and bedridden presence, Tom refused to wear the anorak Mum had bought him, even though the very air was soaked through. Fog and rain had turned the suburbs of London into a dark grey, mud-splattered pit of dirty concrete and squelching grass.

'For a start it's too big,' said Tom, throwing the anorak to the ground. 'Secondly, the zip doesn't work. And thirdly, everyone will laugh at me. You haven't been to school in thirty years. You don't know what it's like.'

'It's an anorak. Everyone else's mums will have insisted they wear one,' shouted Mum, picking it up off the floor and thrusting it back at Tom. 'You don't get picked on because of what you wear. You get picked on for not standing up for yourself.'

'And I'm not going to stand here listening to you. You're not sophisticated enough to know what it's like to be a scholarship boy.'

A week after the birthday party, I came home from school with the intention of going straight out on my BMX and heading over to the woods, where there was a stream in dire need of being jumped over. Then I saw Nev, sitting by our kitchen table, nursing a cup of tea. Mum was next to him. He looked peaceful, serene and frail. It was the first time in two months I had seen him out of his pyjamas.

'Hello, Sturchos,' he said, his old familiar grin back in place. 'How have you been?'

He looked older. Nev had always been a young dad, and young for his age – he was thirty-eight and he could pass for a decade less – but now he looked weathered, reduced. He was extremely thin, like a skeleton rattling about in jeans and a jumper, and the skin was stretched over his knuckles. His curly blonde hair was thin and neat; he must have had a haircut that afternoon. I told him I was fine except that on the day of my birthday the kids at school gave me the bumps – throwing you up in the air for as many times as match your age – and then, when the bell for the end of break went, they all ran off as the bumps hit twelve, leaving me to land on the ground with a thud.

'I'm afraid the same thing happened to me,' he said.

'Boys can be terribly stupid. The most important thing is not to let it affect you too much. You can't control the way other people behave, but you can control the way you respond to their behaviour.'

We chatted about how Nev had been feeling during his two months of serious sickness, as Mum looked at him in a way I hadn't seen before. She wasn't teasing and playful, as she had been with Nev when Tom and I were younger, and she didn't show the resentment and competitiveness that had made the boat trip so tense. She was genuinely concerned about him. There was some kind of affection there, like he was a friend who had gone through a hard time and it was her job to make him feel better. She brought him a bowl of soup as he tried to explain what it had been like to be so ill.

'In a strange way it felt positive,' he said, lightly. 'A lot of it was extremely uncomfortable, but all the pain, and being so sick, made me stop worrying about work for once. It forced me to take a breather. I realized how a lot of things that have been bothering me, such as not having a secretary or not getting my own office, aren't nearly as important as I thought they were. I guess the most significant thing is that it feels as if this illness has been telling me something.'

'Like, don't eat chicken cooked by Penny Lee?'

'I mean it's shown me something about my ego,' he said. 'It was taking over. And at the height of my fever . . . it was either a flash of light or total darkness, but for a moment I felt a sense of release from the weight of the world. It was beautiful.'

'Maybe you went to the Other Side,' I said breathily. I recounted the tale of the Ouija board, and Bartholomew, and the milk hatch flying onto the table. 'Now don't tell me that's a coincidence.'

Nev smiled, but in a strained way. He had been speaking in a slightly fey tone, which I found uncomfortable. It was like when I saw him talking to the burly dad of a friend and was gripped with the fear that he was about to challenge Nev to a fight.

'Anyway, Mum and I have got something we need to talk to you about.'

They looked solemn.

'You're not getting a divorce, are you?'

Mum was sending Nev off to Florida for a month to recuperate, build his strength up, and relax in a stress-free environment. He was to stay with a friend of a friend in a house by a lake in a place called, appropriately enough, Land O' Lakes. The friend of a friend ran the house as something of a retreat, inviting people to stay with them free of charge on the proviso that they use the time there for quietude and contemplation. 'He's not allowed to do any work,' said Mum. 'I'm not going to let him tell the paper where he is. It's going to be a total rest.'

'Sorry to rush off as soon as I'm able to talk to you,' said Nev. 'But this way I'll be able to recover properly and then we can do all kinds of things together. We can climb trees. Have conker fights. Build dens in the woods. Play games on the Atari.'

'I'll tell you what I'd like to do,' I said, thinking of a family ritual that hadn't happened in a while. 'I'd like us to bomb down to Brighton after having loads of spare ribs in the Royal China, spend the afternoon on the pier, have a pinball tournament, play air hockey and go on the beach and try to hit a rusty tin can with a pebble. And then we can stop off at a country pub on the way back to London and you can drink beer while me and Tom have a Coke and a packet of crisps. Can we do that again?'

'Of course we can,' said Nev, warmly. 'That sounds like fun.'

But we never did.

4

Nev Returns

While Nev was off in Florida, I made a new friend. Sam Evans lived in Hammersmith, West London, in a flat. All of my suburban chums lived in houses – not big houses, but houses nonetheless – so a flat seemed terribly cosmopolitan. You walked up a flight of stairs to enter the living room, where Sam's mother Erica slept on a bed that folded out of the sofa. Upstairs was Sam's room. He had a poster of Judge Dredd, a Commodore 64 computer and a large bookshelf with grown-up novels; apart from Tom, I had not come across a boy who had read *A Day in the Life of Ivan Denisovich* or *Animal Farm*. I poked my head into Sam's sister's room. It was phenomenally untidy: clothes piled everywhere, ashtrays – shocking in itself – and posters of David Bowie on the walls.

'Your sister looks cool.'

'Are you joking? Let's go downstairs and get Mum to make us some French toast.'

Erica Evans, who was American and wore oversized glasses and bright yellow dungarees, worked for something

71

called the Institute For Psychic Research. 'We're all psychic,' she said in a matter of fact way as she worked through a pile of papers on the dining table. 'It's just a question of unlocking the power within.' I told her about the Ouija board episode. 'Yeah, you get some pretty restless spirits with Ouija,' she said, nodding enthusiastically. 'Ghosts are dead people who haven't resolved their issues in this world, so they cling on to the living. Best not to mess around with that shit.'

Sam picked up a plastic bag full of white powder that was sitting on the top of a bookcase and said, winking at me, 'Are you selling cocaine again, Mum?'

'I realized this morning we had run out of washing powder and I didn't have time to go out and buy some more, so I asked one of the gay guys downstairs if I could borrow some. He was wearing incredibly tight jeans, and I swear, he had no penis whatsoever. I couldn't stop staring. I hope he didn't notice.'

I was incapable of contributing to this conversation.

It got worse, or rather, better, when Erica had to go out, presumably for a combination of cocaine selling, ghost hunting and the examining of tiny penises. Sam's flat had a video machine and he suggested we watch a film called *The Man Who Fell to Earth*. 'David Bowie plays an alien. Fancy it?'

'OK,' I said.

'It's got, like, a blowjob scene, but it's no big deal.'

'Cool,' I said, with a shrug. What was a blowjob?

It was like moving to a foreign country for the afternoon.

The television was on the floor, under the stairs, which meant that the best way to watch it was lying down.

Perhaps a family's discipline could be measured by the height at which they relaxed. At Will Lee's house, with the exception of the beanbags in the attic, stiff wooden chairs with high, straight backs kept you at a minimum of two feet off the ground at all times, which seemed unfair considering his mother was under five feet tall and had to climb onto them. In our house everything levelled out at a conventional foot and a half. At the Evans's, sitting above carpet level was for the unenlightened.

The film was made up of a series of exotic images, none of which I understood but which stayed with me for years afterwards: David Bowie watching a bank of televisions; wandering around an arid, distant planet; painted figures performing a ritualistic dance in a Japanese restaurant; and a sex scene with the aforementioned blowjob, something that before then I didn't actually know existed. As the months passed those images kept playing back at me, ever more jumbled and confused but still with vivid flashes, and always associated with the first time I saw Sadie Evans.

It was some time near the end of the film when she came up the narrow stairs and into the flat. She must have been about fourteen, the same age as Tom, but she looked older. She had lank reddish hair cut to her shoulders and pale, pimple-flecked skin. She was wearing denim jeans, a denim jacket, a studded belt and a Motorhead T-shirt. She hovered over us, hands on her hips.

'Who said you could watch my *Man Who Fell to Earth*?'

'Who said I couldn't?' Sam replied, not looking up at her.

'You're lucky,' she said with a curl of the lip, 'that I'm in a good mood.' She kicked her brother in the ribs. Sam yelped and called her an idiot. She cocked her head at me and said, 'Who's this?'

'I . . . I . . . I . . . I'm . . . Wuh-whu-whu . . . Will.'

'You will what?'

'That's his name?' said Sam, eyes raised heavenwards.

For some reason this appeared to annoy her, as she stomped off to her room. But halfway up the stairs she stopped, looked at me, and winked. She took the last remaining steps at a slow, steady, sashaying pace.

Half an hour later, the telephone went. It was Mum, telling me it was time to come home: Nev had returned. I left the flat as if in a trance, with only a hazy impression of taking the tube for the three stops from Turnham Green to Richmond, walking up the alleyway at the side of the station and bashing into a man who told me to watch out where I was going, then crossing Queens Road and getting honked at by the oncoming traffic.

I had met girls before. Not many, but I had, and I knew what they looked like and how they sounded. What was it about Sadie, a girl I had known for a total of twenty-six seconds, which caused this strange feeling?

Who could I talk to? Tom was out of the question. Will Lee was unlikely to be of much help. A boy that spent after-school sessions classifying fossils could not be expected to know the mysteries of love. Nev would surely know what to do and what to say. He had intimate knowledge of difficult women and it looked too as though once more he had the strength to take on his paternal duties. After I had crashed through the back door and opened the fridge to glug orange juice straight from the carton, I saw the family, sitting around the table, looking at me expectantly.

74

Nev was no longer a spectre of ill health. He was looking young and fresh in jeans and a colourful T-shirt that said Welcome to Florida, The Land of Sunshine. He was tanned and he had filled out, the edges taken off his angularity. He gave me a stiff hug before presenting a gift: my own Sony Walkman. This was welcome indeed. It meant I no longer had to steal Tom's and risk a beating. Nev got Tom an electronic baseball game. Now I would get to risk a beating for stealing that instead. Nev also had Levi's for both of us, explaining that Rick, the man he had been staying with, worked in the jeans business and gave them to him at a discount.

'But the most interesting thing about Rick is his religious beliefs,' said Nev. 'He belongs to an Indian sect called the Brahma Kumaris. They believe the soul is eternal and our bodies are just vehicles, which we pass through, one after another. They teach that we can return to our natural, soul-conscious state through stillness and concentration, while our actions in this life determine the destiny of the next. They also believe there was no Big Bang, but that the earth always existed.'

'How does that make sense?' said Tom, inspecting his new jeans. 'Everything has to come from something.'

'Oh, I know, it's way out stuff.'

There never was a chance that night to ask Nev what I should do about Sadie – the jet lag took hold and he passed out straight after dinner – but when Mum came in to make me stop listening to my new Walkman under the duvet, I said to her: 'Do you remember you once asked me if I had a girlfriend? Basically, I met a girl today and I really like her, and I think she might like me too.'

'Who is she?'

'Sam Evans's sister. Yes, she's older than me, and she's probably done all kinds of things I haven't, but there was a way she looked at me this afternoon that made me think, well . . .'

Mum took my hand in hers, and pushed my downturned chin upwards. 'You'll see her again soon.'

'Don't laugh, but I don't know what to say to her. I've never been in love before. And the thing is, I don't know what to do, because . . . I'm shy.'

Mum may have not laughed, but she definitely smirked. 'You just need to be nice to her. Give her a smile. Maybe there will be a time when you go round to Sam's that you can sit and talk. You're young. You don't need to do anything else.'

I nodded, and said, 'Thanks, Mum. Oh, and Mum?'

'Yes, darling?'

'What was that business Nev was talking about? Something about the Brother of Kuwaharas?'

'Take no notice. It's one of his fads. It'll be something else in a few days.'

It was after a trip to visit Aunt Angela and Uncle Richard, Nev's older sister and her husband, when I first sensed something might be afoot. After standing around and drinking orange squash on the clipped lawn and neat patio of Angela and Richard's house in Cheam, Surrey, we drove round to the new church the family attended every Sunday. A man with large glasses, a grey buttoned-down shirt and a clip-on tie played 'Amazing Grace' on a keyboard as members of the mostly white congregation clutched their breasts, clenched their eyes, raised their arms and generally looked like something was really wrong. One woman started howling. Another was crying. An old man rolled about on the floor until two young stewards in polyester shirts picked him up and led him away. Then the madness was over, almost as quickly as it began. Everyone filed through to the hall next door and chatted about the cricket.

Under normal circumstances, this would be fuel for our parents to devour in the car journey home; further evidence of the mania raging underneath the carapace of convention. But Nev stared at the road ahead with an odd, wistful air, even after Mum wondered aloud why born-again Christians had to wear clothes that made them look like they had just escaped from a mental institution.

'It's interesting,' said Nev, as we escaped the traffic lights of Cheam. 'All of those people looked so normal, like they could be working in the local tax office, but something happened in there that took them to another place entirely. You could see how whatever they felt was genuine. And yet I felt nothing.'

'It's the Holy Ghost,' I offered. 'When it calls you, there's nothing you can do.'

'What the hell would you know?' snapped Tom, who was slumped deep in the back seat, sullenly operating his electronic baseball game. He was sulking because he had planned to spend the afternoon on his ZX Spectrum home computer.

'I've seen things, Tom,' I replied, feeling a chill at the memory of the Ouija board. 'Things you wouldn't understand.'

That evening, I asked Nev to help me with the long division homework which, earlier in the day, I had denied the existence of. He calmly showed me a fail-safe system for doing it which my maths teacher had failed to explain, in terms which those not naturally gifted at mathematics could understand. He didn't get angry when it took me a few attempts to get the hang of it. 'It's only dull and unimaginative people like me who are good at maths,' he said as we crouched around my overcrowded desk and made space for sheets of long division. 'Creative people like you and Mum are entirely useless at it.'

'What about Tom? He's good at everything.'

'You can't compare Tom to a normal person. He has an enormous brain on a withered, feeble body, like the Mekon.'

Through the open doorway of my room I could see Tom. He was applying a soldering iron to his ZX Spectrum and muttering, 'When are these so-called computer experts going to invent something I can work with?'

Ever since coming back from Florida, Nev had been complaining about the medical trade it was his job to report on. 'They're so materialistic,' he said to Mum the next evening. 'It's like *Brave New World*.'

'What's wrong with that?' she replied, dishing out the sausages and mash while I read a copy of *2000 AD* and Tom scraped the dirt out from under his fingernails with a fork. 'I never understand it when people say *Brave New World* is a satire on a nightmare society. Everything is clean, you don't have children, the stupid people are kept separate and if you feel sad you just take a pill. It sounds ideal.'

'What I mean is, the entire health profession has become a drugs industry. Any kind of holistic approach to wellbeing is rejected as mumbo-jumbo by the medical establishment. It's very frustrating. We all know about the placebo effect, but doctors seem so resistant to accept that the mind can control the way we feel. Suggest that our frustrations, feelings and aspirations have an effect on our health, which I would say is common sense, and you're dismissed as a kook.'

'Like Prince Charles,' said Tom.

'Yes, but also anyone who says our health industry shouldn't depend on drugs alone,' Nev continued. 'It's the same as believing you only need a big house and lots of money to be happy.'

'That is ridiculous,' said Mum. 'You also need a decent hairdresser.'

Nev furrowed his brow. 'Anyway, the good news is that the paper is happy for me to report on alternative health and complementary medicine. Tomorrow I'm meeting a consultant pathologist from the Maudsley called Malcolm Carruthers. He approaches medicine as an art form rather than as a technical issue. The paper asked me to write a piece on twenty ways to save your husband from a heart attack, and I called up Carruthers. Do you know what he suggested? "'Tell your husband you love him."'

'What about twenty ways to save your *wife* from a heart attack?'

'Carruthers is also into meditation. He's asked me to attend a press conference on meditation at Westminster Abbey. This is interesting stuff and nobody is reporting on it.'

'What's meditation?' I asked.

'It's the art of training the mind to change your consciousness. Come on. Let's finish our meals. *Hammer House of Horror* is on in a minute.'

* * *

Nev's burgeoning interest in things that didn't involve spending weekends in tile warehouses didn't make much of an impression on me at first, chiefly because I had more pressing concerns. Sam Evans invited me to spend a weekend at his dad's house in the Wiltshire countryside. Mum forewent her world of work to drive me over to Erica Evans's flat one sunny Friday afternoon, where Erica's former husband would be arriving to pick up the children. Mum even came upstairs and accepted an offer of a glass of wine. Usually, she couldn't get away from her fellow parents quick enough.

'Will tells me Sam's got an older sister,' said Mum, eyes darting about the flat as she sat in the dining area with a raised chin and a professional smile.

'Yes, and she's going through what I believe is known as the difficult stage,' said Erica, as Sam and I collapsed onto the living room sofa bed and disappeared into copies of *2000 AD*. 'Everything I say and do right now is wrong. If I tell her off for smoking, if I tell her to tidy her room, if I dare to suggest that she gets off the 'phone to her friends and does a bit of homework for a change, she says she can't help her bad behaviour because she's a child from a broken home.'

'Oh yes, blame the parents.'

'What Sadie fails to take on board is that I couldn't bear to live with her father another minute.'

Mum sprang into action. 'It sounds to me like you did entirely the right thing,' she said, leaning over the table towards Erica. 'What's this obsession everyone has with families staying together and everyone having to be a couple? It's all so sentimental. As far as I can see, the family is the greatest source of misery and dysfunction in the modern age. I do honestly sometimes wonder why I had children. I suppose Nev and I were too young to know any better.'

There came an angry scream from above. Before we could see her, we could hear Sadie shouting: 'Mum! You *promised* to wash my jeans!'

She stomped downstairs. Gone were the heavy metal T-shirt and the studded belt of only a few weeks earlier. Sadie was wearing a red polka dot dress and had her hair in a bow. When she saw Mum, she stopped frowning.

'If you looked in the laundry basket, darling daughter, you would find your jeans all nice and clean,' said Erica, winking at Mum. 'And by the way, this is Liz.'

She walked over to Mum and held out her hand. 'Hello.'

Mum looked her up and down. 'Nice to meet you. I've heard a lot about you.'

Sadie looked at Mum quizzically and said, 'Really?' She glanced over at me and said, 'That's interesting.' Meanwhile, I hid behind my copy of *2000AD*. Mum said she had better be leaving, taking her big hair and clanking jewellery out of this world of batik tapestries and hanging macramé baskets. As she kissed me goodbye she smiled in an indulgent, almost pitying way and said, 'Have a lovely weekend. And don't forget, you're still young.'

'What's that supposed to mean?'

I never got the chance to find out because the doorbell rang even before Mum left the flat. It was Sam and Sadie's father. I had expected a bearded man in sandals, but the person waiting outside was a tall, stern figure in a dull tailored suit, with grey hair in a politician's wave topping deep lines in the forehead, a jutting chin and an angry nose.

'Well, come on then,' he said hotly to Erica.

'Do you want to come upstairs for a moment? Sadie's still packing.'

'No, I do not. I told you we would be leaving at six sharp and that is the time. Sofia is waiting in the car. It was your responsibility to ensure the children were ready.'

Sadie slouched downstairs with a holdall, hugged her Mum, and said, 'Thanks for washing my jeans. Sorry I shouted at you. I love you.' She pushed past her father.

He tried to take her bag. 'Sadie, I told you that we had to leave by six to miss the traf –'

'Oh, be quiet,' she snapped, as she wrestled her father away. 'The amount of times The Italian has kept *me* waiting.'

'The Italian' was an expensive-looking, chain-smoking woman in her mid-thirties who sat in the passenger seat and stared ahead as we got into the car.

We drove in silence, until Sadie told her father she had started Sociology O-level. He said it was a pointless subject. 'Well, you would say that, wouldn't you,' she replied. 'It helps the world to understand why people like you have taken all the money.'

Sam tried to engage his father in a conversation about politics. The Italian spoke to him in Italian, to which he replied falteringly. All the while, Sadie's hand kept creeping onto my thigh. She twisted her body towards mine and kept asking questions I didn't really have answers to, like, 'Your mother's a good looking lady, isn't she?' or, 'Do you like girls?'

'Stop embarrassing yourself, Sadie,' said Sam, who was staring out of the window, looking disapprovingly at the cars in the fast lane.

'Sitting next to me isn't embarrassing, is it Will, hmm?' she said, pushing my hair behind my ear.

I couldn't actually say or do anything. I was frozen. Close proximity to this impossibly exotic creature rendered me incapacitated. 'Your mother is far too lenient with you,' said their father, as I felt my mouth lock into a hideous rictus. 'The worst thing that can happen to a young woman is she gets a reputation for looseness.'

'Have you ever kissed a girl?'

Of course I hadn't. I was only just beginning to realize they existed at all.

With a sigh, Sadie turned the other way. Sitting in the middle of the back seat, the option of staring out of the window was not available. And The Italian was filling the car with smoke. There was little left to do other than focus on the lines on the motorway, and then on the twisting, hedgerow-shadowed curves of the dark roads that told us we were heading deeper into the wilds of Wiltshire. Eventually, we seesawed up and down on an uneven track and came to a halt.

I didn't have much knowledge of English country cottages, but this one fitted into whatever preconceptions of them I harboured. Its walls were made of Chilmark stone and its wooden porch was garlanded with roses. While The Italian sat in the car, Sam and Sadie's father reached up to a ledge above the door, said something about 'bloody people', and eventually pulled down a key, which he rattled furiously in the door until it creaked open. He went back to get The Italian, draping a coat over her head so the rain didn't put out her cigarette.

'Home sweet home,' said Sadie, throwing a bag and

then herself down onto an old sofa, its red canvas cover frayed and oily.

'It's damp,' said Sam. 'We need to get the fire going.'

As Sam and I built up a fire from old firelighters, yellowing copies of the *Telegraph* and piles of wood, then attempted to light it with sodden matches, I got a sense of the place. The room had worn rugs thrown over a cold floor, a large, soot-encrusted hearth, bookshelves with books that seemed to have grown into each other and a mullioned window looking out into the night. There was a dusty record player with a pile of records, but no television. Next to the living room was a kitchen with a huge sink and a fridge, but no dishwasher. Up the narrow stairs was a bathroom with a chipped, stained tub and a rubber shower attachment, but only two bedrooms. One had a double bed and one had two single beds, all tightly bound with threadbare sheets.

Which meant Sam and I would be sleeping in the same room as Sadie.

Surely two of us wouldn't be expected to share a bed?

'Give me a hand getting down this mattress,' Sam and Sadie's father said, craning his head around the bedroom door. He pulled down an attic ladder of twisted steel. 'You stay there and take it from me.' After disappearing into the black hole for about a minute, and shouting 'damn it and blast' after the sound of something smashing, a thin, ripped, dusty blue mattress appeared.

'Well grab it then!'

I yanked it through and lay it down on the floor between the two single beds. 'There are sheets in that cupboard,' said Sam and Sadie's father, gesturing manically. 'Blankets, eiderdowns and pillows. Can I leave you to it?'

An hour later, Sam and Sadie were in bed and I was on the mattress. And once the light was off Sadie began to perform a striptease. 'Duh-der-duh-da-da,' she went, pulling off her T-shirt before unclipping her bra and twirling it around her head and throwing it across the room. She was silhouetted against the moon shining through the lattices of the window.

'For God's sake, Sadie,' said Sam, pulling the pillow over his head. 'You are a cretin.'

'Will doesn't think so,' she said, poking her leg out from the eiderdown. 'Have you ever seen a woman naked before, Will?'

Twelve years old and thrown into confusion.

Somehow Sadie ended up in her pyjamas, so I felt it was safe to emerge from under the sheet and say: 'What are we doing tomorrow?'

'Tomorrow,' she said, 'I'm going to see my friend Spider.'

Sam and Sadie's father expected us to do the washing up by ourselves – in our family's system of washing, drying and putting away, it was generally assumed a parent would take on the washing role while Tom and I fought over the other two tasks – but this was the kind of unreasonable behaviour I was learning to expect from this man, especially after Sam told me a story about their summer holidays.

'We stay in a nunnery in Italy,' he said, instantly creating a vision of misery, as we washed up after breakfast. 'Every morning we have to make our beds. But then the nuns come along and strip the beds and make us make them all over again.'

'What's the point in that?' I asked, as I battled with an

old sponge and some ineffective washing up liquid to remove the last vestiges of omelette from a frying pan.

'It's meant to teach us responsibility.'

I had never heard of anything so stupid. Sadie appeared, still in her pyjamas. She told me Spider was a hippy who lived in the woods. The only hippy I had come across was a wild-eyed Rasputin type who wandered around Richmond in greasy flares and a corduroy jacket, carrying a broken guitar. It was years later I discovered he was Peter Green from Fleetwood Mac.

'Sounds cool,' I said. 'I love hippies.'

'Yeah, actually I kind of want to go without you and Sam, if you don't mind. So you should probably hang around the house and have a game of Monopoly or something.'

Ten minutes later she was in jeans and Wellington boots, running off into the woods. Sam said he knew where Spider lived. We pushed through dead leaves and broken branches, climbing over logs slippery with moist moss and kicking toadstools into oblivion until we came to a clearing. There was a house made of wood and tin, with a little chimney from which smoke billowed. A large blue van was parked up alongside a static caravan and an old ladder. A wheelbarrow and a few shovels were leaning against the house. At the other side of the clearing was a wooden stage.

'They built that last year,' said Sam, pointing at the stage, 'so they could hold crazy festivals where they all smoke cannabis and take their clothes off and roll around in the mud. Anyway, let's surprise them.'

We crept up to the door of the house, which creaked and groaned in the wind. Sam nodded and counted three, two and one with his fingers. We jumped in.

Sadie was lying on a low cushion/sofa-type arrangement, leaning against a man with an enormous frizz of hair and a Rajasthani waistcoat over his bare chest. At the far end of the room, where the stove was, an incredibly skinny man with dreadlocks and a greyish cut-off T-shirt with arm holes hanging somewhere around the waist was shaking a wok and dancing to reggae. Sadie exhaled a cloud of smoke from a badly made cigarette in our direction.

'Aren't you wondering how we found you?' asked Sam.

'Not really,' said Sadie, nestling deeper into the cushions as her head settled on the frizz-haired hippy's chest.

'Sit down,' said the hippy, making a benign gesture with his scrawny little arms. 'Join us.'

Introductions were made. Spider was on the cushions and a man called Sandra was doing the cooking.

'Why have you got a girl's name?' I asked Sandra.

'We have no genders here,' he said, droplets of sweat trickling from kinky armpit hairs and landing in the wok.

Spider had built the house himself. He spent about half the year on the road, either in Europe or at festivals around the country. He and Sandra were musicians of a sort; there was a guitar, some bongos and a flute lying about. At the front of a stack of records was one with a teenage girl, naked from the waist up, staring out of the album sleeve and holding a toy airplane.

'What kind of music do you like?' I asked.

'Just good music,' said Spider, nodding gently, as he rolled a cigarette.

'I like Jimi Hendrix.'

'Cool, man. What's your favourite record?'

I thought on this a while. '*Smash Hits.*'

'Grub's up,' said Sandra, sticking a bony finger in the wok, licking it, nodding, and sticking it in again. That seemed like a good time to make our excuses and get the hell out of there.

In the evening The Italian sat in the kitchen, reading *Vogue* and smoking cigarettes. Sam and Sadie's father cooked chicken. Sam and I started on a game of Dungeons & Dragons and Sadie spent a very long time in the bathroom before coming downstairs to paint her nails by the fire. When Sam and Sadie's father asked 'you children' to lay the table, Sadie raised her eyes and stomped over to clang down a few knives and forks while Sam did the plates and I did the glasses. Over dinner, The Italian smoked and ate at the same time while Sadie poked at her food and Sam complimented his father on an excellent chicken.

'What do your parents do, Will?' asked Sam and Sadie's father.

'Journalists.'

'Ah,' he said, raising his eyebrows as he poured wine. 'The Street Of Shame. Did they want to be serious writers and not quite have the skill for it?'

'I don't know, actually,' I said. 'I've never asked them.'

'That's pretty rude, Dad,' said Sadie. 'I don't think being a lawyer gives you a right to act all superior.'

'Being a father gives me the right to deserve a little more respect from you.'

'In Italy,' said The Italian, 'children worship their mothers and fathers.'

'Tell that to the Borgias.'

After supper, a miracle happened: everyone went to bed except for Sadie and me. She put a record on the turntable sitting on the floor near the fire: it was *Hunky Dory* by David Bowie. 'This is for sure my favourite record of all time,' she said, gazing at a sleeve featuring a hazy image of a feminine creature clutching golden hair, elbows raised. 'He's a genius . . . listen to this.'

She sat with her legs tucked underneath her, on the rug, holding the sleeve. I nodded solemnly for a minute or so as Bowie sang about the changes we were all going through.

'Sadie, I . . .'

She stopped me before I began, holding up a finger and widening her eyes. Only when the song finished, and she took a deep breath and kept her eyes closed for a good few seconds, did she speak.

'The thing about David,' she said, 'is I've always known he's speaking directly to me. Listen to this song. It's called 'Oh! You Pretty Things', and . . .' she nodded her head rapidly, 'I happen to know he actually wrote this about me. It's a personal message, telling me how people like my dad have had their day and now it's the turn of the switched-on girls to take over the world. Maybe my mum met David at, like, a Buddhist retreat or something.'

Sadie handed me the sleeve so that she could listen in meditative respect with her eyes closed. The album came out in 1971, when Sadie was three. I supposed it was possible he wrote it about her.

'The point is,' she said loudly, somewhere around the second chorus, 'my father doesn't love me. If he did he would never have run away with that awful woman. So why should I listen to him?'

'I'm sure he does really. Maybe he's, like, an uptight square.'

'You've got that right. Oh my God. My favourite song is coming up.'

This was 'Life On Mars', and although I had absolutely no idea what Bowie was going on about, with the story of the girl with the mousy hair, lawmen beating up the wrong guy and sailors fighting in the dance halls, Sadie dissolved into tears. I would have put my arm around her had I dared, giving her the kind of consolation of which only twelve-year-old boys are capable.

'Nobody understands him,' she said through sobs. 'Nobody apart from girls like me. We know how he feels because we feel the same way.'

'I think,' I said, trying hard to look solemn, 'I think I understand him too.'

The only thing disturbing this scene of perfect wonder and excitement was the image of Sadie sidling up to the hippy in the tin hut. I asked her if she had a boyfriend.

'Not really,' she said with a sigh. 'Too much trouble.'

After a pause I said: 'What about Spider?'

'You must be joking.'

If only I could think of something to say. I edged towards Sadie, but the record ended and she turned it over. That meant I had to sit there and appreciate the brilliance of David Bowie's message of love on 'Fill Your Heart' and the wit of his tribute to Andy Warhol, whom I had never heard of, but Sadie said he was a very cool artist from New York, as she explained to me every nuance of every song. After agreeing with everything she said, I resolved to think of a line to move our romantic involvement onto the next level. An older boy at school had told me you could get any girl you wanted as long as you kept the conversation going. She sat on the rug and leaned on one hand with her head tilted downwards, a picture of soulful introspection. She looked thoughtful, serene. Her sad eyes looked up and caught mine. They stayed there for a world out of time. They dropped down. She was younger, child-like, no longer an untouchable goddess but a teenage girl, reaching out for a connection. This was the moment. This was my chance.

I had to say something profound. 'Do you know how much my Dungeons & Dragons starter kit cost? It was almost twenty pounds. I saved up my pocket money for three months.'

Sadie looked at me.

'I think I'll go to bed.'

I decided not to share details of my thwarted romance with anyone, and went home to discover Nev in a state of excitement. The scene was normal enough. Tom, in ripped black drainpipes and a loose white T-shirt he had attacked with scissors, was leaning on the back legs of a chair by the kitchen table. Mum was unpacking an Indian takeaway with one hand and with the other, passing through the pages of the *Sun* in search of her byline. She even managed to kick away the tabby cat that had wandered in. Nev, meanwhile, had a lighter-than-air look, one I hadn't seen before. He was spooning pilau rice onto his plate in a distracted fashion.

'Ah, Sturch,' he said. 'I'm so glad you're back. I've had the most amazing experience. I have to share it with you.'

'Here we go,' said Tom.

Nev explained how he had gone along to a press confer-ence about meditation at Westminster Abbey. The Reverend Edward Carpenter, Dean of Westminster, was in conversation with an Indian swami on the nature of the soul, and they were comparing Christian and Indian mystical perspectives. The swami was expounding on the benefits of a practice called Siddha Yoga, and at the end of the conference there was a meditative chant of the words 'Om Namah Shiva', which translated as 'I bow before the God within'. An acolyte with a squeezebox sat before the swami and made a droning melody that was similar, said Nev, to the one used to invoke the aliens in *Close Encounters of the Third Kind*. Then there was a silent meditation that lasted for five minutes. That's when it happened.

'In those five minutes of silence, a golden red light poured down into the centre of my forehead,' said Nev, wide-eyed at the memory. 'It was absolutely stunning. The bliss that accompanied it was unlike anything I had ever experienced in my life before. It was so concrete. It was like a flower opening out, bright yellow. I could see it, as if it was absolutely there. Tears poured from my eyes. I was transported.'

Nev told us he paced the streets for two hours afterwards. 'When I eventually did get back to the office, I looked in *Gray's Anatomy*. I thought there might be a physical explanation for this. But there wasn't. This thing was like nothing I've ever come across. In that moment it was as if I saw a glimpse of life as it is meant to be lived; as if everything else, from our bodies to our possessions to the earth itself, is just a stage set.'

'I still think you haven't recovered properly from your illness,' said Mum, licking a finger and turning the pages of the newspaper. 'You know your constitution has never been very strong.'

'It's essentially a Platonic idea,' Tom declaimed, his eyes closed and his teeth jutting forwards goofily. 'The world of the senses is the world of lesser men. The enlightened see physical objects as mere shadows of deeper truths. And Socrates taught how reality is unavailable to those that use their senses. The annoying thing is, I always thought if anyone in this family would receive enlightenment and divine flashes of inspiration and open the doors of perception, it would be me.'

I certainly didn't appreciate the significance of Nev's epiphany at the time, and besides, an incident at school convinced me that he was going to forget all about his golden lights and transporting flowers in order to pick me up and throw me against a wall. Ever since the time I got caught copying Bobby Sultanpur's homework I had been waiting for Nev to lose it, to make me wilt under his mighty paternal wrath. This looked like it was going to be the moment.

It was during a game of football. As usual, Sam Evans and I found ourselves cast out as defenders, shivering in the cold mud of the pitch, away from the action, talking about Judge Dredd and hoping the ball didn't come anywhere near us. We were discussing Dredd's recent trip to the mutant wastelands of the Cursed Earth when a boy from a rival school sped past us and swept towards the goal, thereby angering our entire team.

'You're a pair of statues,' shouted the team captain, a boy called Tucker. 'You're untrainable, useless and lazy. And you've just lost the game for us.'

'It's only half-time,' I pointed out. 'Don't be so defeatist.'

He marched up and pushed me over into a puddle of mud. Mr Block, our games teacher, witnessed the whole thing. He was standing nearby, rain splashing off his egg-shaped head.

'Sir!' I shouted. 'Tucker just pushed me over for no reason.'

'Get up, Hodgkinson,' Block shouted. 'Go to the changing rooms and bring out the half-time oranges. And take your 'girlfriend' with you.'

The entire team brayed like donkeys. We ran off and vowed to take our revenge somehow, when Sam suddenly stopped.

'Hey, here's our chance for revenge.'

Between the playing fields and the changing rooms was a copse of trees with a muddy pathway cutting through it. Next to the pathway was an abandoned coil of twine, presumably used for some sort of sporting activity. 'Tucker always pushes everyone out of the way to make sure he's first back to the changing rooms,' said Sam. 'Why don't we give him a little surprise?'

We tied the twine between two trees on either side of the path, about a foot from the ground, and ran in to get the half-time oranges. Sure enough, after we lost the game by letting two more goals get past our defences, Tucker, having punched Sam and me on the arm by way of punishment for our lackadaisical approach to competitive sports, ran ahead of everyone. The plan worked perfectly. He tripped over our twine and fell into the mud, knocked down like a skittle. He raised a grim, defeated head and wiped the grime from his face to see everyone laughing at him – everyone, that is, apart from Mr Block. The laughing stopped. Block told everyone to gather round.

We shuffled towards him, a motley mass of dirtied, bloodied knees and spotty red faces. Some of the boys looked like junior Hulks, subject to sudden growth spurts; others were still twig-like and androgynous. I was somewhere in the middle, a beanpole who had sprouted upwards with no muscle development of which to speak.

'Who did this?'

Nobody said anything.

Block crossed his arms and spoke slowly in his blunt Yorkshire growl. 'Do you know what happens when you play tricks like this? First boy trips over trip wire. Second boy, carrying pointed corner flag, trips over first boy. Result: dead boy.'

'Sir,' I said, perhaps not realizing the seriousness of the situation, 'is that the first or second boy who's dead?'

After Block had grabbed me by my ears and pulled me towards him while telling everyone else we would be doing nothing but squat thrusts and press-ups for every games lesson until the end of term unless the culprits owned up, Sam Evans and I had no choice but to confess to our crime. We thought our teammates would agree Tucker had it coming, but it seemed they were on his side. 'He could have been killed,' said one boy. 'I can't believe you two are so immature,' said another. Tucker himself put it best. 'Just because you've failed in life doesn't mean you have to take it out on those who haven't.'

Our parents received 'phone calls before we even managed to make it home. The word 'suspension' was muttered in authoritarian circles, but it got downgraded to a detention. I could only imagine how Nev was going to react.

Nev was already at 99, Queens Road, which made it worse. Mum was there as well, the tips of two fingers in her mouth. Nev looked distracted, distant, and Mum looked worried, like they had just been discussing a plan of action. Perhaps, if I did all my homework, didn't steal anything, told no lies, went to bed when I was told and didn't even turn the lights back on after I thought Mum had gone downstairs, I could escape the black cloud of shame after a week or so. That was the best I could hope for.

'I know what you're going to say,' I began, holding my arms out as I sat down at the kitchen table. 'And I want to point out that it wasn't my fault. And I've been punished already.'

'Yes, yes,' said Nev, absently. 'We must be careful not to hurt each other.'

Mum looked more worried than angry, which wasn't like her. After it became clear Nev was going to say nothing further on the subject, I said, 'Is that it? Aren't you at least going to shout at me and send me to my room?'

'We all make mistakes, Sturch.'

'Nev's got an announcement to make,' said Mum. 'It's come as much of a shock to me as it will to you.'

'What is it?'

Nev looked extremely pleased with himself.

'I've given up my job.'

5

Enter The Brahma Kumaris

At first, Nev's new status as a willingly unemployed man didn't make a great deal of difference. The main change was that he was at home when I came in from school, in his little study at the back of the house, where not so long ago he had shot a pigeon with an air rifle. And despite no longer having a job or earning any money, he was busy. He was not to be disturbed when he was in his office, which was filled with stacks of loose papers, filing cabinets, and shelves of books on alternative health and complementary medicine. He was, he told us, writing his first book. It was going to be called *Will to Be Well*. It was about the power of the mind over the body.

Beyond providing Nev with the inspiration to give up his job and launch a new career as an alternative health author, however, the experience at Westminster Abbey didn't lead to anything much at first. One weekend Mum and Nev took up an offer by Malcolm Carruthers, the doctor who had originally invited Nev to the press conference on meditation, to spend a weekend's retreat at a

Siddha Yoga centre. 'It was bizarre,' said Nev on their return, as he and Mum took off their matching mackintoshes and paid Judy, our Ouija-board-consulting babysitter, who had taken up the opportunity to look after us for the weekend by inviting thirty other teenagers to the house. 'There were all these people making train noises, and rocking backwards and forwards, as the swami chanted away. I suppose it was about being spiritual.'

'They weren't so spiritual as to not take credit card payments, though,' said Mum, rearranging the messy pile of coats on the hat stand. 'We had to pay all this money to do the course in the first place, and then they charged extra for meals. I hated it. It was so *boring*, not to mention expensive. We won't be doing that again.'

While it was never fully explained to Tom and me, we slowly discovered the rationale behind Nev giving up his well-paid job at the *Daily Mail*. 'After what happened that day in Westminster Cathedral I couldn't possibly go back,' he said. 'It's an arena of empty goals and pointless rivalries, where people jostle for power without even knowing why they're doing it. It's a treadmill of misery. And the *Mail* is a horrible paper in many ways. It panders to and encourages insecurities and prejudices. After seeing a brighter horizon, it felt like I was living a lie.'

'That lie helped pay for this house!' snapped Mum, who was pushing her food around the plate in the manner of a fussy child. And that was another change: the food. Gone were the French-bread pizzas and beans on toast. Now Nev clocked off at around five and spent the next two hours cooking from scratch. We had aubergines and red peppers stuffed with cracked wheat; nut roasts you could build a house with; and lentil stews as murky and as

98

unfathomable as the changes going on about us. Today we were having something called dhal, which was a little like Polyfilla.

The change in food began after Mum came back from a research trip to a factory farm. She described seeing rows of newborn veal calves crammed into cages no bigger than their bodies, kept in darkness and denied everything but liquid feed. The subsequent series of articles she wrote about the experience were key in highlighting the inhumanity of mainstream farming: before then, even free-range eggs were seen as the preserve of cranks. It also made Mum suggest we might think about giving up beef.

'But you hate animals,' said Tom.

'It doesn't mean I want to eat them,' said Mum. 'I feel the same way about meat as I do about giving up smoking. I haven't had a cigarette since the evening of Hugh and Penny's dinner party, and it's been the hardest thing I've ever done. For three months I thought I'd die. But then, suddenly, I wasn't smoking anymore. Now I'm looking around to see what else I can give up.'

There was a health food shop at the end of our street, run by a thin woman the colour of porridge. Nev took me there one afternoon after school. He bought grains and pulses, which were stored in large wooden barrels, by the kilo load. As a special treat he bought me a piece of natural liquorice; a knotty stick you chewed on to bring out the flavour. He also ceremonially presented me with a Carob bar, which was some kind of chocolate substitute.

'Can't I just have a fun-size Mars Bar?' I said, staring bleakly at the promise of nutritional goodness.

Nev gave me a wide-eyed look. 'This is really healthful and positive,' he said lightly. 'And it tastes beautiful.'

The porridge-coloured lady nodded in agreement. 'None of those nasty E-numbers you get in mainstream confectionery enterprises,' she said, leaning against a large cork pinboard offering zero-balancing courses in East Sheen, mother-and-baby yoga sessions in Twickenham, and a free seven-day meditation course in Raja yoga from the Brahma Kumaris in Kew. I pulled this last one off the board.

'Weren't these the people you stayed with in Florida, Nev?'

Nev took the leaflet from me and peered at it. 'So they are,' he said. 'Such nice people. I really must drop in on their centre here some time.' He folded up the leaflet, put it in his pocket, and I assumed that was the last of it.

Two weeks later, Nev announced he and Mum were going out. 'I don't think we need to get Judy, do you?' he said. 'We'll be back by nine.'

They were dressed soberly for a night on the town. Nev had never been flamboyant, but in his dark blue jumper and tweed jacket he looked older, more staid. Mum generally piled on the make-up, volumized the hair, and dress-coordinated as advised by a company called Colour Me Beautiful, but this time she was wearing a long skirt and a jumper in muted shades of beige, augmented by a few pieces of chunky jewellery.

Tom, who had just got one of his ears pierced, was lounging on the chaise longue, reading George Orwell's *Keep the Aspidistra Flying*. 'If we get attacked by burglars,' he said, 'we'll throw last night's lentil bake at them.'

'I see you've got your left ear pierced,' I said, staring at the angry red sore around the little golden stud, such an invasion on Tom's young, unformed flesh.

He made one eye look away from his book. 'I see your powers of observation have improved.'

'Doesn't that mean you're gay?'

He didn't credit me with an answer.

'An earring in the right ear means you're an anarchist,' I continued. 'The left ear means you're a gaylord.'

'It's the other way round, you cretin,' he said, and the book rose over his face.

'You're not going to fight the whole time, are you?' said Mum. We assured her we wouldn't. We would ignore each other like we normally did. As soon as the door closed Tom got up, said, 'I'm going into my room. Keep out, or else,' and stomped upstairs. I went to my own room, put on *Strange Days* by The Doors, and closed my eyes as my head came to a halt on the carpet between two speakers.

It must have been ten minutes later when the door of the bedroom yawned open. 'God, no,' said Tom, baring his teeth in a display of proud contempt in much the same way as a baboon displays its bottom. 'Jim Morrison, the man with the smelliest trousers in rock. They were made of leather and he didn't believe in washing. Disgusting.'

I raised my head. 'What do you want?'

He sauntered over, grabbed me by the arm, and attempted to twist it backwards. Thankfully, Tom's intellectual brilliance was in contrast to his physical strength, and it didn't take much to pull him round and wrestle him to the floor. 'Stop being such a bender,' I said as Tom writhed about on the carpet, looking like a spinal cord with limbs. 'Just because you've got your ear pierced doesn't mean you have to take out your inner gayness on me. Borrow Kevin if you're desperate.'

'So Mum tells me you've got a crush on your friend's older sister. You don't seriously think you stand a chance with her, do you?' His voice took on a tone that managed to convey disgust, pity and amusement. 'You can't expect a hot chick like that to pay any attention to you.'

'What do *you* know? We had an amazing night together as it goes. We listened to David Bowie by the fire and then we got off with each other, with tongues and everything.'

'You're lying, you lying liar. You lie so much you don't even know you're lying.'

'Oh yeah? Well, you're never going to get anywhere near her, except maybe as her hairdresser.'

That infuriated Tom enough to lunge at me. I picked up an enormous rubber snake that St Neots' Granny (our mother's mother, who lived in St Neots') had bought me years earlier on a visit to Whipsnade Zoo and flung it at him. He gritted his uneven teeth and, with a strength that surprised even him, grabbed the snake with both hands and ripped it in two. There was a moment's silence.

'What have you done to my snake?'

I ran at him, screaming, and went for his throat. He shook me off and grabbed the wardrobe, bringing it crashing down. It landed on my stomach and pinioned me to the floor, with only my hands and feet sticking out from beyond its rigid MFI contours. Strangely enough I don't actually remember it hurting very much, but I was wheezing from the shock of it. I felt Tom needed to learn a lesson, so I stopped wheezing, or making any sound whatsoever. There was a moment of silence.

'Will? Are you all right?'

He found it much harder to pull the wardrobe off me than he did it to push it down, but in his panic he managed it. I lay prostrate, making only a faint rasping sound, a little like Darth Vader's breathing.

'I've killed him. Oh God, I've killed him!'

I could hear him running screaming downstairs, and that's when the front door must have opened because Tom was giving a frantic explanation to our parents. Within seconds, Nev had his hands on my shoulders. His reassuring, gentle voice was in my ear, saying, 'Sturch, are you OK?'

'I . . . think . . . I can just pull through . . .'

'What's going on?' Mum said to Tom, the acidic inflection rising in her voice. 'We leave you alone for one moment . . .'

Nev closed his eyes and raised a palm. 'Wait a minute. If we have learned anything tonight it's that fighting solves nothing. You both need to tell us calmly what you have been arguing about.'

We explained. 'But it *is* the left ear that makes you gay, isn't it, Mum?' I said, and Mum told me it was neither here nor there and we should stop acting like silly little children, and if Tom had something to tell her he could do it in his own time. Nev stood in the doorway, holding his long chin in his hands, nodding every now and then. Eventually he spoke.

'There's not enough love in this family,' he began. 'We're so needy, so wrapped up in our own hang-ups, that we have lost all perspective. We fly off the handle at the slightest provocation. You remember that awful boat trip?'

'How could I forget it?' said Mum. 'We were tearing strips of flesh off each other. Strips of flesh!'

'That was symptomatic of our resentful and co-dependent behaviour,' Nev continued. 'We must all learn to approach life with a little more rationality, as if we're actors on a stage, playing a role. I'm going to make sure I spend more time with the boys. I want them to know they're loved. Will was almost killed tonight. This cannot go on. Well, goodnight.'

For the most part, I had no idea what he was on about. But the following evening he revealed that he and Mum had gone to an introductory class with the Brahma Kumaris. A couple of days after seeing the Brahma Kumari leaflet in the health-food shop, Nev had met one of them at a conference and, learning that they were an Indian spiritual group run entirely by women, thought they might make an interesting subject for Mum to write about. She landed a commission for *She* magazine, and went to the suburban house they operated from while Tom ripped apart my snake and tried to kill me. She was there to interview them but, unusually, Nev had decided to go along too.

'It's a very peculiar thing,' he said, as he sliced the bread he had been making all afternoon. I didn't even know you could make bread. I always assumed it came in a plastic bag. 'Liz was there, taking notes and talking to these friendly, gentle Indian women, but I was transfixed. There was something about the vibration of peace, the positivity, which suggested these people have a deep contentment inside them that I'm missing. They have all kinds of crazy ideas about evolution being wrong and time being cyclical, which is clearly a load of nonsense, but it's the *feeling* I got from them that hit me. They teach how meditation helps return us to our natural state, which is soul consciousness, and how all the troubles we suffer through on a daily basis are the result of us getting attached to the physical world of desire.'

'Are you telling me an earthquake that wipes out towns and villages and kills hundreds of people is the result of attachment to the physical world?' said Tom.

'Ah, but how do people react to that earthquake? Do they wallow in misery and want to kill themselves because it's destroyed their homes, or do they accept that physical things are transient and all things must pass? Do they grieve forever for the loss of their loved ones, or do they accept that we all die sooner or later? The Brahma Kumaris have got me thinking completely differently about my approach to life. I'm beginning to see there is a difference between love, which is selfless and giving, and attachment, which is selfish and draining.'

Being only twelve years old, and having been brought up in a household where until recently the closest we got to religious experience was listening to Mum sing along to 'Songs of Praise', I wasn't quite ready to take this in.

'You've got to admit, Nev, if an earthquake came along and destroyed everything and killed everyone you know, you wouldn't be very happy about it,' I said. 'By the way, what's that you're drinking?'

'Elderflower juice. Mum and I have decided to give up alcohol. Just as an experiment.'

The South London centre of the Brahma Kumaris was the front room of a small, modern, semi-detached house in Kew. It looked like the kind of house one of our relatives would live in: crazy paving leading to stone flowerpots in the shape of Roman urns on either side of the frosted-glass door; a small, clean car in the drive; neatly clipped fuschia shrubs and rose bushes forming a square around a front lawn you knew nobody ever sat on and rarely even walked on. Nev had announced we were going to visit as a family, so we could all properly meet the interesting people he had been connecting with recently. Tom had an essay on *Candide* to write and I had a bunch of improper fractions to freeze my brain with, but Nev waved away our protestations with a flutter of the eyelids, telling us we would learn more from a few minutes of meditation than we would from a whole term's worth of education, which was certainly a new concept. Nev rang the doorbell. It made a gentle 'ding . . . dong' sound.

A fresh-faced woman in a white sari answered the door. She had a wide, open smile and her blonde hair was tied back into a ponytail. 'Om shanti,' she said. 'You must be Tom and Will. Please come in.'

The first things I noticed were the shoes. There were at least ten pairs, loosely lined up on the thick carpet next to the wall of the hallway. 'Dadi Janki flew in from India last night and she's already started on the lesson for the day, which we call the *murli*,' said the woman. 'But if you'd like a drink first, we have some squash.'

'I'm cool,' said Tom, raising a palm.

We took off our shoes and went into the living room. There were bay windows, a cheap imitation chandelier, a heavy three-piece G-Plan suite upholstered in brown felt and a polished sideboard with photographs in plastic silver frames of two Indian children. On the wall was a red plastic egg with a pinprick of light emanating from its centre. Sitting underneath the egg, cross-legged, was a small, solid-looking Indian woman. There was no way of guessing how old she was. Her hair was a mix of grey and black and her hands and face were wrinkled, but she had an ageless quality; with her thick black eyebrows under deep-set, calm eyes, perfectly round head and hint of a smile, she looked a lot like Yoda from *Star Wars*. A younger Indian woman sat cross-legged next to her. Both wore white saris.

'That's Dadi Janki,' whispered Nev. 'She's one of the founders of the Brahma Kumari faith. And the woman sitting next to her is Sister Jayanti.'

Sister Jayanti was handsome, regal almost, with a long aquiline nose and sharp features, a sense of intelligence radiating from her. She smiled as we came in, breaking the silence to say hello. Before the two Indian women sat a handful of men and woman, mostly younger than our parents, about half of them Indian and half of them white, with one young black man among them. All were dressed in white. The men wore white pyjama suits and the women, if not in white saris, wore long white skirts and white cardigans. Some turned around to face us; others never moved their gaze from Dadi Janki.

Sister Jayanti gestured for us to sit down. For the first time I noticed there was music playing: indistinct synthesizer notes, devoid of rhythm and made up of gentle washes of sound. I looked to the other members of the family for help. Nev was already cross-legged, focusing with a lighter-than-air look on the pinprick of light in the centre of the plastic egg. Mum was staring at her nails and leaning against the wall. Tom gave me a shrug.

Jayanti started speaking in a slow, calm, disembodied way. 'I . . . am a soul. My body . . . is temporary. I feel . . . release.'

107

I looked over to Nev. I nudged him. 'I don't know how to meditate!' I said in a frantic whisper. He simply turned towards the red plastic egg.

'I . . . let go of the old world. The new world . . . is characterized by . . . purity, honesty, simplicity. I imagine . . . that I am an actor. The scenes of the day have ended. The curtains have been drawn. The role . . . is left behind. It's time . . . to return . . . to my true self . . . the inner being . . . I become still and silent . . . inside . . . I resonate with the silence . . . and the total . . . stillness . . . within.'

Tom decided this was the ideal juncture to pinch me on the arm.

'Get off!' I squealed automatically, causing a number of white-clad people to turn around and look at me. Tom raised an index finger to his lips and said 'shhh' before sitting cross-legged, closing his eyes and making an O with his index fingers and thumbs, which slowly transformed into a V-sign.

The meditation session went on for an extremely long fifteen minutes. How did you know if you were doing it right? And what was the point of it in the first place? I only discovered meditation existed a few weeks previously. And the problem was, I felt no stillness or silence. There was always a part of me that was itching. Images flooded my mind: everything from Sadie by the fireside, so alluring as she curled up with *Hunky Dory*, to the hideous mathematics equations in that night's homework, which I would have to hope Bobby Sultanpur would not confuse with the political turmoil of his mother country when I got him to do them for me the following morning. When the meditation session ended, Dadi Janki spoke – in Hindi. Sister Jayanti translated for her. She was talking about celibacy.

'Mum,' I whispered, leaning over Tom and jabbing her on the shoulder. 'What's celibacy?'

'When people don't have sex,' she replied.

'Gross.'

Dadi Janki seemed be suggesting that the path of celibacy was not only beneficial but essential; only through overcoming sensual desire could we achieve spiritual purity and return to our natural state of soul consciousness. Surely this was madness. How was humanity meant to reproduce, and how was the human race meant to continue? More to the point, how was I to ever pop my cherry?

Dadi Janki's words weren't as worrying as the reaction they got from our parents. Nev was nodding as he listened, like a disciple at the feet of Jesus. Mum wasn't quite so reverential, but she did raise her eyebrows and move her head from side to side, as if weighing up the option and finding it not unattractive.

'There is no greater state than that of the child: purity,' said Sister Jayanti, still translating Dadi's words. 'God has a special place in his heart for those souls that have remained pure of body. Now Dadi would ask anyone who has remained pure to come forward and receive her blessing.'

I turned to look at Nev. He had a wide-eyed, simpleton look about him, and his head was jiggling in expectation.

'Dadi wants to bless you,' he said in an earnest whisper, as if he were a devout Catholic mother whose son has just been chosen for the priesthood.

'What? No way!'

'Go on, Will,' said Tom, loud enough for the room to hear. 'Or you could always come back when you're thirty.'

'Oh yeah, like *you've* done it,' I hissed back. Nev frowned. One moment we're a normal family, and the next I'm expected to go up in front of a bunch of strangers and get a blessing from an elderly Indian woman for being a virgin. I wasn't going anywhere.

Incredibly, two people did go up. One was a man in his early twenties, but when you looked at his greasy hair, bottle-thick glasses, zip-up polyester jacket and trousers that floated about somewhere above his ankles, maybe it wasn't really so surprising. The other was a frail old Indian fakir type.

Because Mum did so many interviews, our parents did have some unusual friends. There was Betty Cowell, a former World War II fighter pilot and racing car driver who became a woman. 'You can't get more feminine than Cowell,' Betty told me once, huskily, on her surname. 'It's a combination of "cow" and "elle".' There was Judy Cousins, a sculptor who made a bust of Dennis Thatcher and was once, like Betty, a man. There was Erin Pizzey, a large woman in her forties who ran a refuge for battered wives and had a twenty-one-year-old American husband called Jeff. But the Brahma Kumaris were quite unlike any people I had met before.

In the end, the combined powers of Nev, Dadi Janki and Sister Jayanti couldn't force me into proclaiming my virgin status to the room, and Tom and I went up to get a normal blessing with everyone else. This involved taking Dadi Janki's hand as she stared at you in a penetrating way, which made you convinced she could read every terrible thought you'd ever had, before handing you a small green square of something sweet called *toli*. It was an extremely sugary, sticky lump of oddness, although

Nev insisted it was 'filled with Yogi goodness' which would enrich our souls.

'Do you know what?' said Mum, as we drove home. 'This celibacy thing isn't such a bad idea. It's one thing to meet a handsome man in your twenties. But when you've got some horrible balding bloke puffing away on top of you when you've got another article to write before bedtime, the whole idea of sex takes on a completely different colour. Personally, I think more couples should be more honest and admit that they last fancied each other about fifteen years ago. Besides, denying men sex is the only way you can truly liberate yourself from them, because otherwise they'll always have some sort of power over you.'

'But Nev hasn't had any power over you for years,' said Tom, chucking his piece of toli out of the window, where it had bounced off the head of a passing cyclist.

'I rest my case.'

It was a school night, it was past my bedtime, and after a lifetime of being told religion was a mythical refuge for those who couldn't face reality we were suddenly expected to take up meditation and believe in soul consciousness, whatever that was. My only hope was that Nev would get over this current fad of his and move on. Three years previously he had become obsessed with the dangers of fluoride, and insisted we only used toothpaste that didn't have any of the deadly tooth-decay-busting stuff in it. Before that he had railed against the horrors of the BCG vaccine, which I was quite pleased about as it meant I was the only boy in my class without a bumpy circular scar on my upper right arm. But none of Nev's campaigns had impacted on our lives in the way this did. None had been as strange and uncomfortable.

'Well,' said Nev, as we passed through the bright lights of Richmond, 'I hope you boys found that a worthwhile experience.'

'I don't get it,' I said. 'What's the point in meditation? It's all about sitting around and doing nothing, which is exactly what you've been telling me *not* to do for most of my life.'

'I have to say,' said Mum, 'I found the meditation excruciatingly boring and I don't like the emphasis on looking as dreary as possible, but I approve of the fact that women run the BKs. It's about time we redressed the balance.'

I did my best to get back to life as a normal twelve-year-old boy, to not even consider the possibility that we might have lost our father to a bizarre cult. The Saturday after the visit to the Brahma Kumaris, Sam Evans and I took a trip to Tottenham Court Road to go to a comics shop called Forbidden Planet. It was an incredible place. Every scrap of wall was covered with rare comics or posters, there were reams of *2000 AD* back issues, and the people in the shop were fascinating: young adults in leather jackets, tight ripped jeans, band T-shirts and unusual hairstyles filled the aisles alongside teenagers, a few boys of our own age, and bespectacled men with ill-fitting clothes and low standards of hygiene. Nev often read my copies of *2000 AD*. He appreciated its star character Judge Dredd and his over-the-top reactions to minor offences, such as giving some poor guy five years in the Iso-Cubes for driving the right way down a wrong-way street. He laughed at the cast of grotesques Dredd fought with, like The League Of Fatties – men and women so enormous they needed belly wheels to stop their overhanging stomachs dragging along the ground – and Pug Ugly and the Bugglies, a punk band at the heart of a craze for looking as hideous as possible. Nev understood that *2000 AD* was an act of subversion masquerading as a children's comic, a celebration of impurity written and drawn by a bunch of misfits laughing at the world. Could its perversions have a place within his new vegetarian, teetotal, meditating, health-food reality? It was hard to see where.

Sam said there was a branch of McDonalds on Oxford Street. This was too tempting an opportunity to pass by, especially as I had a feeling there wouldn't be many family outings to McDonalds any time soon, but just as we came onto Oxford Street a young man approached us. His head was shaved save for a section at the back, he had markings chalked across his forehead and nose, and he was dressed in orange robes. He asked us if we had a minute.

'We're Hare Krishnas,' he said, although there was only one of him. 'We're monks. We work to provide the homeless with shelter and food, and we're trying to promote peace and spirituality through the teachings of Lord Krishna.'

This all sounded rather too familiar for my liking, although this man didn't have the still, placid air of the Brahma Kumaris. He was more like a door-to-door salesman. 'I'd like you to have these, as a gift,' he said, handing us a booklet each. 'They tell you all about the teachings of the International Society For Krishna Consciousness, and they give you an introduction to the important charity work we do.' He folded out the pages for us. There was a photograph of a little girl with the same chalk markings on her face, and there was a painting of an ornate Indian god with blue skin.

I wished he would stop. I was hungry and wanted to go to McDonalds, and the man's way of looming over us was making my head itch.

'I'm OK, thanks,' I said, trying to hand the booklet back to him.

'No, no, I want you to have it. It's free, and I can see that you will really benefit from it. Drink in the holy mystery contained within these words.'

'Oh. OK. Thanks,' I said, and tried to get away. He put an orange-robed arm out, blocking our path with a smile.

'That's a pleasure. Most people make a small contribution to the devotees of the Supreme Lord Krishna when we bless them with our literature.'

Frowning, I dug around in my pocket and pulled out the change. I had two pounds and ten pence left. I gave him a 10p coin.

Still smiling as he took the coin, he said: 'Most people make an offering of at least a pound, so that we can ensure the poor and the needy will always get something to eat when they come to the temple, which, by the way, is just around the corner.'

Sam and I glumly handed over a pound each. They disappeared into the folds of the Hare Krishna's robe as he gave us a toothy smile and said, 'Hare Krishna. Blessed be,' before skipping off towards an old lady with a white stick.

The train journey home was a quiet and hungry one, given that we now had only enough money for one Big Mac and fries between us. I read Sam's comic about a trio of comedy hippies called *The Fabulous Furry Freak Brothers*, in which one of them, a fuzz-faced man called Fineas, did a bout of meditation. I wasn't sure if his method for doing it – naked, on a mountain, smoking cannabis – chimed with Nev's or not.

Sadie was at the flat, in her pyjamas, watching television and eating from a bag of pretzels. Perhaps this was a chance to redeem myself after my disastrous chat-up line about the cost of Dungeons & Dragons starter sets. As Sam darted off into the bathroom I hovered about in the middle of the living room, trying to think of something to say.

'Why don't you stop standing there like a statue and sit down next to me?'

Sadie told me about a place she had been going to see gigs. It was called The Clarendon and it was in Hammersmith, a couple of tube stops away. 'It's *so* cool,' she said, pushing strands of red hair from her face as I sat a few feet away from her, trying to work out how best to arrange my limbs. 'It's really grimy and you get to see all kinds of great bands. It's a good place for people-watching too . . . loads of dishy boys. You should come along with me some time.'

I told Sadie I would love to go there with her. She said she would call me when there was something good on. Sam came in with two bowls of macaroni cheese. An hour later I caught the tube home, thinking how exciting life was turning out to be.

Tom was in the bathroom, holding his head upside down and making a chemical stink with a can of Boots Firm Hold hairspray, which he was using to make his hair stick directly upwards in a shape that resembled a watering can.

'What are you doing?'

'What does it look like?' he said, coughing through the

115

fumes. 'It's called Psychobilly, you moron. I'm going out to see King Kurt at The Clarendon tonight. It's about as different from your patchouli universe of Jimi Hendrix and The Doors as you could imagine.'

'I know all about The Clarendon. Sadie goes there.'

He turned upwards suddenly, and too soon for his vertical hairstyle to set; it collapsed to the side of his head. 'That older sister of your loser friend?' He put his hands together. 'This could be my night. She's bound to be there for King Kurt.'

I should never have said anything. 'I'm sure she's not . . . it's not her thing at all . . . even if she is, I saw her first.'

'You mean when she babysat you?' He marched towards the door, spraying my face with Boots Firm Hold as he went. 'Thanks for the tip, Scum. Have fun meditating.'

As we sat down for a vegetarian thali he'd had spent all afternoon making, I told Nev about my experience with the Hare Krishnas. 'It's outrageous,' he said, hotly, 'that someone could take advantage of a couple of boys like that. And in the name of religion! It's disgusting. They're nothing but a bunch of cranks.'

'I thought you liked all that stuff now,' I said, wondering how much of the thali I could not eat without offending him.

'The Hare Krishnas are just a cult. I feel the same way about transcendental meditation. Any belief system that makes you pay for a mantra should be viewed suspiciously. I can't stand all this hocus-pocus pseudo spirituality.'

I went to bed early that night, after trying and failing to get Kevin to ride on one of the Scalextric cars, reading some Judge Dredd and throwing the Hare Krishna manual in the bin. Nev came in before I turned the lights out. I asked him when he first got a girlfriend.

'I was never very good at that sort of thing. I had a couple of girlfriends before Mum, but nothing serious.'

'You see,' I began, feeling very sleepy but enervated by thoughts of Sadie, 'I don't really know what you're meant to do. Nobody ever told me.'

Nev smiled in a paternal fashion. 'You know the best thing of all to do, Sturch?'

'No. What is it?'

He paused, and gave me a wide-mouthed, wide-eyed smile.

'Nothing.'

I sat up. 'Never?'

He nodded sagely and looked at me in a meaningful fashion. 'It would make life a lot easier. It's nice to have a special friend, but you could find that the true path to happiness, to contentment, is not to worry about . . . girlfriends. If you avoid eating meat, or garlic or onions, which inflame the senses, you can commit yourself to the higher cause of soul consciousness. Honestly, it's the most liberating thing in the world.'

I scratched my head. 'But I want a girlfriend one day.'

He kept nodding, as if he couldn't possibly be wrong in this or in any other matters pertaining to the business of life. 'I'm only just beginning on this journey of discovery, Sturch, and it's taken me almost forty years to get here. If you started now you could be one of the most enlightened men on the planet by the time you're my age. And I've seen your potential. I saw the way you connected with Dadi Janki. You have the divine spark. It's worth thinking about. Well, cheerio then.'

Was that really an option – to completely forget about ever having a girlfriend, ever? Maybe I was punching above my weight with Sadie, but you have to start somewhere, and I certainly hoped the Faint Feeling would turn into a mighty eruption by the time I was thirteen. Nev, on the other hand, was suggesting I become a monk. It was certainly original fatherly advice in late twentieth century Britain. I closed my eyes and dreamed of Sadie, and prayed she didn't meet Tom and end up with him. The only thing that could be worse than that was if Nev left us to join the Brahma Kumaris on a permanent basis, but I knew that couldn't happen. It was simply a matter of time before he moved on. He always did, sooner or later. I hugged my pillow, imagined it was Sadie, and drifted away.

'I need to learn French,' Tom announced, from behind an artfully disheveled paperback edition of *The Outsider*. 'Right now I'm heavily into Camus.'

'Forget it,' I said, tightening the bolts on the back wheel of my bike. 'Why do you need to speak the language just because you like French cheese all of a sudden?'

'That's *Camembert*, you colossal . . . oh, never mind.'

Tom was leaning against the side of the shed, the Psychobilly quiff now deflated and tucked under a beret. Thankfully, the gig had been a disaster. Not only was Sadie nowhere to be found, but also a bunch of Psychobillies had tried to fill Tom's quiff with a mixture of cider and lager called Snakebite and drink from it. At around midnight he had renounced the movement for something more intellectual. Now he was in the garden, a place he generally avoided, because he was doing something wicked: smoking.

'Life is meaningless,' he announced, blowing a smoke ring.

'It will be for you in a minute. Nev's coming.'

Tom swiveled round, threw down his cigarette, and crunched it into the ground. Nev popped his head around the back door, looking rather pleased. 'Ah, boys, I'm glad I caught you. I've got something exciting to tell you.'

Tom was already shuffling down the side alley, covering his mouth and waving the air. 'Later, Daddio. Don't wait up.'

'I've got to get out of here too,' I said, climbing onto the bike. 'I was meant to meet Will Lee at Sheen Bumps ten minutes ago.'

'Do you want me to check you changed your tyre properly?' Nev shouted as I pedaled away. 'I'd never forgive myself if you came home covered in blood because I didn't check your bike.'

'It's fine,' I shouted, and took off down the street. Whatever important announcement Nev had could wait, because after countless times of chickening out I had resolved to attempt an important challenge: to jump over a stream in the woods on my bike. And I had convinced Will Lee to come along with me to capture the moment with his Kodak camera. Sheen Bumps was a gloomy patch of woodland just outside Richmond Park which people went to for two reasons only: to walk their dogs, and to ride bikes on the BMX track boys had roughly formed out of the earth. The stream jump was the most revered jump of all: if you didn't make it your front wheel would hit the bank and you would go flying, possibly into a tree. I had been practising my jumps on dawn sessions, away from the shame of crashing in front of my fellow enthusiasts, and now I felt confident I could get enough air to clear the stream.

We BMX boys tended to stick together at Sheen Bumps, and there was a reason for that. There were rumours circulating about a gang of Casuals – teenagers from the local estate with a love of quality sportswear, whose vanity and fastidiousness was matched only by their fondness for crushing skulls – who went up to Sheen Bumps on mugging sprees. I had never actually seen this marauding mob of label-conscious buccaneers, but there was always someone with a tale to tell about violence at their hands. I couldn't leave Will Lee on his own for long.

Will was there, with his ten-speed racer, Kodak around his neck, frowning in the bright light of the cold October morning. There were no Casuals in sight. 'Where the hell have you been?' he snapped. 'An old lady asked if I had lost my mummy. It was embarrassing.'

'Never mind that. Come with me.'

Will followed me to the top of the hill. The stream looked enormous, the potential for severe and permanent injury significant. That's when I saw them. Heading towards us, on a dubious-looking collection of bicycles that were either too big or too small, was a gang of around ten teenagers. Some had hair streaked with Sun-In, falling over one eye in a style we called a wedge. Others wore box-fresh white trainers, Farah Sta-Prest trousers, Ellesse tennis tops and Fila caps. One of them had a ghetto blaster: it was playing light jazz-funk. There was a girl with them. She had a miniskirt and big legs. It was the Casuals.

'Let's get out of here,' I murmured to Will.

'What are you talking about?' he replied. 'I'm not going

anywhere until I see you jump that thing.' He was never very savvy when it came to survival.

And then it was too late. They had surrounded us, leaning ominously on their motley collection of red-hot wheels.

'Nice bike, mate. Can I have a go?'

'Where d'you get that camera? I could swear I had one like that. Did you nick it off me?'

'Look here,' said Will, wagging a finger, 'if you try anything I'll jolly well tell the parkie.'

This did not strike the level of fear into the hearts of our assailants that Will had hoped for. A Casual grabbed one of Will's 'twiddles' – he had a habit of tying his hair into little knots – and gave it a yank.

'Ouch! What was that for?'

'Right, twats. Off your bikes.'

I had worked too hard for my bike to let it be stolen. It had taken literally weeks to annoy my parents into buying it for me. The Casuals were behind and at either side of us. There was only one thing for it.

I tapped Will on the shoulder, pointed forwards, and shouted, 'GO!' We pedaled with fury mixed with abject terror. Will was right by me, puffing away. We jumped over the stream at exactly the same time. There was a moment, in mid-air, when we looked at each other. The terror turned to joy. We were flying. For that moment, we transcended time and space.

Then we smashed into the ground on the other side.

It took a few seconds to unscramble our bloodied bodies from the confusion of metal and mud and get back on our bikes, but none of the Casuals were going to risk jumping over the stream and come after us; their pathological horror of scuffed trainers wouldn't allow it. We got out of there and cycled feverishly across the woods, through the gates out of Sheen Bumps, down the little path that cut through the cemetery and all the way to Queen's Road, where we allowed ourselves to stop.

'I think we've shaken them off,' said Will Lee, gasping.

'Oh my God. I can't believe we did the stream jump. Are you OK?'

Will inspected his body and his bike. His shirt was ripped and his elbows were grazed, but his bike seemed to have survived the crash. I had a bleeding knee and bruises on my shins where the metal of the handlebars had bashed them, but beyond that, nothing.

Will had to get back home for lunch. Auntie No-Toes was coming. (She really did have no toes. And she was six foot three.) I wanted to get home as soon as possible to tell Nev about my glorious morning. Nev was the most gratifying father a boy could possibly have when it came to things like this. If I told Mum about a new BMX challenge successfully completed, she would reply, 'how is that ever going to pay the bills?' Nev, however, revelled in my achievements as if he had done them himself. 'I was so weedy compared to you, Sturch,' he would say. 'I admire your fearlessness.' Beyond taking it upon himself to ensure my bicycle reached satisfactory levels of maintenance, he never interfered or lectured me on my love of dangerous bike-riding.

I skidded the BMX to a halt in front of the shed. Wait until Nev heard about our daring escape from the Casuals. He'd be so proud. Just as I put the bike away, as I was wondering whether it was reasonable to add that the Casuals numbered around forty and were wielding

122

baseball bats, Nev bobbed his head around the back door, fresh-faced and grinning.

'Nev! You'll never guess what happened . . . what's going on?'

Nev was in some kind of white, Indian-style pyjama suit. On his breast was a metal brooch featuring a red egg with beams emanating from a pinprick of light – the sign of the Brahma Kumaris.

'Sturch, you've arrived just in time. Come quickly.'

'I jumped the stream and escaped from the Casuals. Why are you wearing a karate outfit?'

He closed his eyes and waved a palm. 'Never mind that. I've got an exciting surprise for you.'

Nev made me follow him to the drawing room. He put his finger to his mouth, and opened the door.

Inside the room, within the book-lined walls, sitting on the chaise longue, in the armchairs, cross-legged on the new Moroccan-style rug from Habitat, were two dozen Yogis. In the corner was the young black man I had seen at the BK centre a week earlier, playing ambient music on a little keyboard. Some of the white Yogis had a wispy look about them, as if they could be carried away by a strong gust of wind. Sitting before them all was Dadi Janki.

'Can you believe it?' whispered Nev. 'Dadi Janki is in our house! This is a very special day.'

'The stream jump . . . the Casuals . . .'

'Om shanti, Will *bhai*,' said a small curly-haired man who I had never seen before, in an Australian accent. 'Why don't you come in and make yourself at home? Don't be shy. We can always accommodate one more. You can squeeze in next to Sister Nina over there.'

I found myself being squashed against a German

woman with wild, staring eyes and an enormous frizz of ginger hair. Fiddling with the folds of her white sari was a glum-looking boy of about my age. 'This is my son, Benji,' said the woman. 'You two will have so much fun, meditating together.'

There might be a quick way out of this. 'Pleased to meet you,' I said to Benji. 'Do you want to come upstairs and play a game of Scalextric?'

Benji stared at me with panda-bear-like solemnity. 'Are you mad? Dadi Janki is going to enlighten us on the cycle of rebirths, any minute now.'

All I wanted was for all of them to go away and leave us alone. All I wanted was to have my father back. But I was in there now and the meditation session was starting, and there were half a dozen of them between the door and me, and so I sat cross-legged, and hoped nobody would notice that my chin was wobbling and my eyes were reddening, and I didn't know what was happening to our family.

Years later, I discovered the reason for our house suddenly being filled with meditating Yogis. The centre in the house in Kew, which was owned by Sister Jayanti as part of her dowry, had closed down. Jayanti's father had used the house as collateral in a business deal that had gone wrong and now he had to sell it. Nev stepped in and offered the movement our home for its weekly meetings, although he had neglected to mention this to Mum or us boys. That was why Mum wasn't in the drawing room that day. He had only told her that morning about the meeting. She had responded by telling him that she was going to meet up with her friend Pete and get hideously drunk. Tom was round at one of his friend's houses, attempting to smoke unfiltered Gauloises. I was the only member of the family, apart from Nev, who was witness to the inaugural Brahma Kumaris meditation session at 99, Queens Road.

'I'm so pleased you're here, Sturch,' whispered Nev, just before Dadi Janki's lesson began. 'I feel that we're on this path together.'

Then he stared at the red egg, oblivious to everything else, including me.

6

The End Of The World

So now Nev was officially a Brahma Kumari and there was nothing any of us could do about it. Every day brought seismic shifts. Gone were the Edwardian prints on the walls of innocently suggestive ladies drinking Coca-Cola, replaced by luridly coloured paintings of smiling Indian deities. All remaining meat, mostly in the form of slices of ham in the fridge and sausages in the freezer, left the kitchen. Not so long ago, Nev came back from work trips with I Love New York mugs and Converse trainers. Now he would proudly hand over a T-shirt with a naive drawing of happy children holding hands underneath the words 'Be Holy . . . Be Raja Yogi'.

'This isn't a present,' said Tom, holding up his T-shirt. 'This is propaganda.'

Nev settled into a new routine. He got up at four o'clock in the morning, meditated for an hour, and went off to a six a.m. class at a Brahma Kumari centre in a house in Willesden before returning to start work in the room at the back of the house. He bought a little motorbike on which to get there and back every day.

Who were the Yogis and what did they want from us?

Nev asked if I would mind moving out of my bedroom. 'I'd like to do a bit of rearranging,' he said. 'You can swap with my study. I've got some beautiful plans for your room that I feel would really help us connect as a family.'

It took him a week of working in total secrecy before the new project, which he said would be a 'family room', was ready. All we heard was the occasional yowl of pain as he drove a hammer into his thumb, and all we saw as he emerged from my former bedroom was his red sweating face, covered in paint. Then, one evening after a vegetable curry that contained no onions, garlic, spices or anything else that could inflame, excite or even vaguely pique the curiosity of the senses, he announced that the room was ready for use. He came downstairs and interrupted Tom and me in a game of Trivial Pursuit.

'Which human rights organization won the 1971 Nobel Peace Prize?' asked Tom.

'The CIA?'

It stopped there, because Nev demanded we come and have a look at his new creation. 'It's quite special, actually,' he said, bounding up the stairs in front of us.

'Is this going to take long?' said Tom, who was letting his hair grow and had taken to wearing army surplus jackets and faded black jeans. 'I've got things to do. My friends and I are planning a trip to Stonehenge on the weekend.'

'That will be fun,' said Mum. 'Although I've heard you

can't go anywhere near the stones now. When I last went, on a school trip I think it was, you could walk right among them.'

'When you last went,' said Tom, 'they were still building them.'

Nev opened the door of his big surprise and held out his arms. 'Feast your eyes,' he said.

My old bedroom, so recently dominated by a Scalextric track on the floor, posters on the walls and everything from loose clothes to Dungeons & Dragons figurines to discarded attempts at homework, was now entirely white. The walls and ceiling were white. The floor, its carpet removed and the boards painted, was white. There was no furniture beyond a white mat. There was even a white bookshelf with some white books on it. I picked up one of the books. It was called *Into the White*. Apart from that there was nothing, save for the inevitable red egg representing the light of the soul.

'We,' said Nev, eagerly straining his long, bony, cracking legs into an out-of-shape-person's answer to a lotus position, 'are going to have a family meditation session.'

'You expect me to miss *Coronation Street* for this?' said Mum.

'Let's give it a go.'

After putting on a tape of temperate synthesizer music by Beyond Sound, the Brahma Kumaris' in-house band, Nev instructed us on how to meditate. We were to keep our eyes open, sit cross-legged, and stare at that egg on the wall.

I put my hands on my knees and chanted, 'Ummm mmmm.'

'It's not necessary to do that, Sturch. Just focus on God's light and remember you are a soul.'

'Is that the light in the middle of the egg, or the egg in general?'

Nev did a little head wiggle and a flutter of the eyelids. 'It's not an egg. It's a representation of the divine force.'

'So is the Yogi God the same as the Jesus God?'

Tom raised his eyebrows. 'You are officially an idiot. Yogis don't even believe in Jesus.'

'Try not to insult your brother like that, darling,' said Mum absently as she applied lipstick with a make-up mirror. She was leaning against the back wall of the meditation room, her legs stretched before her.

'I wasn't trying to insult him. I was making an objective statement about Will being an idiot. What's wrong with that?'

'Shut *up!*'

'Boys,' said Nev, his placid face twitching, 'let's think about peace'.

Meditation did take place, but only for about five minutes. I stared hard at the egg on the wall, and did my best to commune with the soul, but all I could think of was that only a week previously my poster of a BMX rider doing a jump over a screaming woman in a supermarket had been in the very position that egg was in. Besides, can you really ever not think at all, and turn your mind into a blank expanse of tranquil nothingness? It seemed unlikely. I looked over at Nev. With his large glasses, side-parted hair, white trouser suit and beatific, vacant expression he looked like a Tory MP in the middle of a nervous breakdown.

Tom farted. He fanned the air around his bottom out into the room while holding his nose.

'Ooh, that's a bad one,' he said. 'The silent killer.'

'This is why I hate living in a house full of boys,' said Mum, slipping into her wedge-heeled espadrilles and walking out of the stinking chamber of God. 'It's so grotty.'

'Well,' said Nev, frowning earnestly as he unfolded his crossed legs by actually picking them up and moving them, 'I think that went rather well.'

'Who can tell me about the Hindus?' said Mr Gaff, who had been given the job of providing us with our education in comparative religion over the space of an afternoon.

'Sir, is it true the Hindus worship sex?' This was Christopher Tobias, who had only recently attempted to make a bomb in the back of his garden and in the process blown off two fingers on his left hand.

Mr Gaff wiped the sweat from his brow, fiddled with his moustache, and leaned against the blackboard in one of the two pre-fabricated classrooms on which our school depended: built in 1948, intended to be pulled down by 1950, and still going strong over three decades later. 'No, er . . . I don't think so. They worship lots of gods, like Vishnu, and Shiva, and the one who looks like an elephant. Now let me see . . . we haven't covered schisms in Christianity, have we? The Troubles in Northern Ireland are between which two Christian groups?'

I knew the answer to this one. 'Sir! It's the Catholics and the Prostitutes.'

It took me a while to work out why everyone was roaring with laughter. 'Settle down,' Mr Gaff shouted, as conventional amusement turned into uncontrollable hysteria. 'Hodgkinson,' he said, eventually, 'you have made what is known as a schoolboy howler.'

That was the first incident of an unforgettably excruciating afternoon, but the second was worse. By the time everyone had calmed down, most of us went back to staring out at the puddles forming on the tarmac of the playground and watching the water drip off the roof of the classroom and splash bleakly onto an imitation briefcase which a child with business pretensions had left out in the rain. Mr Gaff continued to talk in a dreary monotone about Mecca, and Passover, and other aspects of global religious life on which it was completely impossible to concentrate. I worked out that if I leaned on my left hand and held a pen in my right it was possible to look like I was taking notes while actually closing my eyes and having a semi-snooze. I had almost drifted off when I was jolted back into wakefulness by some most unwelcome news.

'Right then,' said Mr Gaff. 'Now, I'm pleased to say that we have a special guest, who is going to tell us about, er . . . a very *particular* type of religious activity. It's called meditation.'

This couldn't be happening.

Nev walked in. And as if that wasn't bad enough, he was wearing his white pyjama suit. He also wore socks underneath sandals. At first, I simply froze. Then I glanced around at my classmates. Initially, they looked as shocked as I was, but it didn't take them long to start sniggering, whispering, and generally making it clear that this was something I would never, ever be allowed to forget. Mr Gaff introduced Nev as my father, who had offered to come in and talk about a new religion that would, he was convinced, help make the world a better place.

'Hello, lads,' said Nev in his new airy tone specially

designed for spiritual talk. He clasped his hands together as he stood upright before us. 'I'd like to tell you about an incredible experience I had. Until recently, I didn't believe in anything in particular. I was happily married, with two wonderful boys . . .'

I clenched my eyes tightly shut. Sometimes, I woke up in a panic after thinking I hadn't prepared for an exam, only to realize I had been dreaming. Sometimes, I started putting on my school uniform, only to realize it was Saturday. Perhaps this too was a dream, and in a few seconds I would hear the familiar, dull sounds of Mr Gaff, talking about matzoh balls.

'. . . And I thought everything was fine. But after getting extremely sick, I had something of a revelation. And I realized: the world is not as we think it is. I have discovered that, through meditation, we can see through to another universe. We can discover our true nature.'

Christopher Tobias put his hand up. 'Excuse me Mr Hodgkinson, but did you take a lot of drugs, like back in the Sixties?'

Nev shook his head with monkish patience. 'I know it sounds quite 'way-out', but all of you boys can see what I saw. It's just a question of being calm, and concentrating, and clearing your mind of thought and going deep within. So now, I'd like us to try meditating.'

'Please, no,' I muttered as a rolled-up piece of paper, which came from the direction of Christopher Tobias, bounced off my nose.

'Does this count towards our end-of-year mark?' asked Sam Evans.

This was nothing less than an act of cruelty on Nev's part. He gave me no warning, surely knowing I would

132

have forbidden him to talk to my class about meditation, under any circumstances, particularly while looking like a cross between Nicholas Parsons and Mahatma Gandhi. All I could think of was that at least I only had two more terms of this school before I would be going somewhere – anywhere – else.

Oddly, the giggles weren't as pronounced as I imagined. After a while, with Mr Gaff leaning with crossed arms against the blackboard, the boys really did go quiet. For a few minutes the room was silent. Some of the boys looked bored, some looked uncomfortable, but a few looked uncharacteristically serene.

'OK,' said Nev, after five minutes of silence. 'Did anyone get anything from that?'

'I didn't like it,' said the captain of the football team, who still hadn't forgiven me for my crime with the trip-wire. 'It reminded me of church.'

'It's bit like being asleep and awake at the same time,' said Christopher Tobias.

'Good. Well, that's all. If you're really worried about something in the future, if you're struggling with revision for an exam, or if you're having a hard time at school, try a bit of meditation. It takes you to a place where nobody can hurt you.'

Christopher Tobias came up after school and said, 'Your dad's pretty cool . . . mine only ever tells me how stupid I am.'

People liked Nev. Will Lee always said that seeing Nev was the best thing about coming round to our house, and Sam Evans, on describing another boy's father, had said, 'Oh, he's great. He's like your dad.' The thing is, I liked Nev too. And that's why witnessing him fall under the spell of the Brahma Kumaris, even if he no longer went purple every time an improper fraction defeated me, was such a difficult concept to get my head around.

As I walked home from school, kicking a stone along the pavement from Kings Road to Denbigh Gardens, I wondered if I would ever again sit with Nev in a pub, or if we'd go fishing together, or scramble along the Cornish coastline, searching for caves.

I was planning to march towards Nev and give him hell for destroying my life, but when I stomped up the stairs and, without knocking, opened the door to his meditation chamber, he was crouched in the corner, concentrating on something. And as soon as I began my speech with 'You had no right to . . .' he held a finger to his lips and pointed to something on the floor.

It was Kevin, standing on the carpet, looking around in his usual pessimistic fashion.

'Don't tell me you've got him meditating too.'

'I have unshackled him.'

Nev said he felt it was cruel to keep Kevin cooped up in his little cage, so he decided to give him the run of the house. We could leave little piles of gerbil food about the place. Kevin had already mastered the art of climbing the stairs – he hurled himself at the vertical carpet, dug in his claws, and scrambled up from there – so he could go everywhere.

'It's a nice idea,' I said, thinking about how my promises to clean out Kevin's cage every week had fallen by the wayside after the second or third time, 'but what about that cat who comes in? And what about Mum? Have you told her yet?'

'Not yet,' said Nev, looking a little rodent-like himself

as he leaned down and tried to stroke the newly liberated Kevin, who bit him on the finger. 'But I'm sure she won't mind. As for the cat, I haven't seen him in months. I'm sure the little fellow will be perfectly safe.'

I heard the scream first. I saw Mum a few seconds later running from the kitchen, where she had spotted Kevin dashing from the swing bin to a hole in the skirting board.

'Liz, it's fine,' he said, raised palms before him. 'I've simply set the gerbil free.'

Mum was so furious that she did an Indian drum roll on Nev's chest, but she had to stop because he was enjoying it too much.

That evening, when Mum had cooled off enough to sit down for supper, Nev answered a few of my questions on who exactly the Brahma Kumaris were. A wealthy diamond and jewellery trader from Northern India called Lekhraj Kripalani began the movement in 1937, after receiving a series of divine visions. Aged fifty-five, Kripalani was at home in Hyderabad one day when the god Vishnu appeared to him and said: 'Thou art that.' A few weeks later, he was in the garden of a friend in Varanasi when Shiva came to him as a luminous orb of light and gave Kripalani a prophecy that civilization was soon to be destroyed by warfare.

Mirroring Nev handing in his notice after his revelation at Westminster Abbey, Kripalani gave up his business and took to meditation to make sense of his visions. He was at home one day when his wife and daughter-in-law went into his room, to see his eyes glowing red and the room filled with light. A strange voice came out of his mouth. It said: 'I am the blissful self, I am Shiva. I am the knowledgeful self, I am Shiva. I am the luminous self, I am Shiva.'

Kripalani became Brahma Baba, a corporeal form of Shiva, to prepare the way for a new Golden Age. He decreed women would run the movement after his death. Only they could lead the world away from the path of violence and destruction it had been following for centuries; the fact that most women were treated as mere chattels in 1930s India was a sign of how corrupted the world had become. 'Shiva Baba has come mainly to uplift women, because they have had to bear injustice for too long,' he announced. Several bright, educated young women from wealthy families found attractive the idea of celibacy, self-empowerment and escape from an arranged marriage; it was a revolutionary possibility that didn't previously exist. In Hinduism, there is no equivalent to the nunnery, of women marrying themselves to God.

Unsurprisingly, the early converts' families didn't find the idea so attractive. The Brahma Kumaris movement was born under the shadow of death threats from aggrieved fathers who believed their daughters had been snatched away from them. Dadi Janki was one of the early followers of Kripalani, aka Brahma Baba, joining a small group called the Om Mandli in a compound in Hyderabad. In 1938, *The Illustrated Weekly of India* reported on the situation.

A delicate problem for a number of husbands in Hyderabad has been set by their wives, who have joined a new religious cult and taken vows of celibacy. They have informed their husbands that they are at liberty to take other wives. The husbands have something to say and they are saying it in no uncertain terms. They believe that the behaviour of their wives is against all the tenets of Hindu law and is contrary to the laws of nature.

The Anti-Om Mandli Committee was set up by the father-in-law of one of Brahma Baba's first female followers, and contained within it several sex-starved husbands worried that they would never get laid again. They decreed that the Om Mandli was an unlawful cult, created by Kripalani hypnotizing his young female followers. Parents prevented their children from attending the school Kripalani had set up to promote spiritual understanding. The centre in Hyderabad was attacked with bricks and set alight. When the case came to court, the Anti Om-Mandli committee claimed that Kripalani was, rather than promoting celibacy, inveigling young women into his cult for his own licentious satisfaction. The Indian government saw no reason to outlaw a peaceful organization, so the committee hired a Sikh bandit to assassinate Kripalani. The story goes that the bandit got into Kripalani's room, and was about attack him with a sword when a blinding light first engulfed then paralysed him. He dropped his sword, swore to renounce his violent lifestyle, and accepted Kripalani's offer of some spiritually pure vegetarian home cooking before going on his way.

After Partition, the fledgling movement set up a permanent base, the World Spiritual University, in the hill station retreat of Mount Abu in Rajasthan, where it remains today. Kripalani became Brahma Baba. His teachings shared similarities with Hinduism – he believed that the soul passes through a series of bodily incarnations – but he rejected the strictures of the caste system and the pantheon of gods. There is but one god – Shiva – and Shiva possesses the religion's female spirit mediums in India to deliver sermons, or *murlis*. These are the scriptures upon which the faith is founded.

As Nev told the tale of the Brahma Kumaris while a nut roast cooked in the oven, I told myself that, however odd it might have been, none of this was particularly threatening. The idea of women being in charge was hardly controversial. Our prime minister was a woman, and there was only one person in charge of our house and it certainly wasn't Nev. Perhaps the idea of reincarnation wasn't as implausible as I had first thought. I always wondered where all of that human energy went after death, and the concept of a Heaven for the good and a Hell for the wicked seemed ridiculous. Reincarnation did follow its own logic, as did the related idea of karma, the idea that all of our actions have a cause and effect, which will determine the outcome of our next birth. There was a part of me that thought I should simply accept these strange people in white saris and pyjama suits, even if they were invading our home and meditating in our drawing room.

What Nev said next, however, was a lot harder to swallow.

'You have to remember, Sturch, evolution is only a theory,' he began. 'In fact, time exists within a 5,000-year cycle and humans have always been a part of that. There are now far more of us than there once were, but we've always been here. And the cycle began with the Golden Age.'

'What do you think about all this, Mum?'

'Don't ask me,' said Mum, who was scowling at a picture byline of Julie Burchill in the *Daily Mail*. 'I was brought up to believe that a man called Jesus, whose mother was a virgin, performed a load of miracles, died, came back to life, danced around a bit, and then spent the rest of eternity floating in the sky next to his father, who is God. All of this BK stuff sounds quite reasonable by comparison.'

The Golden Age, Nev explained, was the Brahma Kumari equivalent of the Garden of Eden. People were so soul conscious in the Golden Age they didn't actually need to meditate. They just drifted about the place as sentient beings, reproducing in non-sexual ways – Nev was vague about how this worked, but he thought it might involve touching fingers – and being happy. There was no sadness if someone died because that was just the soul passing from one body to another and besides, people in the Golden Age did not feel attachment or possessiveness towards one another; just a pure form of selfless love. Getting around was easy too. Everyone had his or her own little pink cloud, which could zip about in the sky and go anywhere. The Golden Age lasted for 1,250 years.

That was the good news. The bad news was that the Golden Age wasn't open to everyone. The population grew as more souls came down from the Soul World – a holding pen for those yet to take physical incarnation – and society got worse with it. Life on earth went through successive periods of increasing decadence and unhappiness. The Silver Age was imperfect but still mostly spiritual; the Copper Age saw the rise of organized religions to take the place of innate wisdom, and the Iron Age saw war, disease, desire and sorrow become the norm. That counted for the suffering that had blighted the earth since the Middle Ages, and now we were in the worst period of all.

'We're in the Confluence Age,' Nev said. 'The Iron Age is complete and we are at the end of the old cycle and at the beginning of the new. The Confluence Age is a period

139

of renewal that lasts for about a hundred years. Right now things are particularly bad because we have to prepare the way for the next Golden Age.'

'How are we going to get there, then?'

'There's going to be a mass apocalypse,' he announced casually. 'Society as we know it will be destroyed. Whether that's through nuclear war, which I am guessing it will be, or a natural disaster I couldn't say. I'd say we'll see it happen in . . . ooh, about thirty two years' time.'

I did some quick mathematics in my head, which came to me much quicker than usual. 'But that's in 2014. I'll only be forty-four!'

Nev smiled once more. 'But Sturch, you won't really die. Your soul will go on. And I wouldn't be surprised if you make it to the Golden Age. That's why I think you need to start meditating and follow the practices of the BKs as soon as possible.'

'And I suppose you're going to the Golden Age?'

He nodded placidly. 'I *know* I'm going.'

'Can't say I'm holding out much hope for myself,' said Mum, from behind the newspaper.

I've never met a religious person, from a Muslim to a Jew to a Christian, who doesn't think they're going to be one of the chosen few. There doesn't appear to be a religious group that suggests, whoever else might be making it to Heaven, it won't be them. This is why it's extremely hard to take religious belief seriously. It is intrinsically self-regarding. How many Catholics are convinced they'll be going to Hell because Oliver Cromwell was right all along?

The Brahma Kumaris were no different. Nev explained that the BKs used an analogy called the Tree of Life. The highest branches represented the greatest distance from God. The limbs of the tree were the great religions, valuable in their own way but removed from the heart of wisdom. The trunk of the tree represented the teachings of Brahma Baba.

Apocalyptic tension fits into this idea of being one of the chosen and it's almost a pre-requisite of small religious groups, although I didn't know it at the time. While, around a weathered wooden table in a semi-detached house in a London suburb, Nev was telling his family about the end of the Confluence Age, the Indian mystic Bhagwan Shree Rajneesh was predicting, from his ranch commune in Portland, Oregon, that two thirds of the world's population was about to die of Aids. That's when he wasn't telling his followers to prepare for imminent global wipeout. Seventh Day Adventists have been shifting the date for the end of the world ever since the Great Disappointment of 1844, when William Miller predicted Christ would return, and Jehovah's Witnesses teach that the current age entered the last days in 1914. The world has been like a shop with an endless closing-down sale ever since it began, but belief in end times never appears to be negated by predicted doomsdays coming and going with life on earth more or less still intact.

When you're only twelve years old, being told by your father that you and the rest of the people on the planet are staring certain death in the face brings up certain questions, like: in that case, can we get fun size Mars Bars again?

'So there we have it,' I said. 'We're doomed.'

'I wouldn't put it that way. There will be a fifty-year period of rebuilding after the apocalypse. Most of the people on the planet will be wiped out, but some will survive, of course, and then we're back to the Golden Age.'

Only a few months ago, what you *saw* was what you *got* in our house, and what you *got* was quality furnishings and all the latest consumer innovations. Religious sects may have been prophesising the End Times for centuries, but not the upwardly mobile. Now the end of the world was nigh.

I scratched my head. 'What about the dinosaurs? They were around 65 million years ago. That hardly fits in with the idea of a 5,000-year cycle.'

'There are a couple of theories. One is that dinosaurs were mutations from a nuclear war, but they were infertile and so they died out pretty quickly. Another is that the fossil record is incorrect. There are huge gaps in our fossil records, and most of what we have concluded on the nature of evolution is based on supposition. There's a strong possibility the dinosaurs simply never existed.'

Nev leaned forward on the table. 'Look at the human eye. Could anything so complex really have evolved from single-cell organisms, like amoebas? The problem is that we now take the teachings of modern science for granted. We don't question it at all, yet science is only what can be proved at this present time. Ten years from now, we'll have a completely different understanding of the world. Science *is* our religion. To question its dogma is to be a pariah.'

Nev's introductory lesson into the worldview of the Brahma Kumaris ended with Mum taking the nut roast out of the oven and dropping it with a thud onto the centre of the table. Mum served it up, hacking at it with a large knife and, when that didn't prove sufficiently destructive, whacking it with a hammer. Then Nev did his latest weird thing: he stared at his plate.

As his eyes went a little watery, he sat with his hands on his lap and meditated on the crushed nut roast. He had a hint of a smile, not of amusement, but of piety.

'What the hell . . .?'

'I'm giving thanks. It's a little like saying grace. We have been extremely lucky in this house in that we have never gone hungry.'

'What about that time Mum tried to make a soufflé and it was too late to get a takeaway?'

'I am taking a moment to appreciate this nourishment for my physical manifestation.'

'I wouldn't take too long over it,' said Mum. 'I want those plates cleared in five minutes.'

As fate – or karma – would have it, there was a TV play on that night that confirmed my worst fears about the apocalypse. It was called *Threads*. It imagined the effect of a nuclear war on a group of people from Sheffield and it was the very normal touches – mums and dads getting up in the morning, making cups of tea, bustling about amid the cheap DFS furniture of Eighties Britain as radiation melted their faces away – that really brought home the horror.

The drama centres on a young man and woman about to move in and build a life together, at the very moment relationships between Russia and the US break down and America launches its first nuclear missile.

The USSR fires a missile at a military base just outside Sheffield, an event the population is woefully unprepared for: people climb beneath armchairs and behind sofas as

143

the blast strikes, blindly hoping for protection against a bomb that razes the city. In the aftermath, Britain undergoes martial law. People are shot for hoarding or stealing food. Their bodies are left to rot in the street, as burning them would use precious fuel, so cholera and typhoid spreads everywhere. The radiation from the nuclear fallout ensures cancer for those who have survived the blast, the death squads and the diseases. Nothing grows on the cursed, irradiated earth. Babies born in the wake of the blast are physically deformed and mentally retarded. The drama ends with the young woman, who has somehow survived against the odds, giving birth to a baby. In the final shot she looks down at her new baby – and screams in insane horror.

Nev didn't watch the programme because he went to bed at around nine o'clock now, but Mum and I did. When it came to an end, I sat and fixed blankly at the screen, not taking in the message that anyone disturbed by what they had just seen could call a helpline.

'You have to remember, darling, it's not real,' said Mum, staring at her nails. 'It hasn't actually happened.'

'But it's going to, isn't it?' I replied in a shaking voice. 'Nev said so.'

Mum swatted away the suggestion. 'You don't believe all that, do you?'

'Don't you?'

She crossed her arms. 'What's the point? If the end of the world really does come there's not much we can do about it. Besides, we all have to die sooner or later, so we may as well get on with our lives while we still can and stop fretting about something that may never happen. Talking of which, I wanted to talk to you about what

144

school you're going to next. Nev and I were thinking Westminster won't be right for you.'

'You mean I won't pass the entrance exam.'

Mum uncoiled her legs from the sofa and sat upright. 'We're all different. We each have different skills. Tom's major skill is being an all-round brainbox. You just haven't found what yours is yet. Nev saw an advertisement in the *Guardian* for a boarding school in Hampshire called Frensham Heights . . .'

I didn't wait for her to finish the sentence. 'I am not going to a Yogi school.'

She waved her hands. 'It's just an alternative for children who are not . . . as academically gifted.'

'So it's a dumping ground for thickos? My God!'

I ran out of the room and up the stairs. The light in Nev's meditation room was on. It was all right for him. He could just disappear into soul consciousness every time things got tough. I didn't have that luxury. I had to go to a school I hated every day, and now they were sending me to a special institution in the middle of nowhere for the intellectually subnormal. On top of that, my father, who had joined a religious cult, had just told me that the world was going to end. I climbed into bed, put the cassette of *Smash Hits* into my new Sony Walkman, and pulled up the sheets.

Mum came in a few minutes later. She sat on the edge of the bed and tapped my head. She said that she would never send me anywhere I didn't want to go, but felt it wasn't doing me any good to be constantly compared to Tom.

'Well, that's true at least,' I sniffed. 'Only the other day Mr Mott said he couldn't understand how one brother could grasp the rudiments of physics so quickly while the other appeared to have more density than mass.'

'It's the kind of comment I'd expect from that pig-eyed Rhodesian still mourning the loss of British rule. Tom may be more academically gifted, and yes, maybe he does have a sharper mind, but you're the good-looking one.' She held my hands and leaned forward in earnest, eyes widening. 'Ultimately, that's more important.'

But what about nuclear war, the Brahma Kumaris, people dressed in white filling our drawing room? The old world was in collapse and I wasn't sure I was ready for the new one. That's assuming there was a new one. After Mum left the room, visions of nuclear terror filled my young mind. I kept hearing the bone-marrow-freezing scream at the end of *Threads*. In quiet terror I lay awake, staring at the glow stars on the ceiling, wondering if, somehow, we could go back to the way we were.

Tom burst in noisily around two in the morning, while I was still awake, being tormented by visions of mutant babies and marauding Yogis.

He had never made it to Stonehenge. He got as far as Twickenham. He had been planning to get a lift down in a van owned by an anarchist road warrior called Diesel, aka Orlando, but when he and some of his Westminster friends leaned out of a window and flicked a sign at the 'pigs' – a couple of policemen in a Panda car from the Richmond-Upon-Thames district – the pigs pulled them over and took them down to the station. Had not Diesel's dad been a QC it could have been serious.

I got up to see what was going on. Mum did too, her hair a Medusa-like mass of black horror and her eyes hollow pits of tired fury. The dressing gown made her look more terrifying than usual. She screeched at Tom from the top of the stairs to keep the bloody noise down.

'It's your fault for being a light sleeper,' he said with a yawn. 'If you wake up because of your neurotic sleep patterns, please don't take it out on *me*. I've already had enough trouble from authority figures below my intellectual capacity for one night.' And with that he went into his room and slammed the door – loudly. For the rest of the weekend, he came and went without revealing where he was going or where he had been. On Sunday night, at three in the morning, Mum woke up to realize Tom wasn't in. She got in the car and drove around Richmond, searching for him without success. By the time she got back home he was in bed, asleep.

At breakfast the following morning I was looking forward to sitting back and watching the show as Tom got it in the neck from our parents, but sadly my entertainment was denied. After Mum shouted at, pleaded with and eventually thumped Tom to get him out of bed, he slouched downstairs in his uniform, opened the fridge, glugged some orange juice from the carton, shuffled over to the jar on the dresser containing Nev's home-made muesli and picked out the hazelnuts and raisins, chewing them in an open-mouthed, cud-like manner. Then he started stapling the backs of the trousers of his school uniform.

'What on earth are you doing?' said Mum, while Nev did his best to appear oblivious as he communed with his cooling piece of toast like a man recovering from electro-shock therapy.

'What does it look like?' said Tom, twisting round as

he turned his shapeless trousers into skin-tight drainpipes. 'I can't walk around for a day more in these monstrosities. I have my image to think about.'

Mum plunged down the cafetière and poured a very large coffee, glaring at Tom with a rage that, I couldn't help but suspect, was mixed with admiration. She had managed to say: 'Your behaviour last night was totally unacceptable . . .' before he put his hands up to stop her.

'I forgot to tell you,' Tom began. 'I got called in for a meeting with my house master on Friday afternoon. He wants me to apply for Oxbridge.'

The anger evaporated from Mum's face. Even Nev stopped staring at his toast, and actually managed to move on to the buttering stage. 'Why, Tom, that's wonderful!' said Mum. 'But isn't it a bit early? You're only fourteen.'

'With pupils of exceptional promise your name goes forward long before its time,' he said, throwing a hazelnut up into the air and trying to catch it in his mouth. It rolled onto the ground and came to a halt by the edge of the dresser, whereupon Kevin poked his head out nervously, looked quickly to the left and right, grabbed the nut in his mouth and darted back out of view. 'That way you can start preparing for the entrance exam and get an unconditional offer. Anyway, the only reason I'm telling you this is that they think it would be a good idea if I go up to Cambridge and have a look round. I need you to drive me, but I'd rather not go in the Volvo. Do you think you can hire a car that would be better suited to someone of my status?'

'How about an arsemobile?' I suggested.

'You are moving into the upper echelons of society,'

said Mum, wiggling about in her seat. 'These are very sophisticated people.'

'Yes, and talking of which, it's probably best if you don't say too much. In fact, don't say anything at all. If someone talks to you, just nod.'

'I don't think I can manage that.'

Tom grabbed his school bag, a canvas bag on which he had scrawled various band names alongside a large anarchy sign, presumably in honour of Diesel the road warrior. He stuffed a piece of toast in his mouth. 'Yeah, well, gotta go,' he mumbled through a crunching sound, before shrieking in pain as one of the staples pierced his thigh.

I had wanted to tell him about *Threads*, and about Nev's vision of a dawning apocalypse, but there was no time. So I shuffled off to school, counting every step along the way and resolving that if I arrived at the school on an even number there would be no end of the world. If I arrived on an odd number, however, not only would nuclear terror rain down on the land, but also Sadie would reject me, Nev would never leave the Brahma Kumaris, and the sweet tin would be filled with sticks of natural liquorice forevermore. The steps came to 1,013.

'Guess that's it, then.'

It turned out half the class had seen *Threads* too. 'It didn't scare me at all,' claimed Christopher Tobias, who had put a ring pull over every one of his remaining fingers and was rapping them with metallic urgency on the surface of his desk. 'I've seen a film called *Mad Max* and that's far worse. People's heads are chopped off.'

'What they didn't show,' said Sam Evans, 'is all the

mutations you get from nuclear fallout. It won't be unusual to see people with two heads, or with enormous lizard-like tails. A lot of women will have three breasts.'

'Perhaps it won't be so bad after all,' mused Christopher Tobias.

After assembly, in which our headmaster made us say the Lord's Prayer and sing 'To Be a Pilgrim' before telling us we would all be punished if the person who drew an oversized part of the male anatomy on the toilet door didn't come forward, and after a particularly chaotic lesson with Mr Gaff which ended up with him chasing Christopher Tobias over the tops of the desks, we sat around a long table in the dining room and discussed our future prospects.

'As long as I do well in the Common Entrance, I'll be going to Westminster,' Sam Evans announced.

'If the head finds out it was me who drew the knob,' said Christopher Tobias, 'I'll be off to Feltham Young Offenders.'

'How about you, Hodgkinson?' said Sam, picking a cooked tomato from his plate and chucking it out of the window.

I didn't really want to talk about it, but I supposed I had to sooner or later. 'My parents have mentioned a school called Frensham Heights.'

Everyone looked up. In the tight-knit amphitheatre of suburban privilege, we knew the options available. If a boy was clever, he went to Westminster. If he was thick, he went to any number of boarding schools in the Home Counties. If his parents were stockbrokers or bankers, he went to St Paul's. If they belonged to the average middle-class, he went to Latymer or Emmanuel. If they had just made a series of disastrous business deals, he went to the local comprehensive. Nobody went to Frensham Heights.

'What?' said Sam. 'Froggam Heights?'

'It's just some place my dad mentioned. I haven't even visited it.'

'Is that because he's gone weird?'

'Yeah, like your family's normal.'

Sam leaned over the table and whacked me, and that was that: a full-on fight. Christopher Tobias wasn't sure whose side he was on, so he punched both of us. Sam's plate of Spam and Smash crashed to the floor. Bobby Sultanpur ducked under the table. I punched Sam twice in the chest and once in the face before Mr Mott came running over and pulled us apart and we were all thrown into detention.

It didn't seem like the day could get any worse. But I got home to find Nev sitting by the kitchen table in a white jumper and beige trousers, a faraway look in his eyes. I stood in front of him; he stared right through me.

'Are you all right, Nev?'

He shook his head and broke out of his state of transcendence. 'Sorry, Sturch. I didn't even notice you there,' he said, smiling. 'Dadi Janki tells us that we should turn everyday routine into meditation, so we're soul conscious even when engaging with the world.'

After shrugging at Nev's explanation and walking on through the house, I saw the tabby cat, which hadn't come into our house for months, playing with something at the foot of the stairs, pushing something backwards and forwards with its paws. I went to stroke this handsome stray until I saw what it was playing with: Kevin.

'Nev!' I screamed.

The cat darted off into the kitchen with Kevin in his mouth. Nev jumped up and chased it around the table, the cat frantically attempting escape as the gerbil swung wildly from its jaws. Nev grabbed the cat. It let out a wail of fury and dropped its shell-shocked prey as Nev opened the door and chucked it out. I crouched on the kitchen floor and tended to my stricken pet. He was on his back, mouth open, twitching. His fur was fluffed up and there was a massive gash across his grey underside. He made no noise.

Tears filled my eyes as I stroked the dying Kevin, and for once he didn't try and bite me. Nev came back in. 'Why didn't you see the cat?' I wailed. 'If you hadn't been meditating, this would never have happened.'

Nev told me to look away. He raised a brown shoe-clad foot and brought it down with resounding crunch onto Kevin. There was a tiny squeak.

'Nooo!' I howled.

'I had to put him out of his misery. He was never going to survive a mauling like that. He's at peace now.'

Kevin looked much the same in death as he had in life, only flatter. He had that defeated look of his, which, if you considered his current situation, was understandable. His little legs were splayed out in four directions. The gash in his stomach had turned into an anatomical drawing of small intestine, liver, kidney and heart.

The least I could do was give him a proper burial. I told Nev I wanted to do it alone. There was a little hand-held fork in the shed. That would do to dig him a grave, somewhere near the bottom of the garden. The ground was covered in a thin layer of frost. I decided on a space between the last vestiges of that year's mint and an

The Hodgkinson family, Richmond, 1973. Proof that Mum managed to make Nev look cool, albeit briefly.

Nev in the South of France, early 80s. Prior to his spiritual awakening, Nev was an irreverent, fun-loving dad.

Mum with two of her favourite things: a glass of wine and a cigarette.

With Will Lee on the Sussex Downs. We're standing by our Stone Age toilet, which Will christened shortly before this photograph was taken.

Aboard the Kingston Cavalier III, scene of the bloodiest episodes in the history of the Hodgkinson family.

Mingling with le tout *Richmond at a bar mitzvah, 1981.*

Salmonella for forty…

… And then parties looked more like this one. Just another Yogi jamboree, our house, early 80s.

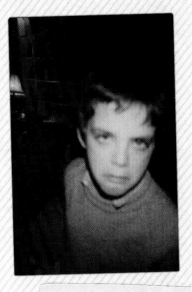

Yogi Père: Nev, Mum and Tom, 1982.

Aged twelve, shortly after being told by Nev that the world was going to end.

Nev at Madhuban, the Brahma Kumaris' World Spiritual University in Mount Abu, India.

Tom, leading the way for the fashion-conscious teen about town.

My first adolescent look, designed chiefly to impress Sadie Evans, unattainable first love, when she took me to a concert by The Stingrays.

On arriving at Frensham Heights, a hug from Gael. A very young thirteen-year-old, I was amazed to discover that sophisticated girls like Gael were the same age as me.

Getting air at Sheen Bumps, Richmond. Often, I would come back from an afternoon's BMX session to find the house full of Yogis.

Polly Russell, 1986. Our relationship coincided with publication of Sex Is Not Compulsory, Mum's case for the sexless marriage.

At Mount Abu, India, aged eighteen. I went in search of that amazing blissful feeling which drove Nev towards a life of meditation and spiritual study, but never found it.

apologetic fuchsia. The ground was so hard that the fork kept bouncing off it in metallic hopelessness. I whacked at it as hard as I could, and the fork snapped. Eventually I managed to scrape off the top layer of soil and scatter it over Kevin. On top of him I put a pile of rotting fig leaves, alongside a few withered sprigs of mint, then patted the whole lot down and went back in to ask Nev what was for supper.

In the morning, Kevin's body had gone. It was when I spotted what could only have been his nose by the door of the shed that I realized how savage his end must have been. His life force stripped of him by the foot of a Yogi, his body ripped apart by feral creatures, he had shown to me that animals live and die and eat each other as cogs in a machine, serving the tapestry of nature in their small purpose. This I could understand. It was the Brahma Kumaris – and now, my father's – rather more meta-physical explanation of life that I was struggling with, not least because of the changes it was bringing to our family. And I was soon to discover just how significant and irreversible those changes were.

7

The Second Party

'I don't want to go,' I said, staring out of the window, waiting for the fake cows on the roof of the Unigate building by the side of the M3 on the edges of West London to come into view. We were driving back from our open day at Frensham Heights.

'Why not?'

'I just don't.'

'You must be mad not to want to go to that school,' said Mum as she pulled into the fast lane and overtook a man in a Porsche with a personalized number plate. 'There are gorgeous girls everywhere, you call the teachers by their first names, there's no uniform. Apart from the fact that you're forced to learn something every now and then, I would have thought it would be perfect for you.'

'Did you see that woman wearing flares? Nobody wears flares.'

'Looks to me like you could have a great time,' Mum continued. 'I must say, I was rather shocked by the squalor of the boys' dormitories, but then that's never been the

154

kind of thing that's bothered you. Besides, given it's in the countryside, there wasn't too much in the way of mud. That's a bonus.'

She was right. Compared to the dreary conformity of the one I went to, this school did indeed look like a bohemian paradise, and ever since I turned thirteen – it was Spring now, six months on from Kevin's passing – I had been noticing girls more and more. But it was also unfamiliar, a further manifestation of our parents' deviation from the norm. Two hours earlier we had driven along a tree-tunneled road where a small, weathered wooden sign for Frensham Heights stood on a corner next to a high hedge in front of large wide playing fields. A scruffy boy of mixed race and about my age, with a loose, messy Afro, a striped jumper and patched jeans, passed unsteadily on a skateboard and waved to us. Two young women walked by, laughing: one wore glasses and had a mass of black curly hair, the other, blonde and big-breasted, was wearing flared jeans, a rare sight in 1983.

The car pulled into another drive, which led through lines of beech and oak. This opened into lawn broken only by a handful of grand old ash trees, and beyond that a patterned, slate-grey balustrade surrounding one of the biggest houses I had ever seen. Soaring windows had panes of dirt-encrusted glass through which there was no chance of seeing. The huge oval oak door did not give you a sense that it appreciated being opened by teenagers. A wild wisteria hung loosely in clumps across the front of this Edwardian mock-Tudor mansion, and reached up to the second set of windowpanes. Puffs of thick smoke billowed from the chimney. It felt like walking into a scene from *Tom Brown's School Days*.

155

The Volvo crunched along the gravel courtyard and halted next to a weathered stone wall. We pushed open the massive front door and walked into a smart, oak-panelled hallway decorated with artwork. The signatures confirmed this was the work of the pupils. There were paintings that captured sadness or doubt, line drawings of nudes that imagined the body in unusual, original ways, and Dali-esque landscapes with ironing boards for trees and apples for bushes. To the left of the hallway was a wide, curving staircase with a red carpet and carved mahogany banisters; to the right, an anteroom with high windows above a window seat, filled with parents and children of around my age. We looked at each other, trying to pretend we weren't, as we took glasses of orange juice and stood around, twitching, moving from foot to foot, waiting for something to happen.

A teenage girl shuffled up and introduced herself as Murphy. She said she would be showing us around. She had a long brown fringe that brushed into her eyes and a round, freckled face. She wore a large oatmeal jumper with a CND badge and a Yasser Arafat-style keffiyeh.

Murphy had one other prospective boy in her group. His name was Will MacCormac. He was as tall and even thinner than me and he had a slightly defeated look, which reminded me of the late Kevin. He told me that he was at a comprehensive in Clapham, but now his parents thought it would be a good idea if he went off to boarding school. 'Can't see the point myself,' he said, 'particularly as I don't really need to go to school. I'm designing a car that I'm looking to get put into production in a year or so.'

He presented this information impressively, factual

rather than boastful. 'How did you learn about building cars?' I asked him.

'It's quite simple, really,' he said with a sigh, as Murphy led us out of the hall. 'All you need to do is study the specs of the world's great supercars. I've got a prototype here, as it goes.'

Will MacCormac pulled out a crumpled-up supermarket receipt. On the back of it was a rough pencil drawing, two inches long, of a shape that, if you squinted, might have been of a car. 'That's called The Jackal. One of its special features is that it can go up to 250 miles an hour.' He stuffed the specifications into the back pocket of his jeans.

'So here are the sixth-form studies,' said Murphy, waving vaguely at a row of small rooms that looked like converted stables. 'The good thing is you're allowed to smoke in here as long as the person you're sharing with doesn't mind. But you can't smoke until you get into the sixth form, which is, like, totally an outrage.'

Murphy took us down a drive that cut through muddy playing fields. 'Hi John,' she said as a slight, balding, middle-aged man in Lennon glasses drove past in a VW camper van. In the windscreen was a sticker with the words 'Nuclear Power? No Thanks!' around a smiling sun. 'Oh John, I forgot to tell you. I can't help out on this year's Un-Sports Day. My mum's having her divorce party.'

'That's a shame, but never mind,' said this man, who had a soft voice and a benign, laid-back manner. 'Are you still OK for our Anti-Apartheid fun run?'

'Oh sure.'

John flashed a peace sign and drove away.

'That's our chemistry teacher.'

157

We went into one of the boys' boarding houses, which was on the first floor of a Tudor lodge-style building surrounding a cobbled courtyard. It smelt of milk and washing powder and had little rooms with three or four narrow beds in each of them. There were pin boards above the beds: some were bare, some had timetables and revision charts, and some had pictures of naked women. The rooms were empty but there were crumpled clothes and tattered homework books scattered everywhere.

'Pretty much everyone has left for the weekend or gone into town or run off into the woods,' said Murphy, picking up a T-shirt from the floor and throwing it onto a bed.

'What happens if you go into the girls' rooms?' asked Will.

'Big trouble. Boys and girls are definitely not allowed to be together after lights-out. It gets a bit easier in the sixth form, but I think the school got terrified of its image as a place of free love and permissiveness. So they clamped down. No more hanky panky. Shame, really.'

Will gave me a nudge, and said in his nasal drawl, 'That's not going to be easy for me. Not with the effect I have on the opposite sex.'

As we came back around to the front of the main building and went into the hall, where there was a grand piano at one end and large windows looking out onto the lawn at the other, Murphy told us a little about the headmaster, Alan Pattinson. He had been a Benedictine monk until, in a reversal of Nev's situation, he lost his faith and turned devoutly agnostic. He had become the new headmaster shortly after Murphy arrived. Pattinson was credited with transforming the school from a pit of anarchy into a liberal centre of learning and enlightenment.

'He's all right, but he goes on a bit,' she said. 'He just seems to take everything so seriously. One time a bunch of us went for a late-night roller-skating session in the dinner hall, which was naughty, but it wasn't *that* naughty. Instead of just making us go and pick up litter after Saturday school, which is the usual punishment, he had to devote an entire morning talk to telling the school what a terrible disappointment we had been to him, and that if only we had asked him first we might have arranged a roller-skating outing for us. Then he burst into tears.'

'Well,' said Mum, surveying the hall with an approving air, 'have we seen everything?'

After a pause, Murphy said: 'Pretty much . . . there is Brackenhill, which is a boys' boarding house, but you don't need to see that. It's miles away. And not very interesting. So, here we are, back where we started. I hope we meet again.' And with that, she was off.

I was wondering why Murphy had seemed so reticent to reveal much about the place called Brackenhill when something occurred to me: Will had not been shown round with a parent. I asked him where they were. 'My dad's over there,' he said, pointing at a dapper, silver-haired man who was sitting in a corner of the hall, lost in a pile of paperwork. Noticing Will, he came over, said: 'Done? Good. Let's go,' and walked off.

'Bye then,' said Will, following in his wake. 'Maybe see you next year.'

Just before we left Frensham Heights, I saw a bleak-looking house hiding behind a line of conifers. It was darker than the houses in the grounds, as if permanently cast in shadow. There was a derelict shed to its side and a blue 2CV, bleached with age, in the drive. The house had its own sign: Brackenhill, Property of Frensham Heights.

An angry-looking man with an enormous, shining dome of a head and little tufts of hair jumping out from either side of it stomped to the front of the house. He was wearing heavy tweeds and had a large beard. He stood with legs apart and hands on hips. Before Mum drove out on the main road and away from Frensham, the man fixed me with a disapproving glare, as if admonishing me for something I was yet to do.

The look was prophetic. The man's name was Jonathan Hughes, and in the years to come both he and Brackenhill would make as much impact on my development, in a rather less spiritual way, as the Brahma Kumaris.

All I wanted, and I don't think it was too much to ask, was for everything to return to the way it was. Even the lack of argument was eerie. Why hadn't Mum put up more resistance to the Brahma Kumaris? She had displayed none of her usual fierceness towards this invading force, even while showing no interest in meditation or indeed any kind of spiritual dimension to life. She had not suggested she wanted to leave Nev, or that she wanted him to leave the BKs. Instead they wanted *me* to leave the house, to live with a bunch of semi-feral hippy children in a bizarre progressive boarding school. No explanations were given. I was simply expected to accept these transformations as not only inevitable, but positive.

That's why I was pleased to discover, on returning to 99, Queens Road, that we were having another party. I wanted to see the house filled with colour again. I couldn't wait to see Sandy, her rich black hair piled into a loose bun, and John, with his aristocratic humility, his bow ties and velvet jackets, once more making witty repartee with our parents. Pete would be there, with another gift from another adventure for Tom and me. It was always entertaining to see Hugh Lee, smiling at pretty women like Nosferatu eyeing up a tasty-looking vein, a glass of red wine in his hand, and Penny, so polite and so kind, so sensible. These were our people.

It was going to be a great party. It was time to hear le Tout-Richmond talk over each other in our drawing room of important things, like where to get a decent bottle of Chablis. I had missed the sound of that.

A pile of bin bags lined the side path of the house. The white metal bars of Kevin's cage jutted out from one of them. Indoors, Nev was sitting at the kitchen table with Sister Jayanti, and the young black man and the pretty, fresh-faced blonde woman I had seen at the Richmond centre. All were wearing white, the women in saris and Nev and the young man in pyjama suits. Nev introduced them. The man was called Brother Malcolm and he was the leader of Beyond Sound, the band that had made the gentle synthesizer music we had meditated to in Nev's Yogi chamber. The blonde woman, who looked older than our babysitter but younger than our parents, was called Clare. I can't say I was particularly pleased at returning from visiting a strange new school to find the house filled with devotees of Brahma Baba, but they did at least prove to be friendly.

'How are you, Will?' said Sister Jayanti, her wide smile reassuring after the uncertainties of the day. 'I've heard that you were looking at a new school. What did you think of it?

'Not sure,' I said, gazing at the polished floorboards of the kitchen and wondering when the real guests would arrive.

'I had to change schools a few times,' said Malcolm, nodding at the memory. 'It never got any less terrifying.'

'Frensham is a very creative place,' said Clare, thereby revealing how they must have been fully aware of my potential move into alternative education. 'And there is something so beautiful about letting the muse take flight.'

'Most important of all,' said Jayanti, 'is that you are happy. In childhood, nothing else matters.'

After smiling with excessive benevolence, Nev told Brother Malcolm I was becoming interested in music. Malcolm asked what kind of music I liked. I told him I had discovered Jimi Hendrix.

'You're starting at the top,' he said. 'He's one of the greatest guitarists who ever lived. If you like Hendrix, you should listen to Miles Davis. He did similar things to jazz that Hendrix did to rock. Talking of music, we'd better get set up.'

I went upstairs and let our parents prepare for the party. Maybe Nev's conversion to the Brahma Kumaris wasn't so bad after all. The organization did appear to attract interesting people. Malcolm was a cool guy. Clare was gorgeous. Sister Jayanti was peacefulness personified, a figure of serenity. It was all quite youthful and forward thinking. Maybe some of them were former hippies who discovered God after having had their minds blown at Woodstock, or Monterrey, or the Richmond-Upon-Thames Jazz and Blues Festival. I could see them getting on well with our parents' old friends at the party. I knocked on Tom's door, heard him say, 'Go away,' and I pushed it open. He was by his desk, staring bleakly at a blackened ZX Spectrum.

'It blew up,' he said, hunched over the ruined machine. He had recently bleached his long fringe with Sun-In; strands of dirty yellow-brown hair flopped onto the keyboard. 'I was trying out a bit of reprogramming when loads of smoke starting pouring out of it. Next thing I knew, it caught fire.'

'What did you do?'

'I smothered the flames with your school jumper.'

He held it up. It was charred and singed. He chucked it at my head. 'You can have it back now.'

I was about to attack him when he jumped on his bed, picked up a book, and said, 'Do go away.' Naturally, this made me want to grab him by the neck and squeeze the life out of him. I was getting ready to perform this terrible act of vengeance, but I thought of Sister Jayanti, and Brother Malcolm, and I stopped.

'Fair enough,' I said, standing upright, pressing my palms together. 'May your dreams be filled with visions of the Golden Age.'

One eye darted towards me. 'Don't tell me they've got you now.'

'Not at all, Brother Tom. Nonetheless, I would appreciate it if in the future you would approach me with thoughts of peace.'

He pulled up his knees and sunk deeper into the bed. 'That's not going to happen.'

Sam Evans and his mother Erica – Sadie was off somewhere – were the first to arrive. Erica, who was wearing an Indian shawl, made a gesture of prayer before Sister Jayanti, and looked around, taking in the posters of multi-coloured Indian deities decorating the hallway. Sam asked if we could go upstairs and have a go on the Scalextric. Mum appeared in her Brahma Kumari-themed look: a white salwar kameez, a white cardigan and white wedged espadrilles. 'I see no reason why you can't be stylish *and* spiritual,' she said to Erica. 'Look at Sarah Miles.'

Soon Anne and Pete were there, and so was Sandy, sitting on the edge of the chaise longue in a long black dress and shimmering necklace. Nev was greeting guests at the door, looking like a gust of wind might carry him away. There were other adults I had grown up seeing every few months or so, talking ever louder about books, newspapers and, most of all, about people. One woman, with a green Bakelite necklace, big teeth and a red slash for a mouth, a novelist whose name I couldn't remember, was talking with Mum while her silent, bearded husband hovered nearby. 'As if sex weren't complicated enough, I read today that we're now all meant to be doing something called 'after play', apparently,' she said loudly, as various white-clad Yogis stood about and smiled in silence. 'Really, it's a bit much. Poor old Nat is still struggling with the concept of foreplay.' Nat nodded obediently.

This kind of sophisticated chitchat was familiar from parties past. This time, however, something wasn't quite right. People were arriving with bottles of wine, and Nev was explaining that it was very kind of them but it wasn't necessary and they should make sure they took the wine back with them when they left. About half of the people in the drawing room were Brahma Kumaris: Indian women looking serene in saris, western women less so, and several people in white pajama suits. Hugh Lee was standing in the middle of the room, staring furiously at his silver beaker of sweet mango lassi. Pete, dressed flamboyantly in a wide-blue-pinstripe three-piece suit, was ruining its shape by sticking his hands deep into his pockets and pouting. Sandy, who never moved from the edge of the chaise longue, looked like a little girl waiting to see the headmaster. Penny stood erect, with her hands behind her back and rocking on her heels, talking to Clare, who was explaining that she had travelled all over India in search of enlightenment before finding it with Sister Jayanti at the BK house in Richmond.

Not everyone appeared so out of place. Erin Pizzey arrived, wrapped in layers of fabric and filling the width of the doorway; she and Jeff were loudly telling Clare how much they liked the idea of a religious group run by women but they couldn't get used to the idea of giving up sex. While Malcolm made adjustments to the keyboard he had set up in the corner of the room, Sister Jayanti nodded patiently as Mum told her how she had been recently to a past-life therapy session, which revealed she was variously incarnated as an Egyptian princess, a high-born lady of the French court, and a pre-Raphaelite muse. How she ended up following this impressive line of rebirths with becoming the daughter of a lorry driver from St Neots, Huntingdon is anyone's guess.

'What do you have to do to get a drink round here?' said one familiar-looking man; I had vague memories of him crashing through French windows at a party much more swinging than this one. Another man suggested going to the pub round the corner. But before they got a chance, Nev flapped his hands, tapped a spoon on the bookshelf, and called the room to order.

It was only then that I realized something: Nev was looking very odd indeed. Because it had crept up on us, I had taken his altered appearance for granted. But to a roomful of old friends, I could see how he must have looked. A few months earlier, he was a typical middle-class, middle-aged man with questionable but essentially accept-able dress sense: tweed jackets, woolen polo necks and smart-casual trousers. Now he was wearing a white pyjama suit with a white jumper over it, with the material of the pyjama top flaring out at the hem, making it look like he was wearing a white miniskirt over his trousers. And on the jumper was an enormous badge with a badly repro-duced photograph of the smiling, silver-haired man we knew as Brahma Baba, founder of the Brahma Kumaris. Then there was Nev's face itself: youthful and handsome, but oddly blank too, as if his intellect had been washed away in order to make space for blind faith.

'Hello everyone,' he began, adding with a chuckle, 'or should I say "Om Shanti", which means "I am a peaceful being". I'm so pleased you could all make it. I've brought together friends old and new to share my wonderful discovery with you. They're called the Brahma Kumaris.'

'If you want a mid-life crisis just climb Mount Everest – or Miss Everest,' said Pete, making a few of the old friends laugh. 'Don't go all Mia Farrow on us, mate.'

Nev batted away the comment with a flutter of the eyelids. 'You could call it a crisis if you like, in that, in the last year or so, I *did* begin to search for something deeper than eating, sleeping, writing articles and drinking wine in the evenings . . .'

'Can't see why,' said John Chubb, Sandy's titled husband. 'Sounds like a perfectly decent way to pass one's time.'

'As you know, I've never been in the slightest bit religious. And the organizations I first encountered, when I started looking for some kind of spiritual dimension in my life, seemed like total phonies. But then I met a group, run entirely by women, called the Brahma Kumaris. They charge nothing for their courses and teach a very simple form of meditation called Raja yoga, which has no chanting or ritual or any kind of hocus-pocus. It was during a meditation session that I first experienced a feeling of intense blissfulness that I can describe only as some sort of enlightenment. This is what I wanted to share with you. Tonight we're lucky to have here with us Sister Jayanti, one of the leaders for the BK movement in the UK. And she's going to lead us through a simple meditation session.'

The BK men and women, who included among their number the ginger-haired Nina and her dark-eyed son Benji, positioned themselves. They sat on the sofa, or on the floor, cross-legged, looking impossibly holy among the demi-monde of suburban London. Sister Jayanti, regal and spiritual, sat on a mat on the floor before them, her long black hair flecked with grey twisted neatly into a single plait that coursed down her back. Erica joined them, owl-like with her oversized glasses and eager, attentive expression. So did Erin Pizzey, sprawled out on a sofa next to her youthful husband. Hugh and Penny Lee, Anne and Pete, the woman who had just discovered after-play, and various other people with loud voices stood at the back of the room. Sandy remained frozen at the edge of the chaise longue, now joined by John, looking, in his bow tie and velvet jacket, like a man whose martini has eluded him and who is beginning to face up to the possibility that he may never find it again.

'It's wonderful to see so many of Neville and Liz's old friends here tonight. We are honoured to meet you all,' Sister Jayanti began. 'True friendship is about extending good wishes and pure feelings towards other people and thinking about how we might benefit them. That will make us happy because we will share the spirit of service. Through meditation we return to our natural state, which is peace, and then we are capable of a friendship that is altruistic, with no other motive. Before I tell you all a little more about what the Brahma Kumaris are trying to achieve, let's get to know each other a little.'

Sister Jayanti was right. We needed to be welcoming to Nev's new friends, even if they did come across as a bunch of white-clad religious yo-yos. I had made no effort to talk to Benji, and yet we had things in common. We were the children of Yogi converts, after all. As two Brahma Kumaris sisters smilingly worked the room with a tray of mango lassis, and as Sandy and John and Hugh and Penny held the lassis with all the ease of a bunch of toddlers given pints of beer, I decided to make sure Benji felt included.

'Cheers,' I said, clinking metal cups and taking a glug.

'Om Shanti,' Benji replied, looking at me solemnly.

'Soooo, what are we drinking to?'

'Soul Consciousness.'

He said nothing more. There must have been something we could talk about. After all, we were both thirteen; teenagers ready for fun and adventure. I didn't know anything about football, but there was music, computer games, television, girls . . . I asked Benji if there were any bands he liked. There was a pause, then, 'Beyond Sound offers a peaceful soundtrack to the world drama.' Apparently, he wasn't allowed to go to the cinema or watch television. As for girlfriends, he stated, with an impressive lack of doubt, he was intending to stay pure for his entire life.

Clearly I was barking up the wrong tree. We needed to talk about the Brahma Kumaris.

'The thing is,' I began, 'I can see the benefits of the meditation and that, but you have to admit, some of the beliefs are pretty fruity. I mean this whole 5,000-year cycle thing . . . it goes against all the evidence. Will Lee here is big into fossils and he can date prehistoric life forms back millions of years.'

'It's a fascinating field of study,' confirmed Will Lee.

Finally, Benji showed signs of animation. 'Ah, but you'll agree that energy cannot be created or destroyed, won't you? So in that case, how could Earth have come into being through a Big Bang, which suggests that something came from nothing? Even physicists struggle to explain it. And if you don't believe in the Big Bang, the whole Darwinian theory is fundamentally flawed. It follows that life hasn't developed from single-cell organisms to the complexity of humanity in the way we think it has. An explanation of time as a cyclical entity actually makes far more sense.'

After a long pause, I replied, 'What's your high score on Space Invaders?'

Beyond Sound hummed away, Nev chatted with Benji's mum, Penny Lee listened with diplomatic reverence as Sister Jayanti told her about the Soul World, and the junior Yogi sisters cleared away the metal plates and cups. My cup was empty of lassi, but I kept putting it to my mouth in a just-developed nervous tic. I turned to Benji.

'How long have you been into the whole Yogi thing?'

He looked at me quizzically. 'Do you mean in this bodily incarnation?'

Before she began the meditation, Jayanti told us how she came to be a Brahma Kumari. She had been intended for an arranged marriage since the age of one, but had gone to a grammar school in London in the Sixties before studying medicine in the hope of assuring she would always be financially independent. It was on a trip back to India in her early twenties that she met Dadi Janki. From then on she knew her calling: to promote peace and equality through the teachings of the Brahma Kumaris.

'When I met Dadi, she was so powerful she awakened the spark of spirituality in me,' said Sister Jayanti. 'And Dadi Janki had been saying to me for some time that a lot of people, not just Indians, want to experience peace. This is what brings us here, thanks to the generosity and kindness of Sister Liz and Brother Neville.'

As Jayanti spoke, I couldn't imagine anyone having a problem with her. I may not have liked the sudden change the BKs had caused to our family, and certainly would have been happier if Nev had gone back to his old, miserable ways, but there was something about Jayanti which reassured you about the strange world of which she was a part. She was one of those benign presences whom it was impossible to feel threatened by.

Nev asked everyone to sit down, to take their shoes off and get themselves into a comfortable but upright position. 'Damned impertinent request, if you ask me,' muttered Hugh Lee, who hovered at the back of the room like a disapproving buzzard, but others complied. Malcolm began playing gentle chords of ambient music on his keyboard, the light of the red egg at the top of the bookcase came on, and Sister Jayanti began.

Speaking in a disembodied voice not a million light years from that of Hal, the evil computer in *2001: A Space Odyssey*, she intoned, 'I, the soul, am a pure, peaceful point of light . . . I am now turning my thoughts inwards to the self, the soul, in the centre of my forehead . . . I leave this . . . physical costume behind and focus . . . on the living energy . . .'

'Stuff and nonsense!' spluttered Hugh Lee, and there was an angry clattering of the double doors leading to the garden.

'Peace, light and love are now my nature. I am no longer the slave, but the master of this body . . . I am able to spread light and purity through the world.'

Jayanti's eyes remained open for the meditation that followed, and I had a chance to do a quick survey of the room. Sandy was looking like she wanted to be anywhere else but here. Nev was wearing his lighter than air expression, perfectly still, cross-legged, giving his best impression of an odourless gas. Hugh Lee had gone, but you could hear a hacking cough coming from the garden. Sister Nina, angular and ginger, and her son Benji, sad-eyed and solemn, sat staring at the red egg, motionless. Erica was sitting in a half-lotus, eyes closed, hands resting on her knees, index fingers and thumbs meeting to make circles. She made a faint humming noise.

The session lasted for about twenty minutes. Sister Jayanti broke the silence by explaining some of the core beliefs of the Brahma Kumaris. The five vices that have caused so much unhappiness in the world, she said, were greed, lust, anger, attachment and ego. The last was the worst. Ego was a form of false pride, and markedly different from true confidence in oneself. Anger was something we could control. We assume our anger is caused by the person or situation with which we are angry, when in fact it's up to us to decide whether to be angry or not in the first place. Rather than be angry with those who do wrong, we should feel sorry for them. In other words, I should feel sorry for Tom every time he annoyed me. The injustice of this was immensely irritating.

'What about Hitler?' someone said. 'Should we have felt sorry for him?'

'Nobody, not even Hitler, believes they are evil,' said Sister Jayanti. 'So, rather than judging others, we should check our own behaviour constantly. Brahma Baba decreed one rule above everything: never contemplate harm to anyone.'

Mum and Nev's friends couldn't have a problem with that, surely?

'Can you explain to me the concept of karma?' asked Erica, leaning forward with palms pressed together. 'I have a few issues with the idea that we get what we deserve.'

'Let me explain it by saying that nothing goes unnoticed by God,' said Sister Jayanti, placidly. 'Every action has its direct consequence, for good or for ill. We must not imagine that our sins will not find us out. When the soul is eternal we can see life as an interlocking jigsaw made of many incarnations, so everything we do in this life has consequences for the next. But this is not a question of crime and punishment. It is a case of cause and effect, as scientific as the laws of gravity.'

'Is it true that the Brahma Kumaris are celibate?' said Pete, looking confused.

'Yes, it is,' Sister Jayanti replied. 'Many of our generation have grown up thinking of religion as the opiate of the people. Today, as fewer people in the west adhere to the religious life, it is sex that we use to create a false happiness. If I want to experience God, the only way is through awareness of the soul. It is much more difficult to be spiritual while continuing physical intimacy with another human being. Also, in the Brahma Kumaris we are promoting equality between the sexes. We believe celibacy is the only way to achieve this.'

'You could be right there,' riposted one man. 'My wife's been on top for decades.'

'Success has existed in this organization because of celibacy,' Sister Jayanti continued. 'The idea of celibacy within marriage has been one of the biggest problems for many people. It can work, though, as Neville and Liz have shown us.'

What?

Everyone turned to them. Mum looked proud, defiant; Nev looked like the non-physical entity he aspired to be.

'What I'd like to know is,' said Pete, with an edge to his voice I had not heard before, 'what do these people want from you?'

Nev explained that the Brahma Kumaris asked for nothing. And it was true. There was no fee for the seven-day introductory course into meditation he and Mum had taken, and no fee to stay at Madhubhan, the BKs' spiritual university in India. The Brahma Kumaris merely offered

173

a lifestyle and a world view. They promoted vegetarianism, celibacy, meditation, renunciation of greed and spiritual study. Most importantly, they promoted peace on earth for all mankind.

That isn't how our family friends saw it. After Sister Clare and Sister Nina offered everyone little squares of pistachio and condensed milk toli, and Brother Malcolm continued to make indeterminate hums on his keyboard, it seemed people couldn't leave quickly enough. 'Quite enlightening!' said Penny Lee, as Hugh Lee stood by the door and glowered at anyone in a sari. 'If you ever want a break from this celibacy lark, you know where I am,' said Pete to Mum, while his wife waited in the car. And Sandy was still sitting on the edge of the chaise longue, her smile tighter than ever, as she clasped her arms around her body, as if protecting it from an invading force.

'Did you enjoy that?' I asked her.

She shook her head.

'Why not?'

She didn't answer. 'But it's always a pleasure to see you, dear Will,' she said. 'You know you're welcome to stay with us for a weekend. Any time you like. Actually, you can stay as long as you like. Should you want to.'

'Very *innaresting*,' said Erica to Nev, smiling and leaning towards him in a way which took me years to understand its significance. 'The lifestyle is a little austere for me, but still . . . *innaresting*. I'd love to talk to you more about it some time.'

'You would be very welcome,' said Nev, clasping his hands primly in front of his chest. 'Might I suggest the Brahma Kumaris' free seven-day course as an excellent introduction?'

*   *   *

'What you have to accept,' said Will Lee, as we played, or rather, as he ruthlessly outmaneouvered me in, a game of chess, 'is that the whole thing is very worrying indeed. Nev's gone completely freaky.'

'What are you talking about?' I replied, as he trapped me into a checkmate after five moves. 'He's not freaky at all. He's just seen the light.'

It was a week after the party, we were back up in the Lees' attic, and Will Lee was contemplating Nev's induction into the Brahma Kumaris. The party had proved to be the worst in the history of the Hodgkinson family; worse even than the time Uncle Richard stood on a table stacked with glasses of champagne and attempted to do a pirouette. I didn't like the way Anne and Pete, Sandy and John, and Will's own father had been so opposed to the Brahma Kumaris. It wasn't that I was all for it. I just didn't want to see Mum and Nev dismissed as cranks by their closest friends. Sandy had called Mum the following day, asking her if she and us boys needed to come and stay with her for a few days, to take a break from it all, get a bit of normality. I later found out that Sandy told Mum Nev had been love-bombed, showered with adulation by a cabal of exotic, witch-like women in order to pull him into their cult. Cults demand two things from a new convert: rejection of previous beliefs and cutting off family and friends. Nev's worldview had already been transformed from a rational to a faith-based one. Next would be the disconnection from the people closest to him. The family would be cast aside. It was only a matter of time.

At the time, I was sure Sandy was wrong about Nev and the Brahma Kumaris. It was disappointing to witness what I took to be a form of closed-mindedness and disapproval. Sandy had always been so . . . *modern.*

Now Will Lee was coming down against them.

Will leaned forward in his beanbag. 'You don't seriously believe in reincarnation, do you?'

'Why not? We've got to come from somewhere.'

'But Nev was always so sensible. How can he really believe the world has only existed for 5,000 years?'

With a sigh, I lay back and gazed up at the skylight. 'I don't know. He just seems convinced about it all. It's funny. Before the party I really wished the Brahma Kumaris would all go away. Since then, I've become rather fond of them. Anyway, I'd better be getting back. We've got a bunch of them coming over tonight.'

The BK sisters didn't end up staying for long. They meditated with Nev in his room for half an hour before we all ate the thali they had brought with them. I had to say, the chapattis, rice, sambhar and sabzi were a definite improvement on our usual diet of nut roasts and dhal stews. When they left, and after Nev went to bed at nine so he wouldn't be too tired for his regular four a.m. meditation session, Mum came in and said goodnight.

'Mum, do you like meditation?'

'No, I do not. It's a complete waste of time.'

'And what do you think about this 5,000-year cycle thing, and how all our ideas about fossils and evolution are wrong?'

'Couldn't care less either way. I've always found fossils to be the most boring things in the world, and as for dinosaurs, who cares whether they existed or not? Why would anyone be interested in enormous lumbering reptiles with tiny brains crashing about in the mists of time? It sounds far too similar to my childhood in St Neots.'

'But surely this suggestion that there's no beginning or end to time is completely far-fetched?'

'No more far-fetched than the argument I'm related to apes, unless you count Uncle Richard.'

'But if you don't like meditation, and you don't really care if the 5,000-year cycle is true or not, how come you're a Brahma Kumari?'

'Who said I was?'

I sat up in bed. 'Then how come you're not against them, like Sandy and John and Anne and Pete and everyone else?'

Mum didn't seem the slightest bit bothered at the mention of the names of all their friends, friends who viewed the Brahma Kumaris as a millennial terror cult and Nev as a brainwashed fool.

'The thing about Nev's experience is that he's got a deep feeling for the BKs,' Mum began. 'And that's something you can't argue with. It's no good believing things with the intellect. You have to feel them with your heart. Intellectually, I've got no problems with the Yogis. I like the idea of karma because it means all the fat and ugly people deserve to be that way, and I'm most definitely in favour of any institution that's run by strong, intelligent, freethinking women. It makes a difference.'

'Why do all our friends hate it?'

'They're scared by it. They don't want their posh life-styles exposed as a hollow sham. They think it's rude of Nev to break rank and sign up for a different approach. Most of the time, people are more conventional than they seem.'

177

'They think you've lost Nev.'

'Who said I wanted to keep him in the first place? It's a bit like falling in love. Most women lose their husbands to another woman. I've lost mine to God. And when I think about it, I could have seen it coming. Nev's always been monkish. He used to say he felt guilty after enjoying a walk in the countryside because he had taken from nature without giving something back. It was only a matter of time before he went religious in some way or another.'

'What about the Morgan? Bombing down to Brighton? The pinball?'

'He was playing at it, tasting other men's pleasures. He was pretending to be the same as Pete Harris or John Chubb.'

'And you don't care?'

She pondered on this for a while.

'Can't see why. Goodnight.'

8

Forest School Camps

By the end of the summer term, it was decided I was to go to Frensham Heights. I changed my mind about the place after returning for the entrance exam, which was shockingly easy. Who doesn't know Christopher Columbus was the first president of the United States?

It was also decided we would not be having a family holiday that summer. With memories of the boat trip still fresh in his memory, Nev felt it would be going backwards to try and force us all together, particularly now that Tom was busy collapsing on beds and sofas across London, Mum was telling anyone who would listen that she saw motherhood as a burden rather than a blessing and Nev was floating about in the Soul World from the comfort of his meditation chamber. I was the only one who bemoaned the lack of a holiday.

'You know what I think we should do?' I said one morning, as Nev gazed in supplication at a bowl of muesli, Tom's head slumped onto the table and in a kitchen corner Mum did a few exercise routines she had memorized from

Jane Fonda's Workout Challenge. 'We should go to America. I've always wanted to go to Disneyworld. How about it?'

'Do they have painkillers at Disneyworld?' moaned Tom, his eyes closed, as a line of saliva seeped out of his mouth and drizzled onto the table.

'Think about it, Nev. You used to love theme parks. Imagine a theme park run by Mickey Mouse! Apparently there's a rollercoaster that actually goes *upside down*. Being on that would be a spiritual experience in itself.'

'You're thirteen now,' puffed Mum as she did squat-thrusts next to the toasted sandwich maker. 'You should be thinking of teenage things, like your choice of career and where best to invest your pocket money. Aren't you a bit old for Disneyland?'

'I will be at this rate,' I said with a sniff. 'I've always dreamed of going and now it looks like I never will. OK, maybe America is too expensive. I just think it's unfair we never get to do the things normal families do anymore.'

'But now we do much better things,' said Nev. 'Why, only last week we had a lovely time at the Brahma Kumaris' non-competitive sports day. And what a meditation session! Those three and a half hours went by in a flash.'

'How about Blackpool?'

Mum sat down by the table and said to Nev, 'Why don't you tell Will what you've got planned for him this summer?'

Accompanied by an impressive display of counterfeit enthusiasm, Nev explained that he had already booked me on a holiday. A suggestion from one of Nev's fellow Yogis, Forest School Camps was, he told me, an amazing experience where you could go rock-climbing and potholing by day and sing songs around the campfire by night. I didn't particularly like the sound of it – if God wanted us to sleep in tents, he/she/it would not have given us the ability to invent houses – but at least it would be something to do during the long holiday before a new life at Frensham Heights began.

Meanwhile, Nev worked on his book *Will to Be Well*. Mum went freelance and earned a lot of money from the *Sun*, the *Daily Mail* and countless magazines, coming up with headlines and then thinking of articles to go with them. Tom became a mostly non-moving presence, slack-jawed, sprawled on his bed in an oversized T-shirt and boxer shorts, deaf to Mum's shrill attempts to get him out of bed each morning. Eventually he appeared at the break-fast table, muttering something to Mum about her being one of Rupert Murdoch's henchmen before demanding she pour him a cup of coffee.

'I'm sick of being pushed around by you!' screamed Mum, hovering over him with a cafetière.

'Go and find someone else to push you around, then,' he replied with a yawn, stretching his arms.

And there were Yogis everywhere. They came to stay, sometimes for weeks at a time. It wasn't unusual for me to come in from a BMX session at Sheen Bumps to see a stranger sitting in the garden, dressed entirely in white, gazing at a daffodil. Nev organized countless family trips to Shanti Bhavan, the Brahma Kumaris' new headquarters in the living room of a house in Willesden, where we sat on a beige carpet and listened to Sister Jayanti. Dadi Janki was there every now and then. I found her terrifying simply because she was so completely without vice or frivolity. There was no small talk with Dadi Janki. You had to stare into her deep brown eyes, shadowed by heavy brows, as they pierced your soul.

'What does spirituality mean to you?' Dadi Janki asked me one evening, through the smiling medium of Jayanti.

I considered this. 'Meditating?'

'Spirituality means having eternal love for another while maintaining a connection with God,' said Dadi Janki. 'You are a soul, and you are connected with the Supreme Soul. He is teaching us, and whatever He teaches we should share with others. This way the quality of our thoughts will be high and we will be filled with positivity and be of benefit to the world.'

She gave me a piece of toli, which she and I held while looking at each other in a spiritual connection known as *drishti*. I tried to have nothing but quality thoughts, but all I could picture was Sadie, running through a field. She was naked, obviously.

I discovered the real reason we weren't having a family holiday that summer. While I was going to Forest School Camps, Nev was heading to India to visit the Brahma Kumaris' World Spiritual University at Mount Abu, Rajasthan. The day before he left he took me to Waterloo Station, dressed relatively normally in white trousers and a blue jumper, with only a small badge of Brahma Baba's smiling face to give away the fact that he had gone mad. We were to meet the Forest School Camps' party beneath the large clock, before the train journey to base camp in the Brecon Beacons.

Looking through the brochure, it did seem like there was potential for good times. My tree-climbing skills, developed over countless excursions into Richmond Park with Will Lee, would come in handy for mountaineering. Exploring caves on pot-holing expeditions would be exciting. Building fires and cooking sausages was fun. However, it was the sight of a big group of kids who all seemed to know each other, who bustled and shouted and seemed to share some codified dress sense and common understanding, that made the skin between my eyebrows pinch together.

'What a nice, lively bunch,' said Nev, as I adjusted the straps of my rucksack and looked on from a distance. 'You should say hello. You'll make friends in no time.'

'I don't know what to say to them.'

I knew that Nev was frustrated by my reticence. I could tell by the way his head was bobbing from side to side. But one boon of the Yogi life was that he wasn't allowed to be angry anymore, so he couldn't shout at me for always holding back, something which he and Mum had accused me of in the past. I never understood what was wrong with holding back. Approaching every new person or situation with fear and trepidation was surely a sensible survival technique.

'Look at that boy over there. He looks friendly enough,' said Nev, pointing to a blond adolescent with a mean, narrow face. 'Why don't you go and say hello?'

Nev insisted this was something I had to do on my own, which I felt was distinctly un-Yogic of him. He told me to have a wonderful time and left, to get ready to fly over to Delhi and join his Brahma Kumari compatriots the following morning. I shuffled over to the group. An Amazonian woman with short ginger hair appeared and, with a bright smile, introduced herself as Frances. She was one of the camp leaders. The other one was a spindly man with a neat greying beard and sensible all-weather gear called Vivian. Frances said that if there was anything I was worried about, she was always available.

That wasn't too bad. Now it was time to meet some of the kids. The narrow-faced boy was by himself. I'd start with him.

'Hello. My name's Will.'

He didn't smile back. 'Julian.'

We stood there.

I looked at him. 'Is this your first time with Forest School Camps?'

'I've been going to them every summer since I was a Woodling.'

'A what?'

He frowned, as if attempting to work out how I possibly couldn't know what a Woodling was, before a big boy with curly red hair came lumbering towards us and picked Julian up in a bear hug. 'Freddie!' shouted Julian, ruffling the boy's hair. 'Where have you been hiding, you git?'

Instead of answering, the boy cocked his head at me and said, 'Who's this?'

'I don't know. Who cares?' They bounded off, knocking into one of the girls and inspiring Frances to give an impromptu lecture about respect for personal space. A few minutes later Vivian announced we were getting on the train, single file, calmly, without any pushing or running. The kids rushed towards the platform like a herd of buffalo. A few of us followed like uncertain ants, stepping up onto the train and obeying Vivian and Frances's orders to put our rucksacks on the racks. Next came a scramble for seats. Everyone seemed to know someone else they wanted to sit next to.

Frances saw me standing in the aisle. 'Will, was it? Right, let's find somewhere for you . . . ah. There we go.'

She led me towards the one empty seat in the carriage. It was by the toilet.

That was fine by me. I had the latest copy of *2000 AD*, a peanut butter sandwich, a carob bar and a piece of toli. The train rolled through the sprawling suburbs of London, past warehouses and rows upon rows of cars outside vast supermarkets, past pylons and rivers, through market towns and into valleys. A mist of rain hung over the land. The granite morning was followed by a grassy afternoon, and it must have been at around three when we got off at a tiny train station, deep in the Brecon Beacons. A rattling minibus drove us to Base Camp, which was a clearing in some woods in a valley. After I failed to work out how to pitch a tent Vivian came along and did it for me, muttering something about pampered London kids not being able to last a minute in the wild. I had never asked to last a minute in the wild. I didn't want to be here at all. Since the family refused to go on holiday with me I would have been perfectly content spending the summer watching television, listening to records, reading comics, riding the BMX and walking (the streets). I'd throw in a bit of meditation if it kept Nev happy. Even that was preferable to being stuck in the middle of Wales with the unfriendly children of the ecologically aware.

I had a strong desire to go to the toilet. I asked Vivian where it was.

'Over there,' he said, pointing to a sheet held up between two sticks speared into the ground. 'If you need to do a crap, make sure you bury it afterwards.'

'Why can't I use the flush?'

185

He looked at me. 'You really haven't done this before, have you?'

The sight awaiting me on the other side of that sheet gave a glimpse into the horrors of life in the trenches during the Great War. The toilet consisted of a hole in the ground about two metres long, half a foot wide and a half a foot deep. It was already filled with human waste and we had only been here for an hour or so. The idea was that you straddled it, a foot on each side of the trench, and relieved yourself in a squatting position, trousers around your ankles. Vivian recommended not using toilet paper because it was bad for the environment, but taking a little bucket of water with you and splashing it up onto your bum instead. That was going too far. There was nothing I could do about having to defecate, but no way was I going to indulge in this level of bottom-based water torture.

It smelt hideous, with flies buzzing about and pieces of soiled toilet paper scattered in and around the ditch. I took some of the paper that hung on a hook by one of the sticks and positioned myself over the trench. One false move and I didn't think I could continue living. I looked up. Standing before me, watching from the edge of the sheet was a little girl. She must have been about five.

'Who are you?' she said.

'Go away!' I hissed. 'This is the boys.'

'No it's not. It's boys and girls.'

'Why don't you wait until I've finished like a normal person?'

'You smell of poo.'

'It's not me, you idiot. It's the toilet.'

'You're not very nice. You're a poo man.'

'Can you leave me alone?'

She ran away, shouting that she was going to tell on me, but she did something much worse. I would never know if it was an accident or not, but she careered straight into the sheet, dislodging it from one of the sticks and leaving it flapping helplessly in the wind. I looked up in horror.

My own mother hadn't seen me go to the toilet since I was six. I locked the door of the bathroom even when there was nobody else home. And now a small army of Forest School Campers, children and teenagers, were sat in a line on the grass, staring at me. There was a moment of shocked silence, before the little girl pointed and started laughing. Everyone joined in.

I resisted the urge to run like hell, hygiene taking precedent over burning embarrassment, and knew that I had to say something. For some reason all I could think of was the episode of Mastermind I had watched the night before. Eventually, I looked straight at those mocking, cackling faces, and said,

'I've started so I'll finish.'

The thrust of the philosophy behind Forest School Camps seemed to be that modern society had made us miserable and we needed to return to a deeper connection with nature. Maybe they were right, but it was this deeper connection with nature that was making me miserable. I liked gravel drives and Volvos, Atari games consoles and toasted sandwich makers. Most of all, I liked flushing toilets. I also liked having parents who were easy to get money out of when they had drunk too much red wine, who splashed out on family holidays, and who filled suburban homes with beanbags and comfortable sofas. It was challenging enough to have all that replaced by meditating yogis and unusual cosmological beliefs. To be forced to live in the Welsh wilderness for ten days as well was a step too far.

After supper we had to scrub our tin plates under a spitting tap, which created a pool of mud around it; the kind of madly pointless activity dishwashers so successfully made redundant back in the 1950s. And there was worse to come. Soon it was time for the ritual at the heart of Forest School Camps: the singing of hearty folk songs around the campfire.

'This is my favourite bit of the FSC experience, said Vivian, passing around spiral-bound booklets of songs. 'Let's start with 'The Wild Rover'. That's guaranteed to get the old vitals pumping.'

I looked around. There were handsome teenage boys with sharp, fine jaws and big teeth, and pretty young women with long blonde hair, elegantly messy in oversized jumpers, ripped blue jeans and weathered Dr. Martens caked in just the right shade of mud. They clutched fingerless gloves around tin cups of hot chocolate, beer and whisky, or they held onto each other as they sang the words of songs with titles like 'Green Grow the Rushes, O' and 'Hallelujah! I'm a Bum'. The sparking, crackling fire illuminated their gilded faces. Every now and then, one of them would look over at me and start sniggering. A pretty girl said, 'Aw, leave him alone,' which made it worse. I quietly crawled away and disappeared into my tent, and told myself that tomorrow could only be an improvement.

* * *

'Right,' said Vivian over breakfast. 'Today we're going on a hike.'

Real country folk jumped into a car to get a pint of milk from the village store a quarter of a mile down the road, but the Forest School Campers' idea of a good time was to walk for as long as humanly possible. With great reluctance, I began a seven-mile hike through the stony paths and muddy tracks of the Brecon Beacons.

'You're posh, aren't you?' said a lank-haired girl in a Yorkshire accent as we marched along a path next to a pine forest.

'Not really,' I replied, truthfully. I was middle class.

'Yeah, you are. I can tell. Do you live in a house with a swimming pool? Have you got a Rolls Royce?'

'It's just a normal house with a shed, thank you very much. And we've got a Volvo.'

Vivian, who had already told me that he worked as a geography teacher at a comprehensive in Acton, appeared to find this amusing. 'Didn't you say you lived in Richmond?'

'Yeah. So what?'

'That's full of stuck-up people. You must be posh.'

He went on to tell me that private education was immoral, muttering darkly about public school bastards going up against the wall come the revolution. That sounded like the kind of thing Tom and his rich Westminster pals bored on about. I quickened my pace to get away.

Thinking about Nev's claim that I always held myself back, I resolved to join Julian and Fred. They were walking in the company of two girls. 'Hi guys,' I said, chirpily. 'This hike is a ruddy nightmare. How far do you think we've got to go?'

'Is that the guy who did a shit in front of everyone?' said one of the girls.

This was highly amusing to all apart from me, so I got away from Fred, Julian and the two girls as well and spent the rest of the hike by myself, seeing how long I could kick a stone along the path before it disappeared into the grass. Eventually we stopped for lunch by the banks of a lake. We sat on logs near the water's edge. I hunched over a cheese sandwich until Fred bashed into me and sent the sandwich careering into the mud.

'What did you do that for?'

'Sorry mate,' he said, as Julian looked on, smirking. 'Accident.'

After taking in a few long, deep breaths, I went up to Frances and asked if I could have another sandwich.

'I'm sorry darling, but we've just run out,' she said, stretching her mighty frame upwards and taking off her CND T-shirt. 'Besides, it wouldn't be fair on the others if I let you have two. Would you like an organic carrot instead?'

I took myself off to a spot near the water under a large weeping willow. It must have been around the third bite of the organic carrot when a remarkable sight appeared. It was Frances, entirely naked. She had a wild bush of bright ginger pubic hair. It was the first time I had ever seen a real, live woman without any clothes on. She disappeared under the surface, taut muscles rippling through the water.

Meanwhile, as if this was the most natural thing in the world, everyone else was getting on with eating lunch. Maybe it was. I couldn't tell anymore.

As I tried to concentrate on a pair of geese flapping

through the rushes, I failed to notice Fred and Julian creeping up from behind. I was crouched down, resting on my knees, and they gave me a push, which sent me flying. I landed face down in the mud.

It only took a few seconds. I picked myself up and ran at Julian with full force, seeing his mocking smile turn to shock as I pushed him backwards over the bumpy grass. Frances was still in the water but Vivian ran over, yelling, 'Hey hey hey!' and pulled me off this boy I had grown to hate over the space of only minutes.

Frances came bounding out of the lake as Vivian held me, red-faced, spluttering and covered in mud. 'I'll handle this,' said Frances, beads of water falling from wherever hair collected on her body. 'Right. What's going on?'

It all came out. As a naked Frances towelled herself dry about a foot away from where I was sitting, and as Julian sat with his head bowed, I told her he seemed to have had it in for me ever since I arrived, and I had only tried to make friends, and all I had been getting from these so-called liberated children was hostility. Being thrown down in the mud was the last straw. When the tirade came to an end, Frances held my gaze.

'I want you to look at Julian.'

Julian had somehow managed to squeeze out a couple of tears during my tale of woe, which looked entirely unconvincing on his weaselly face, with its nasty, thin lips and scheming eyes. Frances, however, appeared to take this as a sign of his deep remorse. She nodded slowly, as if something profound was happening.

'Now I want you to hug each other,' Frances said. She was still naked.

'What?' I barked. 'No way!'

We settled on a handshake. And then we started the three-hour hike back to base camp. This joyless walk through the miserable Welsh drizzle had been for the sole purpose of watching a muscle-bound lesbian go skinny dipping and my being shoved face down into the mud. I walked alone, thinking of the creased lines around Nev's eyes when he laughed, and Mum's indulgent expression after I had managed to convince her to give me money for something I really didn't need, and Will Lee, proposing we take some Bourbon biscuits and milk up to the attic and dig out that David Hamilton book of soft-focus photographs of women without many clothes on, and I decided that I just wanted my old life back.

As I kicked stones into the valley below and we trudged back along the path that cut over hills and through forests, I wondered: what was better? To be teased and harangued or ignored entirely? I decided the latter. A few of the girls linked arms. Three boys in matching waterproof jackets planned the den they were going to build when they got back. Fred and Julian marched on ahead. Frances strode barefoot, smiling broadly, while Vivian fussed over his Ordnance Survey map. I would do my best not to talk to any of them until the whole sorry affair was over.

Somehow the week passed by. I got up each morning and went to war with another day. We climbed up a rock one afternoon and went down a hole on another. And we walked. One day we walked so far that we couldn't go back to base camp, hiking for nine or ten miles through the constant wet before ending up on a flat patch of grassy land outside a wood somewhere, the nearest village a mile away. At least there wasn't any singing around the various campfires that night, but we did all have to sleep in the same big canvas tent with the boys at one end, the girls at the other and the two adults in the middle. I got in early with a copy of *The Secret Diary of Adrian Mole*.

On the last night there was something akin to a fete without money. Everyone was given a handful of beans representing tokens, which you could use to pay for the various fun activities that people set up. One whey-faced girl had overcooked custard to turn it into yellow putty and for a bean you could make a shape with it before handing it back. There was a non-domestic-abuse Punch and Judy show by Frances and a lecture on foraging by Vivian. It cost two beans and took place in the undergrowth.

That night I saw Julian, for a rare moment on his own, by the campfire. I sat down next to him.

'What is your problem with me?'

He looked up briefly, before going back to making circles in the charcoal with a stick.

'Is it because I tried to make friends with you? Because that was my dad's idea. I didn't even want to.'

'No, it's not that,' he said, eventually. 'It's just that there's something about you I don't like.'

That may have been the comment that set me off on a crime spree.

9

Delinquency

Nev picked me up from Waterloo, grinning broadly in his oversized glasses and the same white trousers and blue jumper he was wearing the last time I saw him. I watched the other kids run off towards their parents. Vivian consulted his compass while Frances approached me with an enormous smile, crushing me with the upper half of her body before I had a chance to escape. 'He's been wonderful!' she gushed to Nev. Out of the corner of my eye I saw Julian shuffling towards a cross-looking man, who nodded at him curtly before they set off in the direction of the Underground.

'Was it a proper Boy's Own adventure?' said Nev, as we walked towards the car. 'Did you do all the things you love – climbing trees, making fires and building dens?'

I had promised myself I wouldn't cry. I had succeeded in not crying for the entire holiday and I wasn't going to now. But it was when I got into the Volvo, with its Brahma Kumari egg-shaped air freshener and Brahma Baba bumper sticker, that my heart beat a little too fast, my eyes welled up, and the heat came up into cheeks that so far had remained wet only from the constant rain.

'It was horrible. The kids were horrible. Everything was horrible. I hated it.'

'Oh no, Sturch. I thought you would have a great time.'

'Well I didn't. How was India?'

His face seemed to light up from within. 'It was a transcendent experience. The meditation I practised there unlocked a new level of blissful spirituality that made me realize I've been splashing about in the shallow waters of consciousness until now. Finally, I'm beginning to make real progress on this path I've taken. I've never felt such a strong feeling of arriving at my spiritual home, and . . . oh dear. This is tough on you. The Yogis say . . .'

'I don't care what the Yogis say.'

Nev was silent for a while. I stopped crying as we passed the Porsche showroom at Chiswick roundabout, a sign that home was near. 'I was only going to say that when we work on ourselves, when we no longer feel attachment to others but can offer them something rather than take from them, we find people treating us much better. Perhaps the other kids picked up on something? Perhaps you seemed needy?'

'Perhaps,' I said, gazing out of the window.

'I do think the seven-day course in the basics of meditation might help. When I think of what I was like before I met the BKs, of how much anger, insecurity and ego I had, I can hardly believe I'm the same person. By the way, Mum and I have some exciting news.'

'What? Are we getting a dog?'

Nev chuckled. 'Better than that. I'll wait until we get back before telling you.'

195

There was a For Sale sign outside the house. Inside, tea chests lined the halls. All the books in the living room were packed up. Mum appeared, bouffant reined in by a headscarf.

'What's going on?' I said, dropping my rucksack in the hallway.

'Three guesses,' said Tom, slouching down the stairs with his arm around a girl. He turned to her. 'Oh yeah, I forgot to tell you. I've got a brother.'

The girl introduced herself as Fiona. She had a mane of chestnut hair, nut-brown eyes and a pretty, welcoming smile. Incredibly, she appeared to be Tom's girlfriend. Tom stood there, chomping distractedly on an apple. Nev stood behind him, smiling and bouncing up and down on his toes.

'We've found a beautiful new house,' said Nev. 'You'll love it.'

I stumbled about, looking into the kitchen, the drawing room and the telly room: everything was packed up. I looked upstairs: at least they had left my room alone. I went back down.

'When did this happen? Why didn't anyone tell me?'

'We didn't want to disturb you in your period of transition and growth,' said Nev, softly.

'So you thought you'd just move house instead?'

It took three days to get over the shock of it. On the first day I stayed in bed, emerging only to have a go on the Scalextric and eat supper with the family. Tom's girlfriend tried to hold his hand, but he swatted her off. Mum broke a plate after dropping one of Nev's loaves onto it. Nev held forth on India, Mount Abu and his love affair with the Brahma Kumaris.

'There's a sister there who underwent surgery to have a cancerous tumour removed from her stomach,' he said, signalling amazement with widened eyes. 'And do you know what? She didn't have any anaesthetic whatsoever. She meditated the pain away!'

'Why didn't she just meditate the tumour away in the first place?' asked Tom.

Nev had no answer to that. He described India to us instead. Trains were so crowded that people rode on the roof; monkeys stole your food as you were eating it; and, for those who had slipped through the arranged marriage net, lonely hearts columns in the newspapers revealed a lot about the way people lived. He had clipped one out to show to us. It read: *Shy boy, only slightly disfigured, seeks companionship. Age not an issue but own hair preferred.*

On the second day, I went to Sheen Bumps and stayed there until dusk. A crowd of kids watched as I cleared the stream jump. I told them to put their bikes upside down on the other side of the stream. I would jump over them too.

'What if you land on me bike?' said one boy.

'Who cares? We're all going to die anyway.'

I cleared the bikes. BMX etiquette decreed that you didn't clap when someone did something impressive, but mumbled an understated *yeah*. There were lots of *yeah*s. A boy I had seen around asked if I wanted to come to his place and play video games. I shrugged a yes.

'What do you mean, we're all going to die?' he said as we cycled down the long path, which cut through the cemetery and led back down into Richmond.

'Haven't you heard? There's going to be a nuclear war. It might happen next year, it might happen next decade,

197

but it's coming. Enjoy yourself while you can. There won't be a tomorrow.'

The boy's name was Colin. His house was on Mount Ararat Road, where we had lived before we moved to Queens Road. That had been a happy little home. On our way there we headed down the high street, cycling on the pavement and darting in and out between irate pensioners and mums with prams. We pulled up outside WH Smith.

'I nicked a load of stuff from there the other day,' said Colin, leaning back on his saddle. 'It's easy.'

'Tell me about it. Last week I went in there and stole some bloody . . . fags. Smoked them all and puked up.'

'Yeah, right. Go and nick something now then.'

'Easy.'

Why shouldn't I steal? Nev was more interested in staring at a red egg than he was in his own family. I was being sent off to a hippy school for the educationally subnormal and our parents were moving house to further the cause of weirdness. The only problem was that the old lady with the plastic-framed glasses serving at the till by the chocolate section kept glancing at me, but crime was all about confidence. That's what Christopher Tobias said.

There were a lot of people around. I sidled towards the confectionery racks and picked up a Lion Bar. The old lady behind the till kept looking over at me, frowning. I put the Lion Bar back. Then I saw my moment. She was squinting at the price of a paperback. I grabbed three Milky Bars and stuffed them into my pocket and shuffled nonchalantly out of the shop. It was the fastest nonchalant shuffle that branch of WH Smith had ever seen.

Colin was standing with the bikes outside. 'Go go go,' I whispered.

'Did ya do it?'

'Can't talk here. Let's move.'

We cycled back to the safe house – Colin's bedroom – and unloaded the stash. Milky Bars came in three sizes and I had got the largest. On standard pocket-money budgeting, even buying the middle size felt extravagant. It was a wild, untameable feeling to think that you could have anything you wanted if you were prepared to just go in and take it. Yes, being an outlaw felt good.

Into Colin's room came two girls of about our age. There was a blonde in a denim miniskirt and another with permed hair and a sullen, sleepy-eyed look about her. 'That's my girlfriend,' said Colin, waving vaguely at the sullen one. 'The other one's her mate.' He chucked a Milky Bar at them.

'All right?' said Colin's girlfriend and her mate. They were chewing gum. Eventually, I found out they were called Sam and Emma. They slumped onto the floor in unison, beneath a poster of a tennis player scratching her bottom, took out their gum, stuck it on the wall and split the Milky Bar. Considering they were in a relationship, Colin and Sam exhibited a degree of distance that would have done the Brahma Kumaris proud. Perhaps this was the way of burgeoning teenage romance, because an hour later Emma was officially my girlfriend, although only a few words were spoken and no physical contact was made. The following Saturday we would go for a double date to the cinema.

'Anyway, see you later,' said Emma, as she and Sam pulled the chewing gum from the wall, put it back in their mouths, got up and left.

'Nice one, mate,' said Colin. 'She's a right slag.'

On the third day of my recovery from the shock of the sale of 99, Queens Road, I went with Mum and Nev to the new house. It was in a terraced row called The Paragon and it was tall and thin – five floors if you included the basement – with a big wisteria creeping up its shuttered windows and white plaster façade. It was set away from the busy road that connected Petersham with Richmond, but there were no cars in its drive. As Mum explained, as we walked up the stone steps that led to the dilapidated doorway, the council had refused planning permission for cars on the driveway, considering it too dangerous a road to pull out onto. In fact, they had refused planning permission for anything to be done to the house whatsoever, despite its semi-derelict state. It was Grade II listed and it had to be kept in its original condition. This made it much cheaper than it should have been.

'We're taking a risk,' said Mum as she rattled the door. 'We're getting it for a song, but only because it won't be worth living in if we don't get planning permission to fix it up. Nobody apart from Nev and I were stupid enough to make an offer on it.'

'Why are you buying it in the first place?'

'Fell in love with it.'

If the exterior of the house was bad, it was nothing compared to what lay in wait for us within. The house was squatted. The owner had been living abroad, and an ever-moving stream of Australian backpackers had taken over. Laws on squatting in the 1980s meant that if you hadn't actually broken into a house you had legal rights to stay, so there was no guarantee they would ever move out. An unshaven man with a towel wrapped around his hairy stomach answered the door. He looked at us,

200

grunted, and wandered down a darkened hallway. In the living room, where the roots of a sycamore tree from the garden had burst through the back wall and were now flourishing internally, two other men and a woman were sitting smoking on a broken brown leather sofa amid clothes, porn magazines and piles of video cassettes. None of them said anything or looked at us.

The basement was without light and had a dank, mouldy air. It also had its own toilet, bathroom and kitchen. It was essentially a self-contained flat. 'This is where I'll be based,' said Nev, happily padding about in the gloom.

The garden was an overgrown mess of weeds, but there was a stone path that cut through it and on the other side of the wall was the towpath of the Thames. That was appealing; I could get a little boat and row out to the islands in the middle of the river. At the very top of the narrow stairs inside the house were two attic rooms. I went into the one that looked out onto the river bend below.

Maybe it wouldn't be so bad here. The house was an ancient, creaking ruin, full of imperfections and frailties, but with bags of character. 99, Queens Road was a brick box by comparison. The attic room had a floor which slanted so much you could roll a marble down it. The walls were a mass of bulges. The staircase banisters were broken. The living room had panels that appeared to be moving. It was as if the house were alive.

On the drive home, as she applied her lipstick in the Volvo's mirror, Mum said to Nev, 'We've done it now. You're just going to have to go back to work. And *stop giving money to the yogis.*'

This was the first time I had heard of Nev spending what money he had on something other than the family. At the time, I didn't think much of it. There were more important issues to deal with, such as the forthcoming first date with Emma. I may have been in love with Sadie, but having an official girlfriend – and a slag to boot – would ease the pain.

And then there was crime.

The delinquency moved up a level on the Saturday of the date. That afternoon, Colin and I sat under a tree and discussed the very real problem of how we were to pay for the cinema to which we had agreed to take our girlfriends – Colin said that nobody ever got in a girl's knickers by being a tightwad – when we saw something small, brown and square on the ground. It was a wallet. In it were six twenty-pound notes.

They say money changes people. I felt changed just by looking at it.

'You know I told you my dad is into meditation and shit?'

'Yeah?'

'He believes in karma. Basically, it says that everything happens for a reason. Here we are worrying about money and look what God has put in front of us.'

Colin turned the wallet over in his palms. 'In a way,' he said, 'it would be going against God's will to hand it into the police. Especially as I've been saving up for a hi-fi.'

'And I need new wheels for the bike.'

Colin took the notes out of the wallet, then chucked it into the bushes. He gave me three of them. 'Not a word to anyone. Not even the girlfriends.'

I took a detour to the bicycle shop on the way home and bought wheels at a cost of twenty pounds. I hid them in the shed. Nev was in his meditation chamber. The synthesizer hums of Beyond Sound seeped under the door. I knocked. Nev was inside, cross-legged, staring at the egg.

'Just thought I'd better tell you. I'll be back late so don't wait up for me.'

Nev nodded serenely. 'Have a wonderful evening. And make sure you avoid anger, ego, greed, lust and attachment.'

Colin, Emma and Sam were standing outside Richmond cinema, leaning against a poster advertising *Tootsie*, starring Dustin Hoffman as an out of work actor who starts dressing up as a woman and sees his career take off. It was either that or *Rambo*. Emma and I nodded at each other. She had small eyes and an upturned nose, which made her look, in a not entirely unattractive way, like a pig.

We found a row of four seats near the back of the cinema. Colin and I sang along to the theme tune of Pearl & Dean until Sam told us to shut up. Emma stared blankly at the screen. I thought I had better say something.

'What music do you like?'

'I hate that question.'

An advertisement for a local Indian restaurant consisting of photographs of unappetizingly lurid curries played out on the screen before us. Eventually I said: 'I'm into Jimi Hendrix.'

'Who?'

'Would you two lovebirds put a cork in it?' hissed Sam.

There followed two hours of frozen non-movement in the shadows of Richmond Odeon. Every now and then I craned my neck over to see how Colin was doing, but Sam sat stiffly in her seat, pushing an unending stream of popcorn into her masticating mouth. As for me, I kept thinking about putting my arm around Emma, but the way she was pouting at the screen didn't seem to invite it.

I can't remember anything about the film, except that Dustin Hoffman looked a lot like Auntie Kathleen. When it finished we walked back up to Mount Ararat Road. I asked Emma for her thoughts on BMX maintenance. By the time we got up to The Vineyard, we had stopped talking altogether.

We had just come onto Mount Ararat Road when a door opened to a house a few doors down from the one where we used to live. Four naked people, two men and two women, ran out of the house, waving their arms in the air. They went around the postbox at the end of the road, then ran back into the house and closed the door.

'Bloody hell,' said Colin. 'What was that?'

'Looks like they're having fun,' I said.

'More than we're having, at least.'

I went home without even kissing Emma on the cheek. I think I may have managed goodnight. The date was not the success I had hoped for, but at least I had a girlfriend and besides, I still had thirty pounds left over from the wallet haul. Perhaps this new way of life wasn't so bad after all. Now that Mum and Nev didn't appear to be taking any interest in my wellbeing, education or existence, I was let off the hook. And soon I would be at boarding school. No more would there be tearful recriminations after they discovered I hadn't done my mathematics home-work. No more would they ask me how, after four years of French lessons, I couldn't speak a word of French. I was free, more or less.

The following day at Sheen Bumps, two girls came up to me.

'Are you Will?' said one of them.

'Who wants to know?'

'Yeah, well, Emma says you're chucked.'

I never loved her anyway.

The only time Nev appeared to care about what I was up to was when he wanted me to come to one of the Brahma Kumaris' meetings. It was such an occasion that nearly ruined one of the greatest nights of my life. A few days after the beginning and end of my first romantic involvement, the phone went. It was Sadie.

'Hello, stranger,' she said. Even the way she spoke was sophisticated. 'How do you fancy coming to a gig with me tomorrow?'

This was incredible!

It was a band called The Stingrays and they were playing in the basement of The Clarendon. We arranged to meet outside Hammersmith tube at eight o'clock. I spent the next day preparing. I took the tube, by myself, to a second-hand store in Covent Garden Tom had told me about called Flip, where row upon row of clothes from America's Fifties and Sixties heyday filled two floors of a shop decorated by neon diner signs and truck-stop detritus. For £20 I bought a red-checked shirt and a pair of Levi's.

I had just paid and was on my way out when I spotted a row of classic baseball jackets. There was a particularly nice one: red cotton with elasticated stripes on the collar and waist, nicely worn white leather arms, and emblazoned with a cartoon of a man running along with a hockey stick inside the words 'Coquitlam Ambassadors'. It had a price tag of £60, a preposterous amount. You could feed a commune's worth of Brahma Kumaris for a week for that.

I slipped it on. I didn't look in the mirrors or go the changing rooms. The place was full of people in baseball jackets. Who was to say that I didn't walk in wearing one? The moment of bravery almost left me as I whistled my way towards the door and spotted a security guard, but he was busy chatting up a pretty sales girl. I kept going.

Nobody caught me.

The final flourish was a new haircut. Tom had been talking about getting a flat-top: buzz-cut at the sides, short on top, quiff at the front. There was a barber on Long Acre with a photograph in the window of a similar hair-style, so I pointed to it and told the man to do the same. Shorn was the mass of curly locks that had sat on my head since the age of five. Sadie wouldn't know what hit her.

Mum wasn't there when I got home and Tom was out too, but Nev appeared, bounding forward in a white pyjama suit with that wide-eyed look I was learning to fear. 'Ah Will, there you are,' he said. 'I'm so glad, because we're going to go off on a great adventure together. Dadi Janki is back in England, so I thought we could head off to Willesden on my motorbike and share *rakhi.*'

What he meant was another evening of listening to a sermon on soul consciousness with a bunch of silent westerners and a couple of domineering Indian women, followed by the exchanging of friendship ribbons and an hour's meditation. I explained I had plans, but he batted them away with a flutter of the eyelids. 'Never mind that,' he said, and when I protested that I really did intend to go out and see a band, he said: 'Tell you what. I'll drop you off at Hammersmith afterwards so you can go and see King Crude.'

'They're called King Kurt, I'm going to see The Stingrays, and Nev, I don't want to go to the Brahma Kumaris tonight. I've got to get ready.'

An hour later I was chugging through the streets of West London on the back of Nev's little motorbike. It was red and white, with a high plastic windscreen and a tiny 125cc motor. It had a shopping basket on the back. Nev customized his wheels with a sticker of Brahma Baba and a flag of the Yogi egg, which flapped from the top of the aerial. We chugged to a halt outside the little BK house in Willesden. 'I've been thinking,' he said, taking off his helmet, 'about this unsettling period of global transformation we are going through, and I want to assure you that you don't need to worry, Sturch.'

'What do you mean?'

'You know how I've explained there are new souls, who arrive further down in the cycle, and there are old souls who have been through many incarnations and seem to have within them an innate wisdom, even if it comes with the *sanskars* of many rebirths? Well, I know you are an old soul. In fact, I strongly believe you started your journey in the Golden Age.'

At a guess, this was a compliment, although, given my recent activities, it didn't feel like a deserved one.

'What about Tom?'

Nev mused on this awhile. 'He was probably medieval. My guess is, he was enjoying ale and pig roasts some time before the dissolution of the monasteries. It's why he's so good at Latin, and why he likes going out late, getting drunk, and slumbering in bed in the mornings. He's busy recreating his own Golden Age.'

Perhaps, I thought, as we took off our shoes in the corridor of the little house and laid them in a neat row alongside the others, I *was* around in the Golden Age. A few years previously I had been obsessed with a Japanese TV programme called *Monkey*, which was an adaptation of an ancient Buddhist fable about a monkey king accompanying a priest, alongside a pig and a fish monster, on a pilgrimage from China to India in search of the Holy Scriptures. And I liked the idea of going to India. Maybe I was looking forward to a future incarnation as a Yogi in the Golden Age, travelling about on a little cloud fuelled by mind power, and skipping about with the birds and the animals in joyous harmony? And Nev was definitely right about Tom, who once told me that everything had been going downhill since Martin Luther pinned his *Ninety-Five Theses on the Power and Efficacy of Indulgences* on the door of All Saints' Church in Wittenberg.

As it happened, Dadi Janki's *murli* that day was all about the cyclical nature of life. 'When we accept that the soul is eternal, we ease the passage through to the beginning of the play,' she croaked wisely, as translated by Sister Jayanti. 'Science teaches us that survival is for the fittest, and that chance events have shaped the course of life. This is confusion. We are watching life as it is projected from a deeper reality, like shadows in a cave. Consciousness is primary to the universe and it creates matter, not the other way round.'

It was time to take *darshan* – open-eyed meditation – with Dadi. I stared deep into those tough, unfathomable eyes as Sister Jayanti smiled on. Was this a cult? Surely this was far removed from the People's Temple, whose leader Jim Jones induced his 913 followers to drink cyanide-laced Kool-Aid in Jonestown, Guyana, or the Orange People, whose leader Bhagwan Shree Rajneesh had ninety-three Rolls Royces and whose members had turned sex without ties into a sacred rite and banned mothers from raising their own children.

All the same, the Brahma Kumaris offered the simplified lifestyle that is at the heart of the appeal of cults. The world is a confusing place and new religious movements make it simpler. Moral and philosophical ambiguity is removed; belief is absolute. They come with strict principles on what to eat, how to dress, what to read, how to behave, and most significantly, how to think. Intellectual and scientific enquiry is discouraged in both new and old religious movements; it is not the role of the believer to think they can rationalize the mysteries of the world. Cults also take away the importance of the family and replace it with the enclosed community. Rules governing sexual behaviour in the late twentieth century were ill defined. Who knew what was right or wrong any more? With the Brahma Kumaris it was straightforward: you didn't have sex at all. The BKs offered a set of guidelines on how to think, act and feel.

As we sat in silence in the small white room alongside Sister Nina, Brother Benji, Sister Clare and Brother Malcolm, I knew I had fallen into the physical temptations of the world and it must surely lead to my ruin. Here in this pure room, in this environment where nothing mattered but a reawakening of the soul, was the source of life's deeper meaning. When had Nev last shouted at me? It was before he underwent the process of enlightenment. I had begun my series of bodily incarnations in the Golden Age. Tom only started out in the medieval period, most probably as a pox-ridden pig farmer. That had to stand for something.

If it weren't for the apocalyptic worldview, the boredom of meditation, the white outfits, the dull conversations and the thought that I would be denied wine, women and all the other pleasures of the world before I had even tasted them, I would definitely have become a BK. As it was, I couldn't wait for the session to end so I could run off with Sadie and see The Stingrays.

It was some time after eight when Nev's little motorbike trundled past the line of people standing outside the dilapidated ballroom near Hammersmith tube station that was The Clarendon. Nev putted to a halt.

'What a bunch of weirdos!' said Nev.

'What about your lot?'

'You're not really going in there, are you? Some of those people look terribly degenerate.'

'Nev, please. Maybe I should get off and walk from here.'

Nev didn't seem to mind, so with a quick 'Om Shanti' he chugged off and I hotfooted it over to the station, where Sadie was waiting. Her hair was arranged into Fifties-style ponytail. She wore a baseball jacket over a loose T-shirt, and a leather miniskirt over tights and Converse trainers. Her lips were painted a luscious red.

'Wow. Look at you,' I said.

'Nice of you to notice.'

The Clarendon was divided into three sections: an upstairs ballroom for bigger bands, a ground-floor bar, which had a heavy-metal disco on Saturday nights, and a poky basement for the band we were about to see. We joined a queue, which came halfway down the stairs. The walls were painted black and dotted with the remnants of countless flyers. 'Look old,' hissed Sadie. This was hard when my absorption with those around me was reaching uncontrollable levels. In front of us were two girls stinking of cheap perfume and cigarettes, their hair (one straw blonde, the other pitch black) teased up into some sort of upward motion. They wore purple lipstick and the same outfit of pedal-pusher leggings and black leather jackets, even though the blonde girl was enormous and the black-haired girl was tiny. In front of them was a gang of men in leather jackets with the names of bands on the back. Their hairstyles were similar to mine, only more extreme: the back and sides of their heads were shaved entirely to highlight vertical structures of hair, often dyed green or red, towering high above their heads.

We inched forward. A giant of a man, about fifty, with long, slicked grey-and-black-streaked hair and the complexion of a North American Indian was standing by the door. He wore an overcoat as oily as his hair. Now I could see inside the room. It was miniscule, with a low black ceiling, only inches above people's heads, and a bar staffed by grumpy-looking middle-aged women. There was some kind of a noise resembling music blasting from the stage, which I could just make out. A man in a cut-off T-shirt was leaping about, howling something about 'zombie flesh eaters', as a huge rockabilly next to him slapped a double bass. In the darkness, the crowd at the front of the stage were hurling themselves around and whacking at each other with elbows.

211

'Wow. The band looks pretty crazy,' I squeaked. 'That lead singer is a flipping wild man!'

This proved to be a mistake. Sadie tried to ignore me, hoping that nobody had heard my unbroken voice, but we were right at the entrance, just about to pay the man who was sitting behind a wooden desk with a metal moneybox and a stamp to imprint on hands. The big man with slicked back hair narrowed his eyes and said, in a distinctly non-North American Indian growl: ''Ow old are you?'

'He's with me,' purred Sadie. And then, turning to the man behind the desk, she said, 'You're not going to be mean to me tonight, are you, Mike?'

'Oh baby, how could I?' said Mike, in a New York drawl, spanning out his hands. 'But if I see the little guy at the bar . . .'

We were in. And we didn't even appear to pay anything. The door to the toilets was hanging off its hinges. The carpet was sticky and wet. Beer came in plastic glasses. Everyone was smoking. The very air made your eyes water. The noise level was brutal. And the crowd was cool: a sea of leather jackets, headscarves, hairspray-controlled hair, and denim.

I was the youngest person in the room by years. And they all seemed to know each other, or at least know things I didn't.

'By the way,' shouted Sadie, 'I like your jacket.'

'Thanks.'

'In fact, you're looking pretty cute . . . for one of my brother's friends.'

We were leaning against a black wall, dripping with sweat. Sadie nodded at various people as they went past,

212

but she stayed with me, and when the main band came on she grabbed my hand and pulled me forward into the crowd. The Stingrays featured a drummer who played a single snare drum, a lead guitarist who looked like a Mod, a chubby bass guitarist and a singer with a blond pompadour who, as he leaped about the stage, put the microphone in his mouth, growled, yodelled and made his eyes roll about in his head like he might be on day release.

'Bal's such a nutter,' said Sadie admiringly, as we got splashed with beer. 'Cigarette?'

She held out a packet of Lucky Strikes. I had never smoked a cigarette, but the world was coming to an end anyway so it didn't really matter. I took one. Sadie lit it. I exploded into a hacking cough, just as the song ended.

'Are you all right?'

'Yeah, I'm cool,' I said through the choking. 'I really need to cut down.'

The band was playing a song called 'Come On Kid', and the energy in the room was frenzied. A sort of mania was taking over. It was the exact opposite of the spiritual calm in the BK house in Willesden, and it was . . . not exactly sexual, but heightened, volatile, in the moment. I put the cigarette out and threw myself into the maelstrom in front of the stage. Being rather slight, I ended up being pushed all over the place before slipping in a pool of beer and landing on the floor with a thud. A rockabilly stuck his hand down and hauled me up. Sadie, giggling from the side, jumped in next to me. Holding each other, we half danced, half threw each other around, losing ourselves to the ritual of abandon.

Nev had spoken about the transcendental feeling he experienced with meditation, the sensation of closing

213

down all extraneous thoughts and surrendering oneself to the reality of the soul. Maybe this wasn't exactly what he had in mind, but I felt something transcendental was going on that night with The Stingrays. It may have been closer to intoxication than purity, but the blasts of sound, the sensation of being jostled around, and the reverie-inducing strangeness of being with a girl who had become some sort of fantasy vision all induced in me a moment free of thought; a submission to a power outside of the ego. I felt a great love for everyone in the room. It was a Damascene moment, in fact, in a filthy basement in Hammersmith.

When the set was over and the greasy-haired bruiser got up onto the stage and bellowed 'ten firr-ee, everybody aht', the lights went up and a sense of loss came over me, like I had been thrown back into a lower world. Sadie, smiling, pretty and wan, suggested we go outside for a bit before heading home.

We leaned on the pavement railings, the constant traffic of Hammersmith roundabout on the other side. We talked about how great the band was, what other gigs were coming up, which bands she liked, and how Sam was doing. (He was off to Westminster and, according to Sadie, more of a swot than ever.) I mentioned the move into the house by the river, and that I was off to a strange school called Frensham, and that I didn't know what was happening anymore.

'I never *have* known what was happening,' she said, blowing out a stream of smoke. 'At least your parents are still together.' Sadie ground the cigarette under her shoe. 'I'd better go. But we should do this again soon.'

'Definitely,' I said, shuffling from foot to foot.

We walked towards the station. She would walk up King Street to her flat and I would take the District Line to Richmond. We stopped outside the barriers. I was sweating more now than I was inside The Clarendon.

'Fare thee well,' I said in a mock medieval voice, and regretted it instantly.

'Guess I won't see you now for a while. Maybe you can write to me.'

'I'll write to you every day. I mean every week or so.'

Then it happened – sort of. Sadie leaned forward, and so did I. She was only a little bit taller than me. Our lips actually met. For a second or two there was contact. Then she turned and walked away.

When Nev experienced his blinding flash of light in Westminster Cathedral, on the day that shaped the course of the rest of his life, he told me he was walking around in circles for two hours afterwards, dazed and confused, not knowing whether he was happy or sad, elated or in despair. I felt the same way now. As I waited for the Richmond train I thought only of Sadie's face, and that moment when our lips touched. It was almost too much to bear, like it was going to cause a heart attack.

As I lay in bed that night, ears ringing as a reminder of the excitement of the gig, I felt giddy, intoxicated, in love. Sadie was a lifetime older than me, in both sophistication and experience. The kiss was the feverish climax to a week of finding wallets, stealing Milky Bars and baseball jackets, going on my first date and becoming a style icon without anyone noticing. It was happening as all things – houses, schools, parents – were changing.

Sleep was impossible. I took down my poster of the BMX rider flying over the supermarket aisles. I looked at the Scalextric track. There would be no space for it in the new house. I was a teenager now.

The next morning, neither Mum nor Nev mentioned the fact of my having come in late stinking of cigarettes, beer, sweat, hairspray and whatever else oozed out of The Clarendon at closing time. Instead, Nev was talking about something he had been researching for *Will to Be Well*, now almost complete after a year's work and set to rock the medical establishment to its core. It was an analysis of the effect of magic mushrooms on the brain. It had been discovered that, rather than making the person see things which weren't there, the active ingredient of magic mushrooms temporarily removed the filter that regulates information bombarding the brain.

'It's the same as the experience I've had in meditation,' said Nev, after staring into his porridge for a sufficiently Yogic period. 'I've experienced life as it should be lived, if only the rational part of our brains allowed us to do so. People who have had near-death experiences often describe a feeling of bliss as their life ends and their brains stop working. When people return from these experiences, both from psychedelic drugs and from the edge of death, they realize life doesn't just end at this body.'

'Did someone mention drugs?' said Tom, shuffling into the kitchen in his socks, underpants and a dirty white T-shirt that hung loosely from his puny frame. 'I don't recommend them for breakfast.' He made himself a coffee. Coffee was an important part of Tom's new persona. He looked at me. 'What's happened to you? Your haircut looks like a DIY implement.'

Mum looked up from her copy of Selma James's *The*

Rapist Who Pays the Rent. 'I *thought* there was something different about you. Couldn't put my finger on it.'

'I think it's lovely for you boys to experiment with image,' said Nev in his white pyjama suit.

'It's just a phase we're going through,' said Tom.

'I'm out of here,' I said, pushing my plate containing the crusts of toast made from Nev's homemade bread in the direction of Mum. 'I've got to fit the new wheels on my bike and test them out with some serious airborne punishment.'

I realized my mistake as soon as I opened my mouth. In the old times, any mention that I was going off on my bike prompted Nev to check it was safe to ride, or at least to make sure I checked it was; despite being cavalier in other health and safety issues, Nev always believed the combination of me and a bike to be a potentially fatal one. These days he barely noticed when I came and went. Mum, however, fixed me with a gimlet eye.

'What new wheels?' she said hotly. 'Where did you get the money to buy new wheels? And come to think of it, I've never seen that jacket before. What's going on?'

After a long pause I said: 'I saved up.'

'Yeah, right,' said Tom. Mum pointed a finger and demanded to know the truth. I told her, with rising inflection, that she had no right to tell me what I could and couldn't buy and besides, if they hadn't turned weird, sent me off to boarding school and sold the house without telling me, none of this would have happened. Mum asked Nev to do something about it. He said that he would meditate for half an hour. Then the best course of action to take would be revealed to him by God.

I wasn't planning to hang around and find out what

217

that was. Mum screeched that I was up to something and possibly something serious, and I wouldn't be getting any pocket money until I confessed to whatever it was I had done.

'Leave me alone,' I shouted. 'You're so annoying.' She didn't follow me into the garden shed. I changed the wheels as quickly as possible so I could get out of there and not come back for a very long time. Maybe I'd go to Will Lee's house and tell him about the incredible night I'd had. Maybe I'd cycle over to Hammersmith and ring Sadie's doorbell. In any case, I was getting away from these people who were controlling, judging and asking outrageous questions about my finances.

'Will! Come back here.'

I pedaled away to the sight and sound of Mum, standing by the back door with her hands on her hips, barking away.

It was quarter of a mile down Queens Road when it happened. There was a corner of a kerb which provided a good miniature ramp from which to do a jump, and I must have used it hundreds of times to take the bike a foot or so off the ground. This time, however, I had failed to tighten the bolts of the front wheel, which meant that it came off the moment the bike left the ground.

I don't have any recollection of the actual crash, beyond being aware of a pool of blood on the pavement as I was helped up by, of all people, Tom, who had been on his way to see his girlfriend. He held me as I hobbled back home. Someone else who happened to be passing by carried the bike back. Then it was a vague wash of doctors, hospitals, and long stays in bed. And then it was Frensham.

218

10

Frensham Heights

I still have a shard of enamel imbedded in my upper lip. It's all that remains of my front teeth. After the crash knocked them out of alignment, chipping them and turning them grey, one solitary tooth stuck out in front of all the others. Then, when I was eighteen, I had them replaced by a bridge.

Nev didn't want me to have my teeth fixed. 'They give you a bit of character you haven't otherwise got,' he said, but Mum claimed it was guilt, not tightness, which informed Nev's opinion. 'He blames himself for the crash,' she told me. When I said there was no way it could have been his fault, she replied, 'He thinks he should have checked your bike was OK before you went off on it. It's a classic case of Nev deciding on the right course of action after the event.'

A trip to hospital revealed that my injury looked a lot worse than it was. I had face-butted the pavement with my profile, meaning that if you looked at me from the left, I was completely normal. But if you looked at me from the right, you would see cracked teeth, a lip so swollen it touched my nose, burst blood vessels turning my eye a deep red, and all the skin ripped off to leave the flesh bloody and raw. I couldn't move my right leg, but this turned out to be nothing more than severe bruising and a ripped tendon. The pain was intense. Mum's main concern was that I would lose my pretty boy looks. Now all I'm left with is a tiny scar from a set of stitches next to the corner of my right eye. The new teeth are definitely better than the ones nobody had to pay for.

The only really serious thing that happened was that the baseball jacket, which I was wearing at the time of the crash, seemed to disappear.

Nev was around in the week before I went to Frensham Heights. Tom bought me a copy of *The Velvet Underground & Nico* and Mum brought me soup in bed each day, the only thing I could eat. For the first time, I began to read books. Tom loaned his copies of *On the Road* and *The Dharma Bums* and Mum dug out *Animal Farm* and *1984*. Away from teachers telling you to do it, reading wasn't as bad as I thought. The one I didn't manage to get through was a self-published book, handed over with ceremonial solemnity by Nev, called *Living in Peace: A Beginner's Guide to the Brahma Kumaris*. 'There's some really wonderful wisdom in there, Sturch,' he said, before heading for his room and some final meditation sessions before the move.

By the time Mum drove me to Frensham with my trunk in the boot of the Volvo, my eye was still red and my lip still swollen but for the most part the raw scratches had healed. It was on the drive that I confessed to the discovery of the wallet.

'I know I should have handed it in,' I said, looking out

at the neat Surrey countryside as we drove along a high ridge of a road called the Hog's Back. 'Taking the money seemed like the right thing to do at the time.'

'In what way?' said Mum, but she didn't press me any further. Instead she talked about her plans for the new house. The idea was that Mum and Nev would live together, but not together. Nev would have a self-contained life in the basement, getting up at four o'clock each morning to meditate, and because Sister Jayanti had been forced to sell her house in Richmond, six o'clock morning classes for local BKs would be held there. The basement had its own front door so the Yogis wouldn't bother the rest of us. Nev would also continue to be a normal dad, eating meals with us and so on.

'That's the theory at least,' said Mum, craning her head into the windscreen. 'We'll see how it pans out.'

The Volvo came to a halt outside Hamilton House, the building I would live in for the first year. The first thing I noticed was a notice board with a letter signed by John A, with the A in a circle. That was the anarchist sign. What kind of a housemaster was also an anarchist? The type, I discovered, who let boys and girls lounge around in his front room where there was incense burning, worn rugs of muted colours covering every part of the floor, cushions decorated with red and blue embroidery containing tiny circular mirrors stacked in piles. John A was the chemistry teacher we had seen in the VW camper on the day Murphy showed Will MacCormac and me round the school. I would discover that he ran Hamilton House with an authority that was at once benevolent and absolute, despite his hippy tendencies. He asked Mum and me to come into his study behind the rug-filled room.

221

He said it was completely normal to feel homesick, and that I could always talk to him if something was bothering me. He explained how he liked to make sure all the boys wrote home once a week, and that there was a payphone I could use to call home after homework and before lights-out. His front room was always open to visit, although the rest of his part of the house was not.

Hamilton House had a close, malty smell, which doesn't exist outside of boarding schools. It was both institutional and homely, with hints of milk, biscuits, body odour and cleaning fluids. There was a TV room with several rows of chairs in orange plastic covering, one battered red velour sofa in the wall at the back, and French windows that opened onto an expanse of lawn and the woods beyond the school borders. Sitting on two of the chairs, feet up on two others, was the woman with black curly hair and her blonde friend I had seen on the open day.

They were talking about boyfriends. 'I miss him *sooo* much,' said the one with dark hair, in an American accent. 'I'm going to marry him.'

'But Lara, you mad fool,' said the blonde, who was in an oversized jumper, leggings and army boots, 'you can't get married until you're sixteen. And that's three years away.'

These 'women' were the same age as me!

'Gael and Lara,' said John A, as he led us into the TV room, 'as wonderful as it is to see you both, you need to be over in the main house and getting ready for your first day back.'

'Oh, but John, we wanted to see if there were any cute new boys,' the blonde girl replied in a pleading tone.

'This year, Gael,' he said, with a hint of a smile, 'you

will be concentrating not on "cute new boys", but on your mathematics and chemistry grades. Off you go.'

'You're no fun,' said Gael, as she and Lara pulled themselves up and out of the room. They waved hello as they left and ran off, giggling.

Mum and I went up the narrow staircase, past the fire door with its reinforced glass window, and down a corridor that led to my dormitory. It consisted of three beds, each with an accompanying chest of drawers, and it had a bay window overlooking a section of the garden with stone urns on pillars and a rose garden dissected by a cobbled path. Sitting at the edge of one of the beds, looking up at us with half-lidded eyes was the boy of mixed race with the messy Afro who had been skateboarding along the road on the day of our first visit.

'Don't worry,' he said in a formal tone, 'I'm perfectly sociable.'

He introduced himself as Eugene and, after he asked if I had been in a car accident and I explained I had fallen off my bike, he told me he had been at the school for two years. 'It's not a bad place really,' he said, leaning into the bed with his hands behind his head. 'Some of the kids can be rather annoying, but I guess that's to be expected. Please, take a pew. Join me. Relax.'

I was expecting to be worried or upset when Mum said it was time for her to go. Instead, there was a feeling of relief. I asked Eugene about the two girls I had seen earlier. 'Oh, yes. Them. Lara's always going on about her stupid boyfriend in Yemen,' he said. 'Gael's just a crazy hippy. Both are quite harmless.'

That's when the third member of our dormitory arrived. It was Will MacCormac; a pale, sorrowful vision who appeared to have grown six inches in the months since I had last seen him.

'Are you sure you've got everything?' said Will Mac's father in a distracted manner. He looked at his watch while dumping a trunk onto the one remaining bed. 'I don't want to get a phone call in two hours to tell me you've left your spot cream behind.'

'I'm fine,' mumbled Will, kicking at the carpet.

'Look, you can make friends with them,' said his father, waving an arm in our direction. 'Now try not to lose everything in the first five minutes of being here. I really must dash.'

And life at Frensham began. Eugene, Will and I walked up to the grand house that afternoon, shortly before high tea (there was no low tea), where Gael was playing a sophisticated lament on the grand piano that stood between two tall white pillars in the main hall. A stunning dark-eyed girl was dancing. She was wearing a leotard and legwarmers, a look London had been filled with after *Fame* became a hit movie three years previously.

'Wow. Who's that?' I asked Eugene, as the three of us watched the girl swoop and glide across the hall.

'That's Eva Yiasumi, and forget it. It's highly unlikely she would even look at you or indeed me, even if she weren't going out with the most popular boy in the year,' said Eugene, adding, in his stilted fashion, 'Are you an expert in the field of football?'

'No.'

'In that case, let's move on.'

Eugene said he had yet to do so much as kiss a girl, but he assured us he did have an unusually large penis. 'I don't wish to boast,' he said, walking along the gravel path with his hands behind his back, head bobbing forwards like a learned woodpecker, 'but it's something of a monster. I measured it. It's over eight inches long.'

Will MacCormac didn't make such claims, but he had two major factors in his favour: he was irresistible to all women, and he was an engineering genius. 'She fancies me,' he said glumly, shoulders hunched, as a sixth former passed and gave us a welcoming smile. 'Could be a bit of a problem. Can't say how that's going to go down with my girlfriend. And once I've got the specs for my new car off the ground, harassment from women is only going to get worse. What would you do if a guy built a supercar that goes from zero to sixty in five seconds – and has an ejector seat?'

'What does this machine look like?' asked Eugene, craning his head towards Will Mac.

'Take a look for yourself.'

Out of his pocket, Will Mac pulled a sweet wrapper. On one side of it you could make out the outline of a car, roughly sketched in pencil, if you peered hard enough.

'Careful,' said Will Mac, grabbing the wrapper off Eugene. 'If that gets into the wrong hands I could be looking at losing a cool million.'

It was on that first evening that Eugene wanted to inaugurate us into the boarding school ritual of dormitory masturbation, something in which Will Mac and I, suburban Londoners both, were not keen to engage. After a revelation of a school dinner – there was a canteen where you could have whatever you liked, without anyone shouting at you if you didn't finish everything on your plate – and after an embarrassing shower with a bunch of other boys, we got into bed and talked about girls. I

225

told the others that I had a girlfriend at home (maybe true, maybe not), that she was an older woman (true) and we had talked about doing it but decided to wait until we were older (definitely not true). Eugene said that near his house in Esher there was a place called the Hop where all the girls were pretty much begging for it. He hadn't actually been there yet, but everyone knew the Hop was the place to score.

'The most embarrassing thing,' added Will Mac, bleakly, 'is when mates' girlfriends come onto me. Come to think of it, it's probably worse when their mums do.'

'Hey lads,' said Eugene, 'are you aware of the Faint Feeling?'

I thought it was just Will Lee and me who knew about the Faint Feeling. It turned out to be a hot topic among the boys of Hamilton House, who were split roughly along the lines of those who had only experienced the FF and those who had got to the stage of full-on ejaculation.

'Come on,' said Eugene, heartily. 'Let's have a wank.'

Will Mac claimed he didn't need to masturbate, not when girls were jumping him everywhere he went, and I said it was not the kind of thing I did in public.

'OK, you spoilsports,' said Eugene, 'but don't think about trying to stop me. I'm going to imagine one of the hot sixth formers chomping down on my massive member.'

Eugene insisted we turn the light on because, he said, he couldn't do it in the dark. He sat upright and concentrated on a corner of the ceiling with a look of resolution.

'Do we have to watch?' said Will Mac. 'It's putting me off thinking about my various girlfriends.'

The main thing worrying me, beyond the grubbiness of Eugene's sexual awakening, was the fact that I seemed to be developing at a slower rate than other boys. In the showers, I couldn't help but notice how many boys had forests of pubic hair, where I had a mere sprouting. Some even looked like they needed to start shaving. And now Eugene was making his bed shake. He stared harder at the corner of the ceiling. His mouth was clenched tight, as if he was overcome, not with passion but determination.

'I've done it!' he screamed.

There was a moment of silence.

'I've got an erection!'

I'm not exactly sure what happened to Eugene and Will Mac the following morning, but I ended up going down to breakfast by myself. After marvelling at the choice – there was Corn Flakes, Rice Krispies *and* Alpen – I poured myself a glass of milk from the machine and stood in the middle of a large and noisy dining hall, holding a tray. There were shrieks of laughter from all around. There was a long table occupied by teenagers of about my age: I saw Gael and Lara, and various boys with ruddy cheeks and loud, laughing voices whom I vaguely recognized from Hamilton House.

'You always hold back,' I imagined Nev saying as I stood in the hall, shuffling from foot to foot. So I approached the long table. Then I remembered that first day at Forest School Camps and headed towards an empty space in the corner.

At Frensham Heights, I was relatively normal. Everyone seemed to be the child of divorcees, or had a father who had just announced he was gay, or spent holidays with their diplomat/engineer/ex-pat parents in places of

227

which I had never heard, like Gabon. There were Arab and Nigerian boys and girls possessed of a worldly sophistication and experience you simply didn't get at prep schools in Richmond. The headmaster whom, with pointed informality we called Alan, even though his bearded, bespectacled face terrified us, never bothered telling anyone off or laying down rules in Morning Talk. Instead he expounded on subjects with a passion that was far more effective for instilling discipline.

'What is God?' he said at his inaugural speech as eleven-year-olds sat cross-legged on the parquet floor of the assembly hall and craned their heads upwards, open-mouthed. 'I thought I knew. For fifteen years I lived as a Benedictine monk, in quiet contemplation of the tenets of Christianity. But I lost my faith. To whom does Man turn when the divine order of the universe falls away and all we are left with is chaos?'

Nobody had an answer to that, so Alan moved on. He became terribly upset at reports of a food fight during high tea the evening before, which must have been fairly minor, as I certainly hadn't seen it. 'People in Africa are dying,' he cried. 'And you, you children of privilege, are rolling up bread into balls and throwing it at each other? What kind of madness is this?'

At another Morning Talk, he got quite excited about the way so many pupils threw themselves behind Anti-Apartheid, CND and the Miners' Strike, the last being the latest crisis to benefit from a charity concert organized by some sixth formers who had formed a reggae band called Spliff Riff, but who didn't know how to behave towards one another. 'Yes, it's wonderful that we have raised so much money to help the families affected by the Battle of Orgreave,' he said, a few days after one of the most violent clashes between Yorkshire police and striking miners, 'but why can't we treat each other with love and compassion? Why do I see children laughing at another student because she is dressed in unfashionable clothing?' (I think he was referring to Gael and her flares.) 'Why did I hear two boys describing a girl in a foul and sexist manner?' (This could have been Eugene and Will Mac.) By the end of the talk he was practically in tears.

I didn't go home at all for the first half of that first term. Weekends were spent building dens in the woods or taking the bus into Farnham on a Saturday to wander about, buy sweets, and, when we had the money, go to the cinema. At Halloween, Eugene and I walked into a butcher's in Farnham and asked if we could have some of his left-over guts and offal.

'What do you want it for?' said the butcher, eyeballing us suspiciously.

'It's for our carnivorous pet budgerigar,' said Eugene innocently, his hands behind his back.

Back at Frensham, we headed off into the dense woods which lay at the edge of Hamilton House. A quarter of a mile into the woods were two cast-iron fuel burners next to a tent-like construction of corrugated iron. We had christened the smaller one the Krakon and the larger one the Titan; ancient gods who needed to be appeased lest their wrath turn on us. The Titan was stupid and was largely ignored, but the Krakon was cunning and it would not bode well to anger it. We intended to present the offal to the Krakon as a sacrificial offering; this was the remnant of a virgin we had killed.

'There's one problem,' said Eugene, as we built a fire

inside the Krakon and prepared to throw the stringy, fleshy animal bits onto it.

'What?'

'The Krakon will never believe we managed to find a virgin at Frensham Heights.'

On Sunday afternoons, we rode skateboards down a steep road which ran down behind the school towards a pond, holding on as long as we could until the skateboards started wobbling out of control. On Friday evenings, we sat in John A's front room and watched films. Most of the people in our year crammed in to watch the full-length video of Michael Jackson's *Thriller*, after which Lara burst into tears and announced she would be camping outside Michael Jackson's house in Los Angeles until he asked her to marry him. And once a week John forced us to write letters home. I tended to get mine out of the way on Saturday lunchtimes before doing something more interesting. *Dear Mum and Nev how are you I am fine,* I wrote. *Yesterday we had double maths well must go Will ps can I have a skateboard for Christmas?*

Mum's replies were a little more expansive. *The new house is in a shocking state of squalor and neglect, but with the help of my interior designer I am planning to make it look fashionable yet classic over the coming months,* she wrote. *I was thinking of peach for the living room. Thoughts?*

Nev's letters were of a soulful nature. *I really feel I have only just made a breakthrough in terms of understanding soul consciousness,* he wrote, exhibiting a pattern of only just working it all out that has continued ever since and most probably will continue for the rest of this lifetime and several afterwards. *The spirit within has reached a new level of freedom, enabling me to change consciousness and help the world with the sadness and confusion we see everywhere today. I hope you are remembering to shower regularly. Om shanti, Nev.*

Alan Pattinson, our idiosyncratic headmaster, also suggested that raising one's consciousness is of greater importance than striving for good grades. 'I don't want you to view me as an authority figure, because I'm not,' said Alan Pattinson at one Morning Talk, pacing the floor of the main hall and furrowing his brow. 'I'm trying to work it out like the rest of you. We are all learning, every day, teachers and students alike. So I'm going to sit on the floor over there, next to the Year Ones, and invite anyone with something profound to say to share it with the school.'

Alan Pattinson did indeed sit down, a giant among midgets as he squeezed his long limbs into a cross-legged position and lined up alongside an eleven-year-old, who was sucking her thumb and edging away from him. The problem was, nobody was sufficiently progressive to take Alan's place. This made him angry, negating the purpose of the exercise. Eventually, Eugene got up and sang a section from *Thriller*.

Each week revealed something new. Like the time we had a fancy dress disco. I borrowed one of Pete's old suits and went as a teddy boy. Eugene and Will Mac went as each other. Gael and Lara wore black bin liners and went as punks. A boy called Steve Rose, who was enjoying raised status after having been suspended for sniffing Tipp-Ex thinner and smashing a window in a solvents-fuelled rampage, wore a floor-length red cape and a gold

231

headband. We had no idea whom he was meant to be, and if you asked, he just looked at you gnomically. Eventually, when it was time to be judged on outfits, he walked up onto the stage, spun around, and flung off his cape to reveal thigh high boots, gold hot pants and a red and white corset. Steve had come dressed as Wonder Woman. He won first prize.

I discovered that all the things I used to worry about – being bad at football, struggling with mathematics, being compared to Tom – did not matter here. Even a boy called Richard (aka Dick) Ball, who had only ever once scored a goal and that was for the wrong side, was as much a part of the community as Eva Yiasumi or her football champion boyfriend. And punishments tended to fit the crime. When Eugene went around with a pair of scissors one Spring morning and chopped off the heads of all the daffodils, John A sent him out with a few hundred splints and a roll of Sellotape and commanded him to make them all stand up again. When Will MacCormac claimed he had to miss an entire chemistry lesson because a lorry had blocked his path, he was given a temporary job as a Saturday morning traffic policeman, guiding parents into the car park in an orderly fashion as they arrived to pick up their children. A number of them told teachers how impressed they were that the boy directing traffic had already designed a series of top-of-the-range performance cars.

My own crime wave came to a halt. There was an incident involving a lighter, dry bracken and a section of the woods surrounding the Krakon, but that was an accident. Then there was the time I was skateboarding back to Hamilton House in the dark when a figure on a bicycle loomed up in the other direction, smashed into me, and collapsed into a ditch. It was only while helping up the wheezing man that I realized it was Alan Pattinson.

'You're gated for the next three weekends!' he puffed furiously, forgetting for a moment his belief that the child is father of the man and laying down a power trip of a most unenlightened nature. As he brushed himself off and wobbled into the shadows, I decided to take the gamble he had no idea who I was. I didn't mention it to John A and that was the last I heard of it.

I discovered the reality of girls, really for the first time. Murphy, who had showed Mum and me round the school, gave us glimpses into the life of that worldly and glamorous creature, the sixth former. 'Sex without love is worthless,' she told us during one homework period of which she was in charge. 'Making love is the most wonderful thing in the world. It's important to know the difference.'

'But how do you know?' asked Gael.

'You just know.'

There were girls everywhere. There were girls who became friends, such as Gael, and girls like Eva Yiasumi, whose beauty meant I couldn't talk to them, and there was even a girl who shaved off her pubic hairs, put them in an envelope, and posted them to the headmaster. A sixth former called Ella called me over from the window of her study one afternoon and said she liked my haircut. She invited me into the study, which she shared with three sullen boys. We got talking about music. I said I liked Jimi Hendrix.

'Oh yeah?' said one of the boys. 'What's your favourite song then?'

I struggled to remember the names of tracks I had listened to countless times before.

"Hey Joe," I said, eventually.

'It's only the most famous song he ever did,' he sniffed. Ella, who had a mass of freckles and curly hair, smiled as she leaned her plastic chair back on its hind legs, chewed on a pencil and said that she would lend me her Echo & the Bunnymen tape.

I'd see boys and girls walking along the road to Hamilton House, arm in arm or hand in hand, dressed in patched jeans and old jumpers, and I wondered how they managed to make physical contact look so easy, so natural, when invisible force fields stopped me from any kind of intimacy. The closest I got in that first term was with a girl called Polly. We had been sitting in a classroom, leaning on desks, talking about The Doors. She said she liked Jim Morrison but she didn't like his arty farty poetry. I said that 'Light My Fire' was a good song. Then she kneed me in the balls. It hurt for a week.

During one double maths lesson, Gael asked if she could be excused. The teacher told her no. 'I'll just bleed all over the desk, then,' she replied.

Eugene and Will MacCormac, despite the former's self-proclaimed phenomenal endowment and the latter's irresistible charm, didn't manage to get any girlfriends and neither did I, except for the duration of one week, when a half-Ethiopian, half-Russian girl called Adae became my girlfriend after we passed a series of notes to each other during lessons. We didn't do much during our romance. One evening after prep, we tried out what proved to be the first French kiss for both of us, but mostly we sat side by side on the sloping grass behind

234

the main house as Adae talked about how confused she felt and I nodded meaningfully. This continued until Friday evening, when Adae announced she liked me too much as a friend for us to be together anymore. I took it as a compliment at the time. It was years later I discovered girls only like you 'too much as a friend' when they don't fancy you.

Mum picked me up at half term, and watched as Gael, Lara and Adae hugged me goodbye. 'Who were all those *girls*?' she said, looking at me rather than the road ahead and nearly squashing an eleven-year-old on a skateboard. 'You seem to be very popular all of a sudden.'

'They're just friends,' I said sunnily, waving at Murphy as she walked arm in arm with a handsome sixth former. They were wearing matching army shirts. 'How's everything at home?'

'I have to say,' said Mum as she swerved out of the school grounds, 'Nev's lot are beginning to get on my nerves. The house is full of Yogis.'

Mum wasn't exaggerating. I walked through the corridor of the new house, dragging a suitcase, to be confronted with the sight of Nev in a white jumper, white cotton trousers and the Yogi egg brooch. 'Will, you're back!' he said, and attempted stiffly to give me a hug, jerking from left to right like C3PO of *Star Wars* suffering a bout of malfunctioning. 'It's fantastic timing because I have some incredible news. Dadi Janki is here. In our house!'

'Oh for Christ's sake, Nev, give it a rest,' said Mum. 'He's only just walked through the bloody door.'

Nev exhibited the kind of mild bewilderment of which only those truly sure of their path are capable. 'But this is such a blessing, such a special occasion. Won't you come and meet Dadi? She'd love to see you.'

I hadn't actually seen the house yet, not since it had become our home, and said I'd like to have a look at my new bedroom before engaging in a meditation session. Besides, I was pretty sure Dadi Janki didn't have a clue who I was.

'Come on,' insisted Nev. 'Come and say hello.'

Nev wore that mischievous grin of his, which used to mean we were about to have a fun time. Now it meant we were about to engage in a period of silent contemplation on the eternity of the soul, but at least he was pleased to see me. Besides, I was going to the Golden Age with him, so perhaps this meeting with Dadi Janki was auspicious. As Mum stomped downstairs and put the kettle on, Nev led me into the living room where twenty-three Yogis were sitting cross-legged, listening to Beyond Sound and experiencing *darshan* with Dadi Janki. I waved to Brother Malcolm, Brother Benji and Sister Clare, but none of them waved back; they were locked into open-eyed meditation. Nev gestured for me to sit in the far corner. On the way over my foot got caught in Sister Nina's sari and I tripped, knocking into a man with a tiny head and an incredibly long neck. He came out of his soul consciousness long enough for an irritated tut.

'Turn your thoughts, your mind, to the self . . .' said the young Indian woman sitting next to Dadi Janki. 'I, the soul, am a point of light . . . my physical body is but a costume . . . which I, the living energy, use . . .'

Maybe I was a Brahma Kumari in waiting after all. I found talking to girls I fancied awkward. Being tactile didn't come naturally. And there was some sort of undeniable power attached to Dadi Janki. She made the path of spirituality seem like the right one to pursue, if only one had the discipline to stick to it.

I tried to concentrate on my soulful nature as I sat and looked at Dadi Janki. I was wrong to feel threatened by these people. There was nothing sinister about them. All they wanted to do was transform the world in its final stages before Armageddon. If I felt nothing but a vague sense of discomfort in meditation, it was my fault. The karmic residue of this and previous lives were pulling me into body consciousness and away from the soul. I needed to harmonize my mind in order to control the unhelpful thoughts and sensations that flooded it – like images of Sadie, and the fact that an itch on my right foot needed attention – and a blissful feeling of peace would follow.

I might have actually achieved it too, had not Tom appeared in the doorway and made an obscene gesture involving his tongue and two fingers. I had to make my excuses and get out of there, knocking into the man with the tiny head one more time before finding Tom in the kitchen with Mum and his girlfriend Fiona.

'Have you attained enlightenment yet?' he said as he attempted to push down the plunger of a cafetière.

'I wouldn't expect you to understand,' I said, jumping up to sit on a half-finished worktop. 'When you have come from the Golden Age like me, you are forever hankering after a return to a spiritually pure state.'

'You're about as spiritually pure as my arsehole,' said Tom, provoking shocked but admiring giggles from Fiona. He leaned on the worktop and looked upwards in a toothy fashion. 'Mind you, I suppose it is rather hole-y.'

237

'Tom,' said Mum crossly, as she opened the fridge, 'you've eaten the pizza I was going to give Will for lunch!'

'What did you expect me to do with it? Play a game of Frisbee?'

We sat around the round pine table – one of the few pieces of our furniture to make the move to the new house – and I told them about life at Frensham.

'I hope you're actually learning something for once, given the amount of scribbling I'm having to do to pay your extortionate school fees,' said Mum. 'When I think of the hackery I'm churning out just to cover . . .' but she broke off in mid-sentence. At the sound of heavy footsteps coming down the stairs, she jumped up and rushed into the small room next to the kitchen, for which we didn't have a name but in which the television was installed. 'I'm not here!' she whispered, and crawled behind an armchair.

'What the hell's going on?'

'You'll find out,' said Tom, crunching on an apple.

The Indian woman who had been sitting next to Dadi Janki appeared, smiling brightly. 'Om shanti,' she said as her head darted from left to right. 'Leez, Leez, where are you? You must come and join us for some very special meditation.'

'I think she went out,' said Tom. 'Shall I say you were looking for her?'

'We want to thank her for letting us use her lovely home by giving her *darshan* with Dadi,' said the woman, jumping about in her sari as she searched for Mum, whose black bouffant I could just see sticking out from behind the top of the armchair. 'If you see her, tell to come quickly. Dadi is leaving for India soon.'

Eventually the woman went upstairs and Mum emerged.

'Honestly, they're a bloody nuisance,' she said as she unfolded herself from her hiding place. 'Nev promised me that they would be confined to the basement but they're everywhere, all the time. I keep hiding from them but it doesn't do any good. They seek me out. And Nev's constant meditating is becoming a problem too. This house is costing us a fortune, so while I quite like the fact I don't have a horrible smelly man in my bed anymore, it's time for Nev to start contributing financially again.'

'When *Will to Be Well* comes out, it's going to make us rich, isn't it?' I said.

Tom sniggered. *Will to Be Well* had come out a month ago, after a launch party attended by lots of Yogis but – hardly surprising given that the only drink on offer was mango lassi – not many journalists. Nev's editor had summed up the book's impact by revealing to him his philosophy of publishing: you throw a whole load of shit against the wall and you see what sticks.

'Yes, well, I'm working on my own book now,' said Mum. 'It's going to be called *Sex Is Not Compulsory* and it's extremely provocative. It's about this ridiculous situation we have in which sex outside of marriage is seen as bad and sex within marriage is seen as good, when everyone knows that the former happens all the time and the latter isn't nearly as prevalent as everyone makes out.'

Tom groaned. 'Do you have to? It was bad enough when you wrote that obviously fabricated article about what it's like to have all the men in the office fancying you. And I didn't think anyone at Westminster read the *Daily Mail*.'

I had a look around our new house. While the old one was unremarkable and smart, this was grand and dishevelled and far more romantic. With its winding staircases, uneven floors and creaking panels, it seemed to have a will of its own. Nev's basement was bare and clean; a small single bed in the corner, a white mat on the floor, a painting of Brahma Baba in a gold frame on one wall and the red Yogi egg of light on another. The kitchen was only half-built, and its messiness seemed somehow more elegant than the suburban order of the one at 99, Queens Road. On the next floor was the living room, light and fresh, with imitation Roman urns on round tables, our old chaise longue at one end and wooden shutters for windows that didn't close properly at the other. Immediately above that was Mum's study and bedroom, as busy and as worldly as Nev's basement was monkish and spiritual. Instead of a portrait of Brahma Baba, Mum had framed a photograph of herself. Finally, at the top of the house, were Tom's and my bedrooms.

With Tom safely ensconced downstairs with Mum and Fiona, I poked about in his room. He had a gallery of postcards featuring his cultural heroes: Oscar Wilde, Dr Johnson, Aldous Huxley, The Velvet Underground and The Beastie Boys. There was an ashtray with some funny-looking cigarette butts in it. There were new records in the pile by people whom I had never heard of. Underneath the bed was an empty whisky bottle.

My room was empty. The old Scalextric set was packed up in a cardboard box in the corner. The poster of the BMX rider flying over the supermarket aisles was gone, although my bike, still not fixed since the accident, was in the garden. I didn't know whether I would be using it again. I felt as if I had grown out of it, but at the same time I didn't feel I had grown into anything to replace it.

I climbed onto the roof of the house and looked out onto the Thames below as the orange winter sun sank into the water and shimmered in its own reflection. Sitting cross-legged, watching the river, I made a decision.

Nev didn't bother to conceal his excitement when I told him I wanted to take the Brahma Kumaris' seven-day course. 'You may find that the life of a BK really suits you,' he said as we 'tucked in' (his words) to a buckwheat-stuffed red pepper. 'And I can see that the wisdom you're learning at Frensham is going to help too. Mum said that you had made some excellent friendships with some of the girls. That's great. When we understand we are all souls without gender who just happen to inhabit a male or a female body, we start treating each other equally.'

'Well, cheerio then,' said Tom, picking up his plate and dropping his pepper into the bin. 'We're off.' Fiona followed Tom towards the door.

'Where are you going?' said Nev. 'I thought we'd all have a nice family evening in to celebrate Will coming home.'

'Firstly, that's nothing to celebrate. And secondly, if I've told you once I've told you a thousand times, we've got a party we need to be at. Don't wait up for me. Let's go, Fiona.'

'Thanks awfully for supper,' said Fiona, with an apologetic smile.

That night, some time around three, I vaguely remember waking up to hear Tom shouting at Mum for making him lose his keys and having to ring the doorbell, but that memory is clouded by the more significant thing that followed: my proper, formal introduction into the Brahma

Kumaris. Nev decreed it wouldn't work for a father to give his son the seven-day course, so he arranged for me to take it with the short, curly haired man who had come to our disastrous party at 99, Queens Road. He was a former concert pianist called Tony, who had given up the touring life after discovering the Brahma Kumaris.

Each day over half term, I went to Tony's neat little lodging in a house on Richmond Hill to learn the teachings of the Brahma Kumaris. He told me that the soul has three separate entities: the mind, the intellect and the *sanskars*. Thoughts are created in the mind and they are the basis of our emotions and drives, so we need to be able to harness them in a positive way. The intellect assesses thoughts. The *sanskars*, the personality traits that are built up over a succession of lives, draw us away from spirituality, so we need to train ourselves to be able to purify them.

Tony told me about the three worlds. The first is the Physical World, in which we live now. The second is the Subtle World Of Light, where messages from God are passed down through Brahma Kumari mediums. The third is the Supreme World Of Peace And Silence, where souls waiting to take physical form reside alongside God.

As we sat and drank cinnamon tea, Tony explained in his cheerful Aussie way about the 5,000-year cycle and the stages into which it is split. I told him I was worried about the Brahma Kumari prediction that we only had another thirty years to live before the apocalypse. 'In that case, don't think about it. You don't need to,' he said. 'Anything that produces fear is counter-productive. Concentrate on the state of pure positivity, happiness and soul consciousness we all have within our reach.'

His place was ordered and calm, free of stress. Each day I went away from Tony's feeling hopeful for the future. Even the meditation was enjoyable. Dadi Janki's intense spirituality was beyond my grasp, most of the western Brahma Kumaris came across as brainwashed and unquestioning, and Nev was so humourlessly euphoric about it all that it was hard to learn about the teachings he held so dear without wishing for our old, fun dad back again. But Tony made it accessible. He wasn't distant and he wasn't faking his enthusiasm. He explained the idea of the Tree Of Life: that after the Golden and Silver Ages, other religions appeared. Buddha, Krishna, Jesus and Muhammad are all accepted as important spiritual leaders of one sort or another, and they form branches that grow from the main trunk of knowledge, which is, of course, that of the Brahma Kumaris.

Tony explained that God's teachings, which were relayed in the form of the *murlis*, came through a medium in India called Dadi Gulzar. He told me how consciousness is primary to the universe, how Darwinian selection, with its idea of life forming through chance events and the survival of the fittest, was a flawed theory. I put this to Will Lee one morning when I went round to his house before my daily lesson at Tony's. Will took out a bunch of fossils to illustrate how Darwin was right, but even he couldn't explain how something came from nothing with the Big Bang.

Back home, however, I couldn't stop the conflict between this new understanding of the world, which all made sense, and the fact that Nev, so different from a normal dad, so much like a kid himself, so much one of us and on our side, had left behind foolish things for serious contemplation. The problem was that he'd left us behind with them.

Now there was a chance to be with him again. I couldn't watch a film, go to a football match, talk about girls, play video games, enthuse about comics, eat junk food, go camping, bitch about the world or do a vote on Jimi Hendrix's top ten guitar solos, and I would never be able to go to the pub with him. But at least Nev and I could meditate together.

As it turned out, I didn't even get to do much of that. My new life as a Brahma Kumari proved short-lived because worldly temptations were about to make themselves available, like a feast set before the eyes of a starving man.

11

The Third Party

The most exciting thing that happened in the second half of the winter term, even more exciting than turning fourteen and being only the second ever person at our school to climb the highest tree in Surrey, was getting a letter from Sadie. It came in a small blue envelope covered with drawings of stick people. It was thickly padded, and she had used a series of one and two pence stamps to make it up to first class. She had drawn two lines under my name and followed the postcode with 'England, Europe, The World, The Universe'. I studied the envelope over an entire lunch break. I saved reading the letter for after school, failing to concentrate through an afternoon of French and biology as I pressed down on the folded gem making a square shape in my pocket. And I wasn't going to read this in the dormitory with the risk of Eugene or Will MacCormac bursting in, so I crunched autumnal debris on the forest floor until coming upon a fallen tree trunk, sitting on it and, making sure nobody was around, I opened the letter.

Dearest Wilbur,

*I hope you are settling into your new school and
making lots of friends. Have you met any cute girls yet?
I am revising for my O levels. Yuck!! I still love David
Bowie but now I am sooo in love with Kirk Brandon
from Spear Of Destiny. My friend Charlotte and I went
to see them at Hammersmith Odeon and he is
gorgeous! We even tried to go backstage afterwards but
the wanker security guard wouldn't let us. Then
Charlotte got invited to a party she knew Kirk Brandon
was going to be at and she didn't tell me about it, so
now I'm not talking to her and I've decided that he is
gay. Sam is doing very well at Westminster and being
as annoying as ever. Mum is teaching something called
past life therapy and Dad has married The Italian and
moved to Milan. Good riddance I say!*

It carried on in similar fashion for four pages, complaining
about friends and talking about boys. Reading it was bitter-
sweet. As incredible as it was to get a letter from Sadie, I
confess to hoping she might have alluded to our night
out together. However, she did say that we should go to
another concert some time, and to call her when I was
back in London. That was all I needed to cling onto the
belief that we would, one day, be romantically involved.
I bashed into a tree as I walked back to school and didn't
even feel the pain. I dropped my plate in the middle of
the dining room. I sat down on a chair, failing to notice
that Richard Ball was already on it.

That night, lying in bed and listening to *The Best of the
Doors* on a Sony Walkman to drown out the sound of

Eugene furiously chasing after the Faint Feeling, I thought about Sadie, but also of Nev and the Brahma Kumaris and how I would ever reconcile the two. The Kingdom of Heaven was within reach; all I needed to do was meditate and concentrate on the purity of the soul. At the same time, I gladly would chop off at least one finger for a night of passion with Sadie. I didn't know which way to turn.

The second half of the term introduced history lessons with Jonathan Hughes, the man who had given me such a penetrating, disapproving look on the day Mum and I first came to look around Frensham. He was the house-master of Brackenhill, the house to which I would be going in a year's time. Jonathan was late for our first lesson. After fifteen minutes, a girl called Carol sat in the teacher's chair, which was when he walked in.

Instead of shouting at her, he took a seat at the back of the classroom, folded his arms, and said, 'Continue'.

Carol looked at him with a wobbling chin and jumped out of the chair.

'Return,' he commanded. 'You are clearly giving the lesson today. We are on the unification of Italy.'

Admirably, Carol fumbled through an attempt to teach on a subject about which she knew nothing, while Jonathan sat with his feet up on a desk at the back, giving her sarcastic prompts on key facts like an overeducated schoolboy.

Jonathan had a 2CV he never remembered to lock. One of our favourite tricks was to take the handbrake off and roll the car around the corner from where he parked it, thereby confusing him when he came back to school after lunch in the pub. The 2CV could also turn into an object of fear. We weren't allowed to smoke at Frensham – unless we were in the sixth form – but the woods between the main house and Brackenhill were filled with all kinds of illicit smoking dens. An unlucky teacher was frequently dispatched to break these up and threaten with suspension anyone caught there. Jonathan's approach was to drive his 2CV through the beech trees and rhododendron bushes, terrifying smokers as the headlights came towards them in the dark. Sometimes he ditched the car for territorial missions. Once, three boys were passing a cigarette between them in the pitch black of the woods. Someone handed the cigarette to a tall, rotund figure. He took a drag, let out a long, satisfied exhalation, crunched the butt into the moist leaves on the ground, and said, 'You're nicked'.

Alan Pattinson also used unusual methods to impose his authority. One break time, the entire school was called into the main hall. We assumed that something terrible had happened, a lapse into the bad old Frensham of knife-wielding hippies and teenage pregnancies. In fact, Pattinson just felt the need to berate us for paying too much attention to our appearances.

'I can't believe there are children as young as thirteen in this school who are worrying about designer labels!' he cried, so agitated that he stalked up and down the floor clutching wiry curls of hair. 'This rampant consumerism, this obsession with status, goes against the very values on which this school was founded. What's more important? A childhood lived freely, or the right coat from Jaeger? It sickens me, *sickens* me, to think that all you people care about today is fashionable clothes, your hairstyles, the way you look; as if it matters one iota! What happened to great ideas, to the joy of living in the moment, unencumbered by thoughts of how others perceive us? You should all be running around in the woods and making the most of being alive, not going on shopping trips to Jaeger!'

All anyone could talk about was Pattinson thinking Jaeger was fashionable. And that he pronounced the 'J'!

By the end of the first term, amazing things had happened. I had friends. I discovered it was possible to find teachers not only interesting, but also likeable. And according to my school report, I was officially no longer stupid.

'I really think Frensham has been wonderful for you, Sturch,' said Nev, who was wearing a white jumper several sizes too big, on the first day of the Christmas holidays. 'If I had continued in that conventional, dinner party lifestyle, I would never have opened out to you in the same way and a beneficial move like Frensham would not have happened. There are so many pressures that kids suffer when their journey is distorted by their parents' desires for them, which are really desires for themselves. Thanks to the higher soul consciousness that allowed me to let you be yourself, you now have the potential to be more of a Brahma Kumari than I could ever hope to be.'

Since I had been away Tom had adopted a new look: that of an All-American skateboarding dude. He now liked hardcore punk bands with names like Minor Threat, The Descendants and Hüsker Dü. He wore baseball caps, baggy jeans and sweatshirts. All of this was annoying because Tom had never been on a skateboard in his life, and I had. He even managed to get a holiday job in a skateboard shop.

'Is this what you got a scholarship for? Anyone can get a job in a skateboard shop!' Mum shrieked, as Tom slouched into one of the new chairs from Heal's in the kitchen of our Queen Anne house, reading *Thrasher* magazine.

'I can't see you getting hired,' Tom replied. 'By the way, I'm having a New Year's Eve party and I don't want you and Nev hanging around and cramping my style. Haven't you got somewhere you can go?'

Mum was about to launch off into a torrent of rage – you could tell by the way her bouffant wobbled – when Nev raised a calm Yogi finger and said, 'Actually, Liz, maybe we *could* go somewhere for New Year's Eve.'

'Where could we possibly go? You've alienated all our friends by proselytizing to them the whole time. The last time we got a New Year's party invitation, you still believed the world was round.'

'The Brahma Kumaris are welcoming in the New Year at the Kilburn centre.'

'Oh for God's sake, Nev.'

So it was that our parents arranged their first, post-Brahma Kumari New Year's Eve outing together, leaving the field wide open for Tom's party. Since Nev had not yet decorated the basement our parents said we could have the party down there, on the condition we didn't make too much of a mess. Initially, Tom told me I wasn't allowed to come to the party at all and was to stay in my room and listen to ELO. After much protestation he conceded to my bringing five friends. He would have to vet them, of course. And we must not talk to anyone. Especially girls.

This was also the last year Mum made us Christmas stockings. She said she knew it was time to move on when she knocked on Tom's door at nine o' clock on Christmas morning and told him to get up. He yawned, booted the stocking off the end of his bed, and pulled the pillow over his head.

On Christmas Day, we opened our presents before a festive nut roast in the new kitchen. Tom gave me a *100 Gnarly Wipeouts* video, Mum a pair of kneepads, and Nev a beanie hat with the word 'Insane' in graffiti-style writing over the front.

From Nev, Tom got a tie decorated with little cartoon mushrooms, Mum got *Pearls of Wisdom* by Dadi Janki, and I got a desktop Sellotape dispenser, all presents obtained from a storage cupboard in Shanti Bhavan.

'Thanks, Nev,' I said, picking up the weighty dispenser, turning it upside down, and, after shaking it in the hope that a fifty pound note might be hidden within, added, 'It's just what I always wanted.'

'Actually,' said Nev, eyebrows rising with that old Nevvy mischief, 'if you follow me down to the bottom of the garden, we do have something else for you.'

I was thinking that Nev might have built me a meditation folly, or perhaps he had planted my very own shrub of peace to nurture and learn from. In fact, he had got me an incredible present: a rowing boat. It was big enough for two people. We took it out of the garden and down the steps on the other side of the towpath that led to the water. I climbed in and rowed away. Despite the frantic protestations of our parents from the riverbank, I headed off towards a small island in the middle of the Thames, where I pulled the boat up through the reeds and bullrushes and tied it to a tree. Somewhere in the middle of the island, which was little more than a tangle of weeds and a half dozen silver birch trees, I encountered some geese. Remembering the French boy Dominic's unfortunate encounter with one of these angry creatures on the boat trip, I rowed back home in extra quick time.

At Christmas, Nev usually made us go for a walk in Richmond Park before we were allowed to slump in front of the telly, but this year he had an exciting film we could all watch together.

'Is it the new James Bond?' I said eagerly, knowing that, despite Nev's rejection of almost all other aspects of the physical world, he still had a terrible weakness for action movies.

'Even better. It's the video of this year's BK production of *Grease*. Honestly, it's as good as anything you'll see in the West End.'

Mum broke the silence. 'You're not seriously going to make us watch it, are you?'

Looking a little hurt in his white jumper and Insane skateboard hat, Nev replied, 'Wait until you see Brother Benji play Danny Zukko. He's got a gift!'

Although I was curious to see how the Yogis would treat the moral message of *Grease* concerning the virginal Sandy's transformation from prim goody two-shoes to spandex-clad sex bomb – that, in order to live a happy and fulfilled life, you need to dress like a Sunset Strip hooker – watching a Yogi musical really wasn't anyone's idea of a good time on Christmas Day. Nev rejected our protests with a wave of the arm and a flutter of the eyelids and, after fiddling about with various cables and buttons, got the video working.

'You're in for a treat,' he said, rushing towards an armchair.

The film began with one of the sisters appearing before the camera, looking perplexed. 'Is it working,

Brother Neville?' she said, raising a hand in front of the screen, before saying 'Oh dear' and dashing out of view. The camera zoomed over the heads of people in the auditorium and towards a stage. The curtains wobbled open, and various Yogis, wearing a perplexing mix of white saris, pyjama suits and Fifties-style scarves, baseball caps and sunglasses, formed into some sort of dance routine. From then on it was indeed a production of *Grease*, but one that managed to incorporate within it the central tenets of the Brahma Kumaris: one song, 'Shanti Bhavan Dropout', was about Sandy, a young BK, questioning the path she was on. Benji, in a patched-up baseball jacket that looked suspiciously like the one I nicked, made for an unlikely Danny Zucco, the bad boy with a heart of gold. There was a rousing finale about the eternity of the soul, during which the cast bumped into one another as they attempted to dance in a line without actually touching. Then the curtains juddered together again.

Initially, Nev ignored our increasingly hysterical giggles. But when Tom said, 'Andrew Lloyd Webber, watch out', he lost his temper as much as is possible for a Yogi.

'If you're not even going to give it a chance then I don't see why I should sit here with you,' he puffed, taking the video out of the machine.

'Oh, come off it, Nev,' said Mum. 'That was awful.'

'It was fantastic!' he said in a high-pitched squeak. 'It was top quality! Everyone at Shanti Bhavan put so much work into it and all you do is laugh. I'd like to see you pull off something so professional and yet so meaningful.'

'So there we have it,' said Tom, picking up a copy of the *NME*. 'Four years of intense meditation and spiritual study have made absolutely no difference whatsoever to your ability to take a joke.'

Nev was about to go off for a sulk, or, as he put it, a meditation, when I decided to interject. Thinking of the wisdom I had learned on the seven-day course and repeating it verbatim without actually being quite sure of what it meant, I said: 'Some people – Mum and Tom, for example – are not drawn to the spiritual path. It is hard for them to see the value of the profound. Perhaps, Nev, it would be better to focus on your own process of trans-formation. A river feels no need to urge people to drink its water. Likewise, make your spiritual efforts so attractive to others that they are drawn to it naturally. Don't seek praise; it will not come. Instead, be of the intention to be of service to others. Change yourself first. Then you can change the world.'

Nev stopped in his tracks, just by the double doors (which Mum claimed were a unique original feature) leading to the kitchen. He nodded. He adjusted his Yogi egg brooch and arranged his scarf.

'Do you know what, Sturch? You're right. Using the approval of others as a source of wellbeing can lead to great pain.'

'That's why,' said Tom, ripping apart a festive satsuma, 'you shouldn't be upset when we tell you your musical stinks.'

Some time before lunch, Mum sat at the kitchen table and poured herself a large glass of sherry.

'What are you doing? I thought you weren't allowed to drink.'

'Who says?'

I thought about this. 'Nev?'

254

Mum closed her eyes and took a sip. 'I'm sick of him checking up on me the whole time. And he gives me that holier-than-thou look whenever I do something he doesn't approve of, which is pretty much anything apart from floating about in white. Why is it that every single bloody thing the Yogis do or say is wonderful and everything anyone else does is awful?'

By the time Nev emerged from his meditational bliss, Mum had let the nut roast turn into a smouldering lump. Nev chugged off to Shanti Bhavan on his little motorbike some time around the Queen's Speech. It wasn't easy being a good man in a bad world.

Our parents left us with strict instructions about the running of the party. Nev suggested we would have a lot more fun if we stuck to non-alcoholic drinks and played charades, but Mum conceded it was OK, now Tom was sixteen, if he got in a few beers. Smoking was out of the question and the whole thing had to be over by one o'clock.

'Don't forget, boys,' said Nev, as he stood in his little basement, 'this is a spiritual centre. Please respect this space. As we enter into the New Year, the party might also be a good opportunity to share a few of the BK's teachings with your chums.'

'What, like the world's going to end?' said Tom. 'Do you mind if I take down that picture of the white-haired Yogi man? It won't go with the mood of the party.'

Tom handed Nev one of the invitations he had made with the help of a few pulp fiction covers and the photocopier in Mum's study. There was a drawing of a man and woman standing under a street lamp, smoking. 'SIN after SIN after SIN' read another section of the black and white collage. A lurid drawing of a knife-wielding hoodlum in a leather jacket snarled out of the invitation. Next to a line drawing of a Lolita-like temptress were the words, 'She was too much for one man, but not enough for two!' Nev studied it all, frowning.

'I suppose this line, "they lived for today, not worrying about the future and forgetting the past" is in line with Yogi teachings about non-attachment to the material world,' said Nev, 'but otherwise this is a bit much, T. What kind of a party is this?'

'It's got a beatnik theme.'

I was particularly excited about the party, because I had invited Sadie and she had accepted. Even if I had been thinking along Brahma Kumari lines, even if I knew that love sought externally could only ever cause deception and sorrow and that one must turn within and nurture a relationship with God and the soul, this was fantastic news. Sadie was the perfect teenage girl. She had a gap between her teeth. She smoked Lucky Strike cigarettes. We had gone to see The Stingrays. She had written to me.

I had also invited Sam Evans, Will Lee, Steve Rose, Will MacCormac, Gael, Adae, Richard Ball, two Pollys (the one who had kneed me in the balls, and another with frizzy hair and wide metal-framed glasses), a few other people whose names I wasn't sure of and Eugene, who couldn't come because the Esher Hop was having an all-ages New Year's Eve special and he fancied his chances with the sister of the guy DJing. I did have every intention of sticking to Tom's five-friend limit, but somehow word just got out.

By nine o' clock, there must have been fifty teenagers packed into Nev's Yogi basement. By midnight, it was over a hundred. I remember the next day, when Nev was going around his former temple of serenity in a daze and saying things like, 'but *how* did the beer get on the ceiling?' and 'breaking the banisters is one thing, but the stairs?' I wish I had some answers for him, but I was not witness to any of the acts of carnage that happened that night, least of all the one that resulted in us having to rip up the carpet after someone had built a fire in one of its corners. I was in too much of a fog to notice the destruction. All because of Sadie.

It had started well enough. In the few weeks since I had last seen him, Will Lee had transformed from a fossil-collecting child with a bowl haircut and brown corduroy trousers that stopped around his ankles to a floppy-fringed heartthrob with amazing rhythmic skills. Sam Evans had matured into a bookish youth with long hair and a scruffy trench coat. After Tom's hardcore punk mix tape was ejected from Nev's cassette player in exchange for Sadie's party favourites, Will Lee commanded the floor with his best Mick Jagger strut to 'Sympathy for the Devil', Gael jumped about to 'Stay Free' by The Clash, Will MacCormac leaned against a wall with a beer in his hand and slurred 'she fancies me' as any girl walked past, Tom and Fiona poured the drinks and people sat in little groups, cross-legged, smoking and drinking.

I found Richard Ball, swigging from a bottle of Baileys, slumped next to the groin-kneeing Polly and Steve Rose as they stuck tongues down each other's throats.

'I'm a disaster area,' he scowled, eyes downcast behind his standard-issue National Health glasses. 'I'm never going to get a girlfriend. Look at Steve there. All the girls love him.'

'Sure you will,' I said. 'You were runner up in Junior Brain of Croydon. What's Steve done apart from dress up as Wonder Woman and smash a window, out of his head on Tipp-Ex thinner?'

'It's all right for you. I'm a social leper. Bits of me fall off at parties.'

Just then, a large girl in a ra-ra skirt and a diamanté tiara stumbled towards us. She looked at Richard Ball, narrowed her eyes, stubbed a cigarette butt out onto the wall, said, 'You'll do,' and dragged him off towards a corner of the room. He looked like an acne-ridden rag doll in the grip of an overgrown sugar plum fairy.

Adae wandered into view and asked if I wanted to go outside and join her for a cigarette.

I had only ever smoked that one cigarette with Sadie and it had made me feel sick, but I joined her anyway. We sat on the little bench in the garden, facing the Thames, and as she passed me the cigarette I took drags and let the smoke sit in my mouth for a while before puffing it out again. It tasted disgusting.

'So let me get this right,' said Adae. 'Your father is a science journalist but he doesn't believe in evolution?'

'What's wrong with that? Evolution is only a theory,' I said, remembering Nev using those exact words to describe it.

'So does he think God created Adam and Eve?'

'No, he believes in reincarnation, and so do I. We are all souls.'

'Hippy.'

'You're repeating yourself.'

'I've never called you a hippy before.'

'I mean you are literally repeating yourself, word for

word, action for action. Because time is cyclical, this moment has happened countless times before. We're just actors playing a part in the great drama of life. And we shouldn't worry too much about the outcome because everything is predetermined anyway.'

Adae took a drag on the cigarette and looked at me meaningfully. 'So,' she said, eyes half closed, 'what do you think happens next?'

It was cold on that starry night, and although Will MacCormac compromised the serenity of the moment by stumbling out of the house and vomiting into the gunnera, Adae's face took on a look of tender profundity. She put her hand on mine. 'You know, when I felt that our relationship couldn't go any further I had a lot on my mind, a lot of confusion. But I'm beginning to think we have a special understanding. I feel like you *know* me.'

A few months earlier, a blonde girl with an upturned nose chucked me after I had paid for her to see *Tootsie*. Now a stunning Ethiopian-Russian with long black curls was inches away from me. Frensham Heights was a wonderful school.

'There's a strong possibility,' I said to her, 'that we knew each other in a past life.'

She inched closer. Her lips parted. The spirituality line appeared to have worked wonders. Inside the packed basement, scores of teenagers were shouting the countdown to midnight. I inched closer too . . . and then I saw Sadie. Her arm around some guy. Who the hell was he, and what was he doing at my party? He was tall and handsome with a black quiff, a green lumber jacket and Levi's 501s with big turn-ups. An idiot, in other words.

'I'll be back!' I shouted to Adae, and ran down to the

end of the garden before Sadie and the wannabe Elvis disappeared from view.

Midnight struck. I turned to see Adae going into the house. I stopped for a moment. All I had to do was run back and kiss her, but Sadie was heading off towards the river with some guy. I opened the garden gate and darted from left to right on the towpath before spotting them. There they were, under a weeping willow in the moonlight, kissing each other. It was disgusting.

I ran over and stood before them, panting.

'Oh, hi Will,' said Sadie, looking cooler than ever in a red cardigan over a black and white polka dot dress and a red ribbon in her hair. She made no attempt to take her arms off the bequiffed hunk molesting her, which would have been the decent thing. Instead, she held him tighter. 'Great party.'

'It was until the Jolly Green Giant turned up. This is a highly exclusive event and it's not open to just anyone! Who the hell are you, anyway?'

Sadie stared at me. 'His name is Jim and you're being rude. What's got into you?'

To make matters worse, Jim was not only handsome, stylish and about twenty-three; he was nice too. 'Don't give the little guy a hard time, Sadie baby,' he said, extending a hand for me to shake. 'You're right. We should have told you I was coming. And you should know that Sadie thinks the world of you.' He gave a manly chuckle. 'By the way, I was beginning to get worried. Thought I might have some competition for her heart.'

I didn't want to shake his hand. And what was this 'Sadie baby' business? I wanted to tell him to fuck off. But, with confrontation never being my strong point, it came out as a question. 'Fuck off?' I asked, much too politely, before realizing the only thing left to do was run away.

I would sail off in my little boat, finding solace in the still waters of the river under the black night. I jumped over the prostrate body of Will MacCormac crossing the line of the garden gate. 'She fancies me . . . or he fancies me . . . whatever . . .' he moaned. I went over to the garden wall against which I had left the boat after its inaugural journey on Christmas morning, to find that it wasn't there. Someone had stolen it.

I pushed my way past all manner of teenagers to get into the basement, where 'What Difference Does It Make?' by The Smiths was blasting out of Nev's little stereo, people were coupled off in corners, and a friend of Tom's from Westminster, who went on to become a famous television presenter and documentary filmmaker, had managed to fall asleep with his head in the toilet after vomiting all over it. Tom was dancing with a bunch of his friends, a bottle of wine in one hand and one of the badly made cigarettes people were smoking in the other.

'Hey, it's my brother!' he said brightly. He even put his arm around me. 'Happy New Year. Great party, eh?'

'No it isn't, because two things that can never be replaced have been stolen from me. First my heart, and then my boat.'

Tom stopped dancing. 'Someone stole your boat?'

'And my heart.'

A large, drunken, rugby-playing type standing nearby must have heard us. 'Hey, I just went for a ride in a boat,' he slurred. 'Found it at the bottom of the garden. Might have left it in the river, come to think of it . . .'

261

Tom did something that surprised me. He pushed the boy, who was a lot bigger than him, up against the wall and shouted, 'You stole my brother's Christmas present! That's all he got apart from a Sellotape dispenser! You're going to get that boat right now even if you have to wade through the mud to do it!'

The boy held his arms up and said, 'I am so, so sorry,' and ran out to the garden. Five minutes later he came back, dripping wet, carrying the boat on his shoulders. I went to thank Tom. He was in a corner with his pretty girlfriend, both looking cool and sophisticated in their matching berets and striped tops as they leaned against the no-longer-white wall of Nev's meditation basement.

'No worries, brother,' he said, as Fiona gazed at him with the look of love. 'If anyone else gives you trouble, send them my way.' He offered me a puff on one of his badly made cigarettes. I took it with a shrug. If I was to be a real teenager I had to inhale like everyone else did. The problem was this homemade cigarette tasted even worse than the normal ones. It was like smoking the contents of an herb garden. I exploded into a fit of coughing.

'Gah! I feel sick.'

Fiona, doe-eyed, said, 'First time?'

'Oh no. I've felt sick lots of times.' I took another drag just to show how hard I was. This time it stayed down. 'Well, the boat's back. But I'll never fall in love again.'

I explained to Tom and Fiona the situation with Sadie, of how we were meant to be together, and how our destinies were entwined, and yet here she was, at our New Year's Eve party, under a willow tree, kissing a gigantic rockabilly. Fiona said that there were other fish in the sea and that it was normal to fancy someone older, someone unattainable, before you found your first real girlfriend. This was the kind of advice I should have been getting from Nev, but if I had gone to him and poured out my romantic problems he would have just told me to be celibate for the rest of my life.

'Besides,' said Tom, 'who was that gorgeous girl I saw you talking to earlier?'

'My God. Adae!'

I had abandoned her at the crucial moment, and now that cigarette had made me feel extremely light-headed. A rising sense of panic developed. I had messed up my one big chance of copping off with a girl, and I might have caused irreparable damage to an important part of my brain as well. With the chaos of teenagers getting drunk and groping each other everywhere, this was a bad situation. My body felt odd. There was something wrong with my arms. They kept rising involuntarily. They must have belonged to someone else. I had to get out of that basement. I had to find Adae. I was heartbroken. Everything had to stop.

I ran over to the hi-fi, pressed stop, and put an end to a bunch of public school boys in eyeliner waving their arms about to 'She Sells Sanctuary' by The Cult. Amid a chorus of groans I stood on top of Nev's bed, accidentally put my foot between the heads of Richard Ball and the big girl in the tiara, and said . . . nothing.

I couldn't remember what I was doing, why I was standing on Nev's bed, or what I was planning to say. I looked around the room.

Finally, the words came.

'Why are you all staring at me?'

263

Then I experienced what I later discovered is called a whiteout: a blinding flash of cold, sick, shivering energy that sends you in a spin. Without knowing it at the time, I was stoned. I collapsed. The next thing I knew I was lying on my bed, being glared at by a black-haired gorgon in an expensive red coat, who – it took a few moments to realize it – was my mother.

12

Florida

It was at the beginning of the summer holidays, after a year of life at Frensham Heights, when Mum announced she and I were going to Disneyworld in Orlando, Florida.

'All of this Yogi stuff has been hard on you,' she said, hair suppressed by a headscarf as she stood on a chair with a feather duster and attacked the spiders in the corner of the kitchen ceiling. 'Nev thinks it's all so wonderful, but it means you've missed out on a lot of normal family activities. He's off to India again this summer so I thought I'd treat you. You always said you wanted to go to Disneyworld.'

I could hardly believe I was hearing this amazing news. 'What about Tom? Doesn't he want to go?'

'I wouldn't worry about him,' she said, hopping off the chair. 'He's got other interests these days.'

I looked over at Tom. He was asleep on the floor of the room with the television, where he and some friends had been celebrating the end of their O-levels the night before. There was a cigarette butt glued to his forehead.

There was a caveat to the Florida trip: we would be with the Brahma Kumaris. Mum explained that Rick, the man who Nev had stayed with when he was recuperating from his near-fatal chicken poisoning, had invited us to his house/retreat in Land O' Lakes, Florida. Although I had more or less made peace with the Brahma Kumaris and accepted the huge changes they brought to our lives, this did temper the excitement of the holiday somewhat. We would be expected to meditate every day and talk about soul consciousness. Soaring deep into Space Mountain and having our photograph taken with Goofy at The Magic Kingdom was one thing. Sitting around in silent contemplation and staring into the eyes of elderly Indian women in saris was quite another. Still, this was an amazing opportunity. Like any kid growing up in 1980s England I had always wanted to go to America. If that meant wearing white and eating a bit of toli every now and then, so be it.

So it was that Mum and I flew on Florida Airlines to Orlando. On stepping out of the airport the heat hit us like an anvil, but we were soon protected from it by a remarkable invention I had not come across before: air conditioning.

'This is incredible!' I said, as Mum navigated her way out onto the Bee Line Expressway in a hire car, momentarily forgot that Americans drive on the right, and mounted the central reservation just in time to prevent an oncoming platoon of honking cars from smashing into us. 'It's baking out there, yet it's freezing in here.'

'Welcome to America,' said Mum. 'You can go from your air-conditioned house to your air-conditioned car to the air-conditioned shopping mall, and the reality of the weather barely needs to affect you. It really is a wonderful country.'

What they said about America was true. Everything, from the cars to the buildings to the people, was bigger. Fifty-foot cypresses towered over four-lane highways. Hotels with palm tree-lined drives supported entire civilisations of people in shorts. How strange, I thought, that the Brahma Kumaris should have a place in this brash land of plenty.

We took a turning off the expressway and headed into prettier territory: sycamore trees, bumpy roads, ranch-style houses with wood-cladding and rope swings hanging from branches outside. 'This must be the place,' said Mum, spotting an aged wooden sign painted with the familiar Brahma Kumari egg. We went down a narrow track through marshy woods that led to a big house surrounded by a series of bungalows. A great egret flapped past. A rangy man with a ponytail drove ahead of us on a miniature tractor. There was a row of cars near the house and beyond that a wide, still lake. Mum parked the car, next to a pick-up truck with wheels that were at least as tall as Will Lee.

Mosquitoes buzzed around in the simmering heat, but there was another, more mechanical buzzing sound too. I walked onto the decking at the edge of the lake: near the other side was a speedboat pulling a person on water-skis. That looked like fun. I guessed they must have been Rick's neighbours. But as the boat turned around and came closer to us, the waterskiing figure came into view – and she was wearing a sari.

'Hey, you must be Liz and Will,' shouted the boat's driver, after he killed the engine and steered the boat up

267

to a jetty near the big house while the woman in the sari sank into the water. 'I'm Rick. It's so great you're here! Give me a moment to help Sister Waddy out and I'll be right with you.'

Rick was a trim, bearded man in Wayfarer sunglasses and cut-off denim shorts. If it weren't for the little Yogi brooch pinned to his tie-dye T-shirt there would be no way of identifying him as a Brahma Kumari. After tying the boat against the jetty he and the waterskiing Sister Waddy bounded over to us. 'Om shanti,' he said, in a broad American accent. 'How are you guys doing?'

Mum already knew Waddy. She was an Irish woman who had lived in London until moving out to Florida to set up the Brahma Kumaris' centre in Miami, and she had dropped over to Rick's for a spot of waterskiing. 'I must admit,' she said, wringing out folds of white cotton, 'I was a bit nervous about being attacked by one of the alligators when I first had a go, but Rick tells me they're quite harmless. The peaceful vibrations of this place seem to have had a positive effect on them.'

'You've got alligators in that lake?' I asked, backing away.

'Of course. We're in Florida, after all,' Rick confirmed. 'Hey, here comes one now.'

Sure enough, an alligator no more than a metre long climbed out of the water and onto some decking not far from where we were standing. It smiled up at us in an expectant manner. 'This one's the baby of the three,' said Rick, hands on hips. 'He normally comes up here when he's hungry, but you mustn't give him anything to eat.'

'Like one of my legs?'

'English sense of humour!' said Rick, pointing at me. 'OK, guys. Let me show you around.'

Rick introduced us to his girlfriend, a black-haired woman called Sandy. Whether they followed the Brahma Kumaris' rule of celibacy or not, I didn't ask. 'Well, hey,' said Sandy, who was blending a frothy pink concoction in the enormous kitchen of the big house. 'Looking forward to going on some of our Florida rollercoasters? We've got the best in the world.' She handed us two huge strawberry milkshakes in the kind of metal tins other BKs served mango lassis. 'Make yourselves at home. If you need anything just ask. We are so honoured to have you here.'

'I must say,' Mum said to Rick, as we walked through the gardens and past friendly-looking hippy types who said 'Om Shanti' while giving us the peace sign, 'you make the Yogi life look a lot more attractive than they do back home.'

'You know what?' said Rick, as he opened the door of our bungalow, 'if you gotta be good, might as well be good in style.'

The bungalow was a perfect mix of American comfort and Yogi simplicity: two rooms, plain wooden walls, Native Indian rugs on the floor and neat beds covered by multi-coloured quilts. The room I was to sleep in had a television and a videocassette recorder. There was a tape of *The Karate Kid*, which had only just come out in cinemas in England. And I would get to watch American TV, with its rumoured fifty-six channels and never-ending advertisements! While Mum unpacked and had a shower, Rick suggested I join him for an early evening meditation session.

We walked around the corner to another bungalow. Inside were six or seven Yogis dressed in a mix of white saris, white pyjama suits, and Hawaiian shirts. I got into a cross-legged position, preparing myself to spend the next hour or so meditating. It would be wrong to offend our host by refusing, after all. I had just settled into something resembling the correct posture when Rick said:

'Wow. I felt a deep connection with the soul, right there. Good work, guys. Well, see you tomorrow morning.'

After our meditation session of approximately forty-eight seconds, Rick asked if I would like to join him while he headed into Orlando on a couple of errands. As his enormous station wagon rolled out onto the highway he told me a little about himself. He left school at fifteen, barely able to read or write, and built up a chain of jeans stores that made him a millionaire by the time he was thirty. He also had five kids and an ex-wife. 'I had succeeded in the eyes of the world, but I felt something was wrong. We weren't put on this Earth just to make money,' said Rick as we cruised along the wide road. 'Then I met the Brahma Kumaris and everything they said and did made sense. That was ten years ago. I'm proud to say I've been a devout BK ever since. Hey, do you like arcade games?'

We headed over to an arcade in a shopping mall and sunk quarters into *Star Wars*, *Defender* and – a favourite of Waddy's, according to Rick – *Battlezone*. Then we dropped by a store to stock up on Reece's Peanut Butter Cups and Mr Goodbars.

Rick was the best Brahma Kumari of all time.

Each morning I swam across the lake – the alligators never bothered me – before Mum drove us off for one adventure after another. Disneyworld was surreal in its innocence. It was gentle and old-fashioned, despite its dedication to commerce. The Haunted Mansion and the Jungle Cruise gave a sense of reassuring wonderment. The Swiss Family Treehouse belonged to an America slipping from view, even in 1984. Walking along Main Street, I dropped an ice-cream wrapper. One of the Seven Dwarves darted over and grabbed it before it had a chance to reach the ground.

One day at the Yogi ranch, Rick taught me how to waterski while Mum, having been convinced by Sandy that the alligators wouldn't be tempted to jump out of the water and take a bite out of her, sunbathed on the decking by the lake. In the evening at sunset I went out on a rowing boat with the rangy man with the ponytail. He worked as Rick's gardener. His name was Ed.

'See over there,' he said in a low growl, pointing towards some bullrushes as the water lapped against the sides of the boat. 'That's the big 'gator. She's grumpy as hell right now.'

She was a six-footer, and she sank into the water in the way alligators are meant to: furtively, with a hint of amusement, as if about to get up to no good. I asked Ed if it really was safe to swim in the lake. 'Sure it is,' he replied. 'But even spiritually inclined 'gators can be nasty when they want to be. Stay away from those bullrushes and you'll be fine.'

As the orange sun's reflection shimmered in the water and the alligator slithered silently into the glades at the edge of the lake, Ed asked, 'You a Yogi?'

'Not exactly,' I told him. 'Are you?'

'I'm just Ed,' he replied, chuckling. 'They're good people,

and I like peace as much as the next guy, but a lot of it doesn't make sense to me. They're vegetarian. OK, I can understand how you don't want to harm animals. But the Brahma Kumaris' – he pronounced it *koo*-mar-ees – 'they don't even eat eggs, and eggs is unfertilized. That little egg ain't ever going to grow into a chicken.'

From then on, Ed treated me as the son he never had. We shot basketballs in the hoop round the back of his bungalow. We caught crabs in the mangrove swamps. He loaned me his collection of Marvel comics, which I read in a plastic wicker chair outside Ed's bungalow one evening while he sat nearby, smoking cigarettes, drinking whisky and telling me about his troubles with women. 'My current girlfriend is a nice lady, I guess, but she's feisty, always complaining,' he said, puffing plumes of smoke out into the still air as I tried to concentrate on Captain America's tribulations with the Red Skull. 'And once women start complaining, they never stop.'

'Have you got any more of that Mountain Dew?'

'It's in the fridge. Now my old girl Cyndi . . .'

The following afternoon, Rick and Sandy took Mum and me to a roller disco in Orlando. There we met Rick's son, a curly-haired teenager of sixteen. I asked him what he thought of the Brahma Kumaris. 'OK, I guess,' he said with a shrug, before asking me if it was true that people in England still lived in caves. To the sounds of Queen, Prince and Led Zeppelin, American youths skated around the oval rink as coloured lights flashed above them. Mum sat by the side and gave a huddle of other mums her views on the Florida lifestyle.

'There's a reason why you're all so fat,' she told them. 'You drive everywhere and you eat junk food all the time.

I'd be the same too if I lived here. Good thing I'm stuck in dreary old England, I suppose.'

'She says it like it is!' exclaimed one of the women, before telling Mum to join them for a Margarita. Strangely, Mum's less than diplomatic observations went down a storm in Florida. And for all her protestations on how she hated childish things, she spent a fortune on letting me be a kid for a little while longer. Each day brought a roller-coaster, a water park, or, at the very least, a trip to the mall. There had been no attempt at including anything of educational value, unless you counted the afternoon we drove to St. Petersburg to see a man having a fight with an alligator.

Our two weeks in Florida were over too soon. I said a tearful goodbye to Ed, Sandy and Waddy, and after Rick took us to his jeans warehouse and told us to stock up on whatever we could fit in our suitcases, Mum and I returned to Orlando airport. Unfortunately, in the week we had been away, Florida Airlines had gone bust. No compensation was offered. British Airways announced those of us with return flights could buy a seat back to London for the full fare that night, but otherwise we would have to wait for two weeks in Florida before replacement flights were found.

'We're not doing that,' said Mum as we stood in the overcrowded departure lounge, alongside 200 stranded British tourists in flowery shirts. 'You've got school on Monday. I'll just have to buy a couple of seats on my credit card. Spend now, worry later. That's my new motto.'

While our British Airways aeroplane waited on the burning tarmac of an Orlando runway, I asked Mum why she had splashed out on the holiday.

'I was thinking about all the transformations we've been going through,' she said, looking out of the window as the airhostess located the emergency exits of the Boeing 747. 'And I thought to myself: Will's going to be fifteen in a few months. It's now or never. Better take him while I still can, because you never know how life will change from one day to the next.'

Family life was indeed about to change once more. This time, however, it wasn't Nev who instituted that change, but Mum.

13

Sex Is Not Compulsory

As much as life at Frensham proved there was no such thing as a normal family, there were fundamental differences between the Hodgkinsons' post-Yogi worldview and that of everyone else I knew.

Until a couple of years ago, we had been subscribers to the modern orthodoxy. It wasn't shocking for the Monty Python generation to be irreligious. Quite the opposite: it was archaic, unfashionable and potentially even offensive to *be* a practising Christian in 1980s liberal Britain. For a generation that grew up in a period of much greater material comfort, meritocracy and scientific understanding than the one before them, Christianity was associated with oppression, superstition and imperialism. From some time in the late Seventies, the conventional, quasi-intellectual, middle-class mode of thought in this country was to be anti-racist, anti-sexist, to preach that everyone is equal while personally being very ambitious and wanting to make lots of money and, most importantly, subscribe to a materialist, scientific approach to life that made no

275

allowance for the fantastical or the mythical. Heroes of the new rationality like Stephen Jay Gould and Richard Dawkins were waiting in the wings, sharpening their claws against the snake oil merchants of the old beliefs.

At the same time it was entirely acceptable to have a Buddha on your mantelpiece, to do a few relaxing 'om's after your weekly hatha yoga class and to feng shui your living room before ordering a new set of curtains, because all that fitted into a sophisticated, slightly exotic, attractive lifestyle. In 1968, The Beatles went to Rishikesh and studied meditation under the Maharishi. In 1986, the inhabitants of London's well-heeled suburbs were only too happy to incorporate the trappings of mind expansion into their comfortable, socially aware lives. A touch of Eastern spirituality complemented the Osborne & Little wallpaper. What was not acceptable was genuine free thought and inner revolution that implicitly questioned the choices of everyone else.

Nev had rejected contemporary scientific rationality, put spirituality before materialism, and subscribed to a worldview rooted in the distinctly non-liberal tenets of Hinduism. The Brahma Kumaris do not preach equality in this world. Alongside declaring that everything in the drama is fixed and inevitable, they present a vision of perfection available only to an elite, spiritually conscious few. They teach us that karma decrees our positions in society and hierarchy is inevitable and necessary, that seeking recognition or praise for our efforts, which is the carrot on the stick of western achievement, will only deplete us, and that attempting to understand the world through the intellect will lead to a sense of emptiness. Above all, the Brahma Kumaris reveal the pursuit of wealth and status to be a shallow endeavour, which only takes us away from our true nature. By embracing all this, Nev was suggesting that his and Mum's old friends were suffering under a cloak of illusion and had made all the wrong choices. Looking back, it's not really surprising the Meet the Yogis evening at 99, Queens Road wasn't a smashing success.

Being teenagers, Tom and I were a lot more open to this kind of pioneer thinking. After all, we had nothing to lose. We were yet to make any real choices, nothing about our beliefs and opinions was fixed, and we were in a position of great privilege. Our financially aspirant mother's ferocious work ethic and high earnings allowed us to live in a beautiful house and go to the top schools in the country, while our meditating father gave us a much wider, deeper perspective on the nature of reality by turning received wisdom on its head. Their selfishness, typical of an educated, post-war generation that put the individual above all else, played into our hands too, because apart from the times when Tom came in at three in the morning and shouted at them for having the audacity to wake up, our parents didn't particularly know or care about what we were up to. That allowed us a lot of freedom.

After initially feeling threatened by the Brahma Kumaris, I was finding their idealistic, unconventional, radical approach rather attractive, especially after seeing just how much fun the BK life could be in Florida. It was all rather Sixties and even a little bit groovy. You focused on the soul, looked into other worlds and challenged the status quo. A year into my time at Frensham, I stopped being embarrassed by Nev and actually became quite proud of this father who went off to India twice a year and provided all kinds of unusual beliefs for me to argue about with my friends. However, there was one aspect of our new family set-up I would much rather have kept private. That was sex, or rather, a lack of it.

I did manage to have a girlfriend of sorts before *Sex Is Not Compulsory*, Mum's case for the sexless marriage, was published in 1986, but only after a long time in the desert.

A year earlier, Nev and Tom came with me on my first day at Brackenhill, the boys' boarding house run, if that is the word, by our mercurial history teacher Jonathan Hughes. The Volvo pulled up on the drive. At first I thought the conifer trees lining it were there to give the house some privacy from the world, but I realized later they were designed to protect the world from the house. The clue was in the pale blue Y-fronts caught in one of the trees. They had belonged to Eugene until he decided it was better to liberate than wash his pants after two weeks of unbroken usage. They stayed in that tree for the next four years.

Brackenhill had a square central area with dormitories on the ground floor and an upstairs gallery running around the house. It was on the latter that Jonathan Hughes first appeared, as Nev and I dragged my chest up the worn carpet of the stairs and towards the dormitory that would be my home for the next year. Jonathan was wearing brown brogues, knee-high socks with garters, beige shorts and a paisley smock. With this ensemble complemented by his beard and enormous cranium, he looked like a scoutmaster on his way back from Woodstock.

'You must be Jonathan,' said Nev, puffing away at the

top of the stairs. 'Pleased to meet you. This is Will's brother, Tom.'

Jonathan looked at Tom. 'I can see that,' he said, and marched off to stop Eugene from swinging off the gallery bannisters and jumping onto the pool table below.

On that first night, Jonathan gave us instructions on the rules of the house and how we should behave. He called us all into the central area and said: 'Bedtime is nine o'clock. Stay away from girls. They will only cause you pain.' Then he disappeared into his living room, which, unlike John A's, was not open to the rest of us. Sometimes we did manage to sneak in. Rows of dusty hardbacks with titles like *The Tudor Mind* and *My Part in the Crimea* lined the walls. His kitchen, with its porcelain sink and formica table, had the air of a 1950s bachelor pad, right down to the stack of dirty plates in the sink and the encrusted jars of Colman's mustard and Gentlemen's Relish on the worktop. The living room consisted of a free-standing lamp with a brown heavy fabric shade, two high-backed armchairs and piles of papers that turned out to be homework, much of it unmarked and dating back to the Seventies.

We had assumed Jonathan was locked away in his quarters that night until we were woken, a little after eleven, by the sound of his 2CV squealing into the drive and grinding to a halt as he rammed it into one of the conifer trees. We watched him stumble out of the car and into the house. A few minutes later, the doorway of our room framed a silhouette of a dome-like head with tufts of hair sticking out from either side of it.

'What's going on?'

We blinked as the neon light blinked with us. 'I leave

you for five minutes and there's pandemonium,' said Jonathan, as we rubbed our eyes and sat up in our beds. 'This is highly irregular.' He picked up a pillow that happened to be lying on the floor, threw it at Eugene's head, and stormed out.

This was around the time I accepted it was unlikely to happen with Sadie, and that Adae's brief moment of interest in me at New Year's Eve was not likely to return, and I gave up on girls entirely. Jonathan mentioned something about wanting us to have a shower at least once a week, but he was not one to enforce that kind of thing and I regularly forgot to wash for a month at a time, meaning no girl in their right mind – not that there were too many of those at Frensham – would want to come near me. Under Jonathan, 'Brackenhell', as it was widely known, became a paradise for teenage boys with an aversion to hygiene but a no-go zone for anyone else, reaching a state of such decrepitude that even the cleaners refused to venture in there. The last straw was when one boy decided getting up in the middle of the night when he needed to go to the toilet was too much of a chore, so he simply rolled over to the side of the bed and relieved himself on the floor.

Prudence was a neat-looking woman with her hair in a bun, who blasted into Brackenhill and spoiled all our fun.

She was parachuted in to impose order on our lawless universe. All of a sudden we were expected to wash regularly, go to bed at lights-out, and no longer roll up slices of Mother's Pride bread into little balls and flick them at each other. 'Let's clear the air of all those farty feety smells,' she would say as she woke us up in the morning, briskly throwing open the curtains and shaking our duvets, impervious to what might be revealed beneath.

It was the first time that house had ever seen its inhabitants get up at the proper hour. (Brackenhill boys were notorious for being absent at breakfast.) When the layer of grime left Brackenhill, however, something of its soul left with it, and Jonathan resented this zero-tolerance one-woman swat team invading his empire. One night, after lights-out, he came in and lay down on our dormitory floor. He said it was the only place he could get away from her.

'Her husband had the right idea,' he said, bony knees in the air.

'Didn't he die?' said Eugene.

Despite the suffering it caused, Prudence's reign led to a revelation: when I no longer smelled like I had gone mouldy, girls no longer sought to avoid me. And by then, the Faint Feeling had developed into the real thing. Then, on one typically boring Sunday afternoon, me and Polly – not the Polly who kneed me in the balls, but the one with frizzy hair and wide metal-framed glasses – went for a walk in the fields below the school. She took off her glasses, and I realized how pretty she was. We ended up kissing one another. We were fifteen.

We were unsuited to each other. I was developing an increasing obsession with underground rock bands, while the only records Polly had were *Dream Melodies* by Klaus Wunderlich and 'Do They Know it's Christmas?' by Band Aid. I thought my new outfit of drainpipe trousers and paisley shirt made me look like one of the Velvet Underground. She thought it made me look like a malnourished pipe cleaner. My goal in life was to meet

281

Lux Interior, lead singer of The Cramps. Polly's was to be a total swot, to the extent that when she got to the sixth form and found herself sharing a study with the most popular kids in the year, she asked to be moved in with all the squares in order that she could better concentrate on her studies.

Our relationship never made sense. Polly liked rugby-playing types with heavy stubble, limited vocabularies and vast future earning potential. I liked shallow, appearance-conscious fashion victims. At fifteen, my body had as much muscle definition as a twig. Polly ate an apple a day and little else. When we got together it was like two skeletons locked in a casket and pushed off a cliff. Our conversation consisted of her insulting my stick legs and me telling her I didn't believe her stories about being chased after by chinless wonders with names like Cosmo Tufton-Bufton. She was like the sister I never had.

'Imagine if we actually ended up together,' I said to her one afternoon, as we sat on the hill outside the main house. 'It would be a disaster. You'd be throwing one of your awful dinner parties and I'd be coming in from a gig at two in the morning.'

'Oh yeah, like you'll still be going to gigs at the age of thirty.'

Polly became my first girlfriend to be exposed to our parents' weirdness. Polly lived in Richmond too, alternately with her mother in a house near the station and with her father in a house in Kew, and she came over one Saturday afternoon. We were watching *Tommy*, Ken Russell's film version of The Who's rock opera about a pinball-playing deaf, dumb and blind messiah, when Mum appeared.

'Who's this?' Mum demanded.

'This is Polly,' I said as, on the television in front of us, Ann-Margret slithered about in a roomful of baked beans. Polly politely said hello.

'You're not his girlfriend, are you? What do you see in him?'

For a moment, Polly looked confused. 'I'm really not sure,' she replied.

Mum raised her head, as if addressing an imaginary auditorium. 'Why do people have this obsession with coupling off? You see these bright, intelligent young women and before you know it they've popped out a couple of babies and become dreary mums pushing prams up and down the high street. Anyone can reproduce!'

'It hasn't quite come to that, Mum. We're only fifteen.'

'I don't know what's happened to the sisterhood. Until women decide to not have sex at all they'll always be under the power of men. When we were young, we thought the Pill would be this great liberating force. Little did we know it would give men the opportunity to run around sleeping with whoever they wanted while we were left at home, literally holding the baby. I really thought the next generation would have learned from our mistakes, but it seems there is still a lot of work to do. When are women going to stop allowing their bodies to be used as receptacles for men's desperate desire to spread their seed and lay claim to them once more? Are you staying for supper, Polly?'

Nev appeared.

'Ah, you must be Will's friend. It's so nice to connect with you. Mum told me that Sturch had invited his friend over. It's good to have friends.'

While Mum assumed Polly was already up the duff, Nev acted as if she and I were about to skip off and play

283

a game of hopscotch in the primary school playground. I'm glad he managed to look away from the sight of Ann-Margret slip-sliding about in tormented baked bean ecstasy. It might have put him off his stuffed aubergine.

'Wow,' said Polly after supper, when Nev retreated to his meditation chamber in the basement and Mum disappeared back into her study upstairs. 'Am I right in assuming your parents don't sleep with each other anymore?'

I didn't answer her. We continued watching *Tommy*, slumped up against each other on the sofa. We saw that film over and over again. We sang its songs together as we walked through Richmond Park on weekends home from school, harmonizing to the words *What about the boy?* as we stomped through the bracken. It was the one thing we had in common.

Polly chucked me six months later. The only thing that changed was that we stopped awkwardly groping each other in the brief period between the end of the homework period and the time we had to return to our respective houses. We actually saw each other more after we were no longer romantically involved, and for a brief period Polly developed enough of an interest in the Brahma Kumaris to take the seven-day course, although she admitted later that she only did it because she had a crush on Nev.

Meanwhile, away from home, I forgot about the disciplines of Brahma Kumari life and the strange ways of the family and concentrated on being a real teenager, complete with French kisses in the woods and notes passed furtively under desks during double maths.

That was before *Sex Is Not Compulsory* threw it all out of the window.

* * *

It was a Saturday night. We were crammed into the TV room at Hamilton House, which Eugene, Will Mac and I had left for Brackenhill a year earlier. We were waiting for John A to hold one of his intermittent film nights – I think he had a video of *An American Werewolf in London* – when a chat show came on. The host was talking about introducing a married couple who were staying together but no longer sleeping together.

At first I didn't notice. I was at the back of the room, having an arm-wrestling match with Gael, when someone said, 'Hey Will, isn't that your mum and dad?'

To my horror, it was. Mum, legs crossed and hair bigger than ever, and Nev, stiff-backed and clad in white, were sitting opposite the chat show host. 'But you're both young, good-looking people,' he said, holding his arms up. 'If you love each other and you're married, why on earth don't you want to sleep together?'

'There are many forms of love, and the purest are not physical,' said Nev, gently, with raised eyebrows.

'I've had enough of the idea of my body being owned by someone else,' trumpeted Mum. 'And I've had enough of him humping up and down on top of me. When I was growing up, there were two options open to a woman who wanted to escape from her family: prostitution or marriage. Turns out they were the same thing!'

When the roars of dissent died down, someone in the studio audience suggested Mum and Nev were only celibate with each other, a point both parents refuted. 'I'm not saying it's for ever, or for everyone,' said Mum. 'I'm just saying that not having sex can lead to a lot of liberation.' She held up the book and added, with a toothy smile,

285

'As the title of my controversial and much-talked-about tome points out, sex is *not* compulsory.'

I shrank deeper into the vinyl covering of a Hamilton House chair and peeked through my fingers in horror as a dozen fascinated teenagers swivelled round and looked at me.

'So are your parents really celibate?' said Gael. 'Does that mean they live together but they don't sleep together? And does that mean you're celibate too?'

'Yes, yes and yes, although I'm hoping to do something about it as soon as possible.'

'All I can say is it explains a few things,' said Adae, getting up and leaving the room.

'If those were my parents,' said Lara, 'I'd die. Simply *die.*'

'Personally, I think you're lucky,' said Gael. 'Once people become parents, the kindest thing they can do for their children is to stop doing it because that's something nobody wants to imagine. Let's hope your mum doesn't change her mind later on in life and start having lots of hot sex with old men.'

The dormitory at Brackenhill provided some sort of a refuge, particularly as I now had a Sony record player and tape deck and a handful of albums offering escape into other, more attractive worlds than the one involving questions about Mum and Nev's extremely public private life. That evening I put on *Meat Is Murder* by The Smiths, pretty much the only band I liked that you might have a chance of seeing on *Top of the Pops*. The Smiths' gladioli-wielding lead singer Morrissey was celibate, apparently, joining Pope John Paul II, John Ruskin, Sir Isaac Newton and my parents on the short list of people who turned

286

not having sex into a badge of honour. Listening to The Smiths' 'There is a Light that Never Goes Out', and realizing the inspired lyrics came from the first-ever pop star to make a virtue of a lack of interest in sex, provided some comfort. Then Richard Ball came in.

'Oh, I'm Morrissey, I'm so depressed,' he said, skipping about the room and limp-wristedly flapping his hands in the air, 'so I'll sing about getting killed by a ten-tonne truck and make everyone else miserable too.'

'But you're always going on about how depressed you are. Why don't you like The Smiths?'

'Because I'm desperate for a shag. The last thing I want to hear is someone going on about not getting any. Besides, why would anyone want to listen to The Smiths when you've got the Quo?'

It was probably a good thing I was isolated at boarding school for the next few weeks, because according to Tom, life at home went haywire. The idea of a married couple not having sex, even if Mum did claim this was the unspoken reality of the vast majority of married couples in Britain, was deemed outrageous and unacceptable. Oddly, the more conventional the person or organization, the more disgraceful they seemed to think celibacy. 'It is at once hot-headed and pernicious,' said the *Catholic Herald*, who you might have thought would have been all for it. Our relatives announced they would disown Mum forever, or at least until the next family reunion. Film crews came to the house on a weekly basis. *Sex Is Not Compulsory* became a big hit around the world, with as many people – married women in particular – coming out in support of it as decrying it. We didn't read many newspapers at Frensham Heights, thank God, but Mum

287

assured me you couldn't open a paper without seeing an article by her or an interview with her – and, for reasons that are best known to her, she felt the best way to promote celibacy was by looking as foxy as possible in every publicity shot.

'You're not given permission to be celibate in marriage,' I read Mum proclaim in a magazine I had the misfortune to pick up on the train back from school one Saturday afternoon. 'But since this book came out, I've spoken to so many people who tell me they haven't had sex with their husbands or wives for years. The attraction peters out and nobody mentions it because we all collude to keep the myth going. Then people start having affairs, and then they associate their lover with glamour and excitement and their wife or husband with drudgery and nagging. Besides, you can easily have friendships lasting a lifetime, but as soon as you have sex with someone then jealousy, possessiveness and insecurity take over. It's not a good situation.'

Nev was wheeled out in his white pyjama suit whenever necessary. 'If I want to experience a true relationship with God, the only way is through awareness of the soul, and that is much more difficult while having intimate bodily contact with another being,' he explained gently on one television show. 'The Brahma Kumaris have true equality between men and women and it is celibacy which allows for that.'

I wasn't entirely convinced there was equality between the sexes in the BKs. It was pretty obvious it was the women who were in charge. When the community began they had succeeded in liberating themselves from men, creating a chance for Indian women to escape the entrapment of marriage for the first time in India's history. They were hardly going to surrender the upper hand for which they had fought so hard. When Nev first got interested in spirituality, I thought it might be to escape from being henpecked. Just as so many men disappeared into the garden shed to get away from their wives, Nev went off to his meditation chamber every time Mum started yelling about how much money they needed to earn to renovate the roof or pay our school fees. Nev's subsequent embracing of the BKs could be seen as an extreme form of hiding away in the garden shed, but it backfired terribly. Instead of finding the solace he craved, he found himself henpecked by thirty Indian women in saris.

As for Mum, she loved it. She loved becoming almost famous. She loved the attention, good or bad. She was never happier than when throwing a provocative idea out there and watching the sparks fly, and when *Sex Is Not Compulsory* was translated into twenty languages and caused her income to double, it was a win-win situation. 'What people don't seem to understand is that I might believe in something else entirely tomorrow,' she said one evening, when I asked her if she minded all the gnashing of teeth her book had caused the sex-mad moral majority of Britain. 'I'm not thinking of celibacy as a lifetime decision. I'm thinking of it as an interesting avenue to explore at the moment.'

I couldn't have been happier when my own celibate life came to an end six months later, quickly and inelegantly on the floor of one of the sixth form studies, with a girl whose seductive green eyes and enormous breasts proved so exciting that I had only just worked out where to put it when it was all over. I was sixteen. I went back to the dormitory that night and told nobody, not sure whether or not it had really happened. I cannot claim to have been in love with her, but I do remain grateful to this cheerfully accommodating beauty who bestowed upon me the gift of carnal knowledge when the sight of my parents talking about the joy of no sex on a prime-time chat show was still fresh in the collective memory of pretty much everyone I knew.

One evening at Brackenhill, over the phone, Mum told me her father had died. 'A black cloud has been lifted from that house,' she announced, but when I asked her what she meant and how Granny was taking it, she pretended she hadn't heard and began detailing her plans for landscaping the garden of The Paragon instead.

I never found out why our mother hated her father so much. John Garrett was an ill-tempered, childish man, given to temper tantrums and gargantuan sulks – he once refused to speak to Tom and me for an entire weekend because we wouldn't spend the Saturday in the bar of St Neots Rowing Club with him, which was a bit much considering we were only seven and five at the time – but I didn't see evidence of anything truly sinister. He had certainly had a few punch-ups with Uncle Richard, but when I asked Mum if he had ever hit her she said: 'He wouldn't *dare*.' Her tone suggested she was still challenging him to give it a try.

We went to the funeral a week after the phone call. 'You should have divorced him years ago,' said Mum to Granny as we sat in the crematorium, watching the coffin disappear behind the curtain.

'Now I don't have to, do I, dear?' Granny replied, with typical practicality.

Then it was down to the Rowing Club, where men in blazers with Brylcreemed hair and nicotine-stained fingers propped up the bar, drank frothy pints of ale, and talked about cricket. When I commented to Uncle Richard that it seemed to have more of a party atmosphere than a funeral and nobody seemed particularly upset, Uncle Richard drew heavily on a Rothmans, exhaled philosophically, and said, 'Well, he wasn't exactly a paragon of virtue, was he?'

Meanwhile, Nev's parents benefitted, in minor ways, from their son's expanded consciousness. Initially, Pa barely noticed and Min naturally assumed Nev had been abducted by one of the sex cults she had been reading about in the *Daily Express*, and they certainly didn't trust his views on alternative medicine. She and Pa were on a cocktail of drugs for a smorgasbord of ailments but principally for old age. They had reached the stage of taking one drug to counter the effect of another drug, then taking a third drug to deal with the second and so on. Pa, never the most adventurous or courageous of men, decided to deal with the situation by taking our other grandfather's lead and dying, but Min kept going.

'He never let me do anything or go anywhere,' she said at Pa's funeral, as chatty, healthy old ladies bustled about while their decrepit husbands sat and watched helplessly from their wheelchairs. 'Now I'm going to make the most of my freedom.'

That freedom turned out to be ten years in a care home in Angmering, West Sussex, but she did do one thing that would never have happened while Pa was alive: she allowed

Nev to talk her out of having an operation to remove her gallbladder. Somehow he convinced her to go for an alternative treatment, which involved drinking an explosive mix of castor oil and bicarbonate of soda, thereby turning herself into a human blunderbuss. Min was cured of her gallstones, but the porcelain at the bottom of her downstairs toilet was never the same again.

Nev went back to work. He was appointed science and medical correspondent of the *Sunday Times* and Andrew Neil, the paper's editor, supported his coverage of alternative medicine, cutting-edge science, the self-interest of the pharmaceutical and medical industry, quantum theory, and a series of articles questioning the link between HIV and Aids. Mum and Nev were both well paid and busy with conventional, respectable careers, leaving Tom and me in the position of exploring the jungle of adolescence without interference but with the security of a family to fall back on.

A great discovery of mid-teenage life was finding it possible to tell the school I was staying with my parents for the weekend, and tell my parents I was staying at the school, and stay at neither. The result was the opportunity to come up to London and go to all the places I really wanted to be. One weekend a friend and I crashed a party in a squat in Kentish Town occupied by the members of My Bloody Valentine. Sometimes we would go to all-night horror movie sessions at the Scala Cinema in Kings Cross, and more often than not we would end up at the bohemian townhouse off Brick Lane in East London where Will MacCormac lived with his architect father, his father's girlfriend (the severely glamorous interior designer Jocasta Innes), and various offspring from various relationships. We would sit in Jocasta's large kitchen, with its stone floor, Aga cooker, stencilled walls and artful blend of decadence and domesticity, and we would smoke roll-ups, listen to The Rolling Stones and take nips from the bottles of whisky we passed round until three in the morning. You fell asleep wherever you could, a bed if you were lucky but more commonly a sofa or a pile of cushions in a corner of a room. Somebody was always coming or going. I remember Chloe, Jocasta's serene youngest daughter and a future girlfriend, lighting a cigarette and sitting with us one evening when she was twelve. Jocasta came in, turned up the corners of her mouth in wry amusement, said, 'Naughty Chloe,' and glided away.

It was a world of exploration where the adults never quite knew what we were doing because we didn't tell them. After being stung by spending twelve pounds on a vacuum-sealed block of wood, we learned how to buy lumps of hash on Portobello Road, standing outside the betting shop until someone turned up and offered it to us. One sunny Sunday in Richmond I took LSD with Peter Taylor, a fresh-faced American boy from Frensham whom all the girls liked. As we wandered through the pretty streets, marvelling at how Richmond looked like a toy town with all the colours so much brighter and everything seeming to be made of plastic, I wondered if this expansion of the consciousness was similar to the one Nev experienced in meditation. After I spotted my old mathematics teacher from Kings House stumbling out of a pub, and convinced myself he was a deadly poisonous alcoholic spider coming to get me, I concluded it wasn't and stayed away from drugs thereafter. Nonetheless, I'd gained an understanding that existence contained far greater depths than were apparent on the surface.

We must still have been tripping when Peter and I returned home and sat around the dinner table in dilated silence, as Mum expounded on the hypocrisy of long-term couples pretending they had active sex lives when they didn't and Nev stared at his carrot masala in spiritual thanks. I don't think they noticed.

Not long after losing my virginity, I was with Tom in his room. He had returned home for Christmas from Cambridge, where he had started on an English degree three months earlier.

'I'll probably do the whole religious thing once I've had enough of hedonism,' said Tom, drawing heavily on a roll-up. 'Maybe I'll get into Christianity. There's a rich mystical tradition right under our very noses. You don't have to run off to India to find it.'

'On the whole, I like the BKs,' I said. 'I'm not sure about the whole anti-Darwin thing, though. That's a lot to take in.'

'I don't see why. DH Lawrence was against evolution. We can't prove it either way. My problem with the BKs is that I've never really experienced this amazing blissful feeling you're meant to get under meditation. What about you?'

For the last year or so, Nev's suggestion that I was a child of the Golden Age had made me think that one day I would indeed become a Brahma Kumari. I admired young men like Benji and Malcolm, who seemed so sure of their path that they could sacrifice the pleasures of the world and cut off all attachments to pursue a state of spiritual awareness. Everything Dadi Janki said made sense. 'Weakness invites negative thinking,' she had pronounced on my last visit to Shanti Bhavan. 'Love, peace, purity, wisdom: the more you think of these things, the more you will become them.'

I could only agree with her — the wisdom of her message of peace was inarguable —but neither had I experienced that amazing blissful feeling.

'Only a bit,' I said, in answer to Tom's question.

'I sometimes wonder if Nev was always going to end up like this,' Tom continued. 'He's never really enjoyed good living. In the Middle Ages he wouldn't have bothered getting married at all. He'd have gone straight to the monastery.'

'Where do you think that leaves Mum and Nev?'

Tom puffed smoke into the air, leaned back in his chair, and rested his arm on the messy pile of books covering his desk. 'Their marriage can't go on like this forever,' he said, eventually. 'It's only a matter of time.'

He was right, of course. Unfortunately, I had just settled into the idea of living in a world of moneyed spirituality when it proved to be as fleeting as all things of the flesh. The Brahma Kumaris were about to claim more than just our father's soul.

14

Surrender

I was on holiday in Spain with Adae and her boyfriend Marco, the son of a rich Italian restaurant owner, when my A-level results came through. After countless teachers had told me I was on a much lower intellectual level than Tom, after a childhood in which my only real achievements were to jump over a stream on a BMX and climb the highest tree in Surrey, I got two As and a B. It came as a surprise to everyone.

'It's very annoying,' said Tom, when I spoke to him down the line from Marco's marble-floored apartment on the Costa Del Sol. 'I always used to think you were so much less intelligent than me. Now I've discovered you're only slightly less intelligent than me.'

While I was living the high life with Marbella's nouveau riche, our parents were moving into separate flats. In the last few months, two events had happened that brought about the end of our unconventional family arrangement and took Nev beyond the point of no return with the Brahma Kumaris.

Without telling Mum about it, Nev went to a solicitor to see if he could draw up a rather unusual will. He wanted to make an arrangement that if Mum died after him a large percentage of the proceeds from the sale of the house would still go to the Brahma Kumaris. As it turned out he wasn't legally allowed to do it, and that would have been the end of the matter had not the solicitor, fearing Nev had been taken over by a bizarre cult, broken professional conduct and told Mum about the meeting.

'It's turned me off Nev forever and made me determined to get divorced from him as soon as possible,' said Mum, when I got back from Spain. She had moved into a pretty maisonette in Ladbroke Grove and Nev into a featureless flat in Kensington. We were in her new living room, sitting on cream-upholstered armchairs. 'By trying to leave the money from the sale of the house to the BKs after I die, he was hoping to control me from beyond the grave. Nev was furious that the solicitor had rung me up and told me about it, but I'm jolly glad he did. It opened my eyes to the level of Nev's commitment to the Yogis.'

'What does Nev say about it?'

'He says he was in a weird frame of mind,' she replied, getting cross as the thought of it. 'All I can say is that his frame of mind wasn't so weird he couldn't go to a solicitor and try to bequeath to the BKs the money I wanted you and Tom to have. He went behind my back. He says he still loves me. But he's made our life together totally impossible because there's no compromise on his part whatsoever. I didn't want to tell you about it when it happened because you were in the middle of your A-levels, but now that you've finished school it can all be out in the open. Nev and I are *over*.'

Mum could put up with almost anything, it seemed, apart from someone interfering with her cash. 'But he's always been a good dad,' I told her. 'And a good husband.'

'That's true,' she said, stretching her legs out along the newly fitted carpet of her luxuriously appointed flat. 'But there's something important you need to know. The BKs come first in Nev's life. You and me and Tom will always play second fiddle and there's a reason for that. If you look at religious cults, the one thing they have in common is they have to replace the family. That's the strongest bond in a person's life and so it may threaten the cult. And cults will have an unconventional approach to sex. You may have to have sex with lots of people or you may not be allowed to have sex at all, but it's going to be different from the norm. Nev may not think of the BKs as a cult, and they would certainly claim they don't break up families, but you can't deny the similarities.'

Whether the Brahma Kumaris were anti-family or not, it was Mum who called halt on our own family life, even if it was Nev's act of subterfuge which convinced her to do it. It was a chance event, meanwhile, that allowed her to do that.

While I was in my final years at Frensham Heights, I was unaware that the old arguments had returned. The house was in need of constant and expensive restoration and Mum and Nev were spending money quicker than they were earning it. To make matters worse, Nev was giving a chunk of his monthly salary away to the Yogis.

'It's not the amount you're giving away that bothers me,' Mum said over Sunday lunch. 'It's the fact that we need every penny we've got to fix up this house.'

'I've given enough time, energy and money to you and

the kids!' Nev replied in spirituality-supported indignation. 'It's quite right that I should give my support to the BKs now. They have treated me extremely well.'

'As far as I'm concerned you might as well have told me that you've got another girlfriend, she's had a baby, you need to support her, and she's great in bed so it's all worth it,' Mum snapped back.

Nev poked at his lentils. 'It's a preposterous comparison.'

'In real terms – in money terms – it's exactly the same.'

Eventually, my girlfriend broke the long silence that followed in the way only a well brought-up young woman like her knew how.

'This home-made bread is gorgeous.'

At the same time, Nev had just won a three-year fight with the council to be allowed to park a car on the street outside, and to make interior and exterior alterations to a house previously condemned by preservation laws to a state of eternal decay. As a result the house doubled in value, almost overnight. Then one Saturday afternoon, when Mum was at home by herself, the phone rang. It was the owner of a local art gallery who said she had heard our house was on the market. It wasn't. The woman said it was her dream home and asked Mum how much she would be prepared to sell it for.

'I honestly don't have a clue how much it's worth.'

'How about half a million?'

It was 1988. Half a million pounds was a ludicrous amount, five times more than our parents bought the house for – and enough for them to buy separate homes and get divorced. But when Mum mentioned the offer to Nev when he returned from work, he said that they were not selling. He didn't want the family to split up. They finally had planning permission to do all the things they wanted to do, and with him in the basement and Mum upstairs, the arrangement was working well. He had gone for a walk along the river with an old friend who said he would be crazy to sell, just when the house was coming together after being a slum for so many years.

The following morning, Nev chugged off on his little motorbike to the Brahma Kumaris centre in Willesden for his six o'clock class. Dadi Janki and Jayanti were there. When he came back he said to Mum, 'We'll sell.'

The Yogis, the only people with any real power over Nev, had changed his mind. He had asked Dadi Janki and Jayanti what he should do. They told him, 'You must do what Liz wants.'

All of this went on without my knowledge. But when I came back from my last term at school and Mum and Nev sat Tom and me down and told us the news, we reacted in a way that might seem strange: we welcomed it.

It was for pragmatic reasons as much as anything. I hated Richmond by then. It was boring and sterile, and every time I went to a concert I ended up missing the last train and having to walk for an hour and a half along the pollution-encrusted dual carriageway from Hammersmith. I was soon off to university in London, and it would be ideal to have a flat in Ladbroke Grove to stay in when I needed a break from life in halls. We had long got used to the idea that our parents weren't together in the conventional sense, and as far as I was concerned I had left home when I first went to Frensham and hadn't suffered pangs of homesickness five years earlier. For Mum to have a crash pad in the place I had first scored a block of vacuum-sealed wood seemed like an excellent idea.

Tom was already living another life. We all were. Will Lee was now a handsome art student at Camberwell. Whenever I went round to his shabby flat above a kebab shop on Denmark Hill, bohemian art-school girls were pouring him glasses of cheap red wine before taking him off to a pub called The Hermit's Cave and admiring his nihilistic pronouncements on the death of God, or why cheese-and-onion crisps were better than salt-and-vinegar, or the way he stared bleakly out of the pub window and said 'moo' in such a poetic fashion. Gael became a full-on hippy. Adae was a face on the London club scene. Polly was heading off to the wilds of Louisiana to study Cajun cooking. Eugene drifted through Southern Africa, where the Zimbabwean secret service made an ill-fated attempt to recruit him (he decided to take a job in a backpackers' bar instead.) Will MacCormac continued to be convinced that every girl fancied him with the result that a few actually did, and he spent the next few years sitting at Jocasta Innes's weathered dining table with one hand pressed against his cheek and the other drawing up his latest pioneering automobile design or revolutionary hi-fi system on a scrap of paper, a female admirer never too far away.

I hadn't seen Sadie since our New Year's Eve party, but one day Tom came back to Mum's flat to announce he had spotted an extremely attractive girl by a bus stop in Hammersmith whom he vaguely recognized. When he got up the courage to talk to her, she recognized him too. It was Sadie. She was working as a DJ in Brighton. Tom forgot to ask her whether she was still going out with the would-be Elvis, but at least he suggested we all meet up some time. Then he lost her number. I never saw her again.

*　*　*

Nev was alone in his flat in Kensington. It was only much later he told me how the years after the break-up of the family were the worst of his life; how he felt that, rather than him choosing a life away from us, we had chosen to be with Mum and to cast him out. He certainly didn't give any indication of his loneliness at the time, but one of the problems of the spiritual path is you are forever meant to be learning and growing, not wallowing in misery. Meanwhile, Mum was busy discovering that while sex may not be compulsory, it can certainly be appealing after a long time in the desert, and she got herself a new (grumpy, sixty-something) boyfriend.

It was around then that I began to reflect, more than I was expecting to, on the teachings of the Brahma Kumaris. I decided I had to find out properly whether this was the life for me, as Nev so deeply hoped it was.

The supposed freedom of university turned out to be a big disappointment. The food fights and high jinks of so many young people let off the leash for the first time just seemed like an average evening at Brackenhill. I kept away from it, spending most of my time with a Puerto Rican-Italian-American called Alexa who quickly became my girlfriend. Her rich father had run off with a Swiss woman, and now the pair of them lived a peripatetic life in Europe's finer hotels – her family life was as odd as my own. When I wasn't with Alexa, I worked: for Jocasta Innes as she set up a paint effects company, as a cleaner in an old people's home, in a health food shop off Portobello Road, and, for a few memorably disturbing nights, in the bowels of University College Hospital where I had the task of making notes on the provenance of various human brains, hearts and livers medical students had dissected, before putting them into plastic bags and throwing them into an incinerator. On one occasion I bagged up a brain too hastily. I chucked it towards the flames, only to see a plastic bag floating in the air. I looked around, wondering what had happened to my brain. Then I looked down. It was on my foot.

All of this meant I had a bit of money, not a common situation for a student, so when Alexa announced she would go to back to New York to stay with her mother at Christmas I decided to make my own journey: to Madhuban, the Brahma Kumaris' World Spiritual University, on Mount Abu, India.

Nev was overjoyed. His greatest wish was for us to follow him to that blissful place to which meditation opens the gates. Nev had gone out earlier, so I flew into Delhi by myself, arriving at night and taking a grand old Ambassador taxi from the airport through seemingly endless swathes of homes made of mud and tarpaulin, to the Brahma Kumaris' centre at New Rotak Road, New Delhi. This was a middle class area but you would be forgiven for not realizing it. I had never seen so many people sleeping on the street, some in narrow wicker cots and others on mats on the dusty ground, next to the huge open drains that separated the busy road from the houses. The hot smell of the place was a cloying blend of diesel and petrol fumes from the thundering trucks and little auto-rickshaws streaming along the road, cooking oil from the food stands still open along the street, and raw sewage. I had to wake up a man to open the gate on the metal fence surrounding the BK centre, while another man in a dirty blue dhoti, with no hands and an eaten-away face, presented his stumps and asked for baksheesh in a low pitiful murmur.

When a BK in a white pyjama suit welcomed me into the building, also white, built on two floors around a courtyard and fringed with banana and palm trees, I could do little more than sit in the dark, drink water from a tin cup and listen to the singing of the cicadas.

The following morning, the environment seemed more familiar, less threatening. I recognized the childlike paintings of the Tree Of Life, and of the smiling blue baby Krishna playing with a pot of ghee, and I knew the significance of the red egg, which groups of Indian men and women, dressed in white and swathed in shawls, stared at during their morning meditation in the courtyard. The man who had opened the gate, a cheerful young BK called Mahesh, took me into the centre of Delhi and taught me how to haggle with a rickshaw driver, how to fill in an endlessly complex form which would allow me to buy a train ticket to Mount Abu, and how to cross the road at Connaught Circus without getting killed. He donated to me a white pyjama suit, which made sense in this country of heat and dust in a way that it never did in Richmond and Willesden. We bought bhelpuri from a street vendor for a couple of rupees, Mahesh shouting at a monkey that tried to take it from us in a manner far more assertive than any of the western BKs would have dared exhibit.

After a few days with Mahesh I was ready to travel down to Mount Abu. Sleep on a second-class berth was interrupted every time the train pulled into a station and the vendors made their eerie, drone-like chant of 'chai, chai, coffee, coffee' as they pushed clay cups through the metal bars of the carriages. At one point in the night a group of men in saris and makeup waltzed onto the train and started shouting and singing with a camp rolling of eyes and tossing of hair, to the terror of the passengers who proffered rupees while shielding their children. They were hijras, eunuchs, treated with a mix of fear and respect in Hindu culture, and – although I didn't know it at the time – they were putting horrific curses on anyone who didn't give them money. One hijra angrily clapped his hands and put his lipstick-clad face right up against mine, so close that you could feel the stubble. It was intimidating, but no more so than being harangued by a transvestite in a London nightclub. I ignored him until he and his friends eventually went away.

Then it was Mount Abu. This hill station in Rajasthan has been a holy centre for centuries: Brahma is said to have done penance there with the goddess Saraswati. It's a lush oasis built around a lake, amid a desert land of tribal villages and rocky expanses, and a former outpost of the British Raj which has remained popular with Hindu pilgrims and Indian honeymooners. Madhuban is a grand, temple-like building, long and low, with a wide span of stone steps leading to its entrance. Outside, with its white turrets and rows of windows, it looks like Brighton Pavilion. Inside it is both chic and spartan: it may have an ashram-like sense of emptiness and space but everything, from the marble floor to the huge paintings of the Brahma Baba on the walls, speaks of wealth and comfort.

Madhuban also feels like a spiritual holiday camp. It has five hundred permanent residents and tens of thousands of visitors each year. You can walk through foxglove-filled gardens from Universal Peace Hall to the Tower Of Peace, a pillar under a canopy which serves as a memorial to Brahma Baba. The garishly painted World Renewal Spiritual Museum takes you through the stages of the world cycle, and if you fall sick there's always the Global Hospital in which to recover. Once you are better you can watch dances on the hedge-lined lawns of Peace Park, experience the calm of solitude in the Forest Of Peace, or have a look at statues of gods and goddesses in the Spiritual Art Gallery. Madhuban has everything for which a peace-loving Yogi could hope, not least the Majestic Diamond Hall, capable of holding meditation sessions for an astounding twenty thousand people at a time.

It was here Nev's journey was leading him to. A sari-wearing sister took me to his cell-like stone room after I told her I was Brother Neville's son. It had nothing more than a single bed, a desk and a window with no glass but two wooden shutters to stop the monkeys from getting in and stealing all your toli. Nev was sitting by the desk, reading a *murli*, looking like he wanted for nothing.

'Sturchos!' he said, gripping me by the shoulders and giving me the old Nevvy grin as he jumped up at my arrival. 'I can't believe you're here! I'm so pleased. Right then, let's get you settled in.'

After I was given my own small stone room, and after visiting the vast food hall and getting a plate of brown rice, vegetable curry, chapatti and salad – all remarkably similar to the food served in the London Brahma Kumari centre – Nev and I went for a walk through the Forest Of Peace. We talked about the chaos of Delhi, of how it felt as if a thin thread of control was always just stopping the whole thing from falling apart, and I told him about university life, without too many details of what exactly I was up to and no mention of my girlfriend. We must have been talking for an hour or so, walking side by side in our white pyjama suits, when I asked Nev about the incident involving the solicitor and the will that had proved the final straw for Mum.

He stared at the dusty ground. 'Oh look, a gecko,' he said, but when I didn't respond, he answered my question:

'You know, I . . . I was very stupid in that regard, Sturch. And this is where the religious thing can become dangerous. A teacher had come over from India and mentioned a story about someone who had died regretting they hadn't made a will to make sure the BKs got something. I was about to fly out to India, and I thought, what if I die in a plane crash and none of my share of what we had worked for all these years goes to the BKs? I dropped the idea when the solicitor told me it wasn't possible to leave a chunk of the capital from the house to the BKs when Mum died, but it looked very bad when she found out.'

'She certainly thinks so,' I told him, thinking of Mum's anger when she recounted to me what had happened.

'It was a turning point,' Nev said, nodding reflectively. 'But the thing is, I had reached a stage in my journey where I wanted to surrender to the BKs. I had to do it to move on. When you burn your bridges, you protect yourself against straying from the spiritual path.'

The idea of a believer completely giving up his or her own will to a higher power is not a new one. In the Gospel of Luke, Christ talks about the emptying of self to allow God to live through the person: 'If any man come to me, and hate not his father, and mother, and wife, and children, and brethren, and sisters, yea, and his own life also, he cannot be my disciple.' The word 'Islam' is an Arab word for 'surrender'. In the *Bhagavad Gita*, Krishna tells Arjuna

307

that freedom from the cycle of rebirths comes from surrender. The belief must come first, before everything and everyone else.

And what about the surrender of all those Brahma Kumaris who filled our house day after day, who took the place of old friends we never saw again? Of the early English converts, only Nev remains. Brother Malcolm of Beyond Sound is married with children and working as a psychologist. Brother Benji also renounced the faith, and according to Nev he's extremely bitter about the whole experience, feeling he wasted the best years of his life on something that ultimately served no purpose. Sister Clare, Tony, those earnest young men and women who crowded into our elegantly appointed suburban drawing room in white pyjama suits and saris to tell Sandy and John and Anne and Pete and Hugh and Penny how they should renounce their materialistic ways and embrace the Yogic path . . . all gone. Nev said the struggle of maintaining spirituality in a body conscious world defeated them. But if these people no longer believed, who had spent so much time lecturing me about the metaphysical reality and ulti-mate truth of the Brahma Kumari worldview, then how can anyone be qualified to tell someone else how to live their life? It makes you ask yourself if faith is something that can ever be recommended or imposed.

After pacing through the forest for much of the after-noon, Nev and I went to the Great Hall for an early evening meditation alongside a few hundred other Yogis from around the world. Everywhere you looked there were people, all dressed in white, with serene smiles, moving in slow contemplation, sitting on chairs, leaning against walls, cross-legged, gazing out in silent engagement, rarely talking to one another. If I didn't experience the transcendental pull from the divine here I was never going to experience it, so I decided to do everything I could to clear my mind of extraneous thoughts and concentrate fully on the soul. We sat down on little white mats and stared at the red egg on the wall, with its white and red beams of light emanating in all directions. Now was the time for revelation. Now was the time to feel whatever it was that Nev felt.

I needed to achieve soul consciousness. I had spent years listening to Nev telling me how the physical experience of incarnating through a series of bodies had caused me to lose sight of the spiritual life, but that deep spirituality lay within. I needed to truly believe the soul was eternal in order to experience the blissfulness Nev felt; blissfulness so profound it replaced the world. I could hear the message of Dadi Janki: God gives us everything. All I had to do was concentrate.

Here I was in this beautiful place, with my father. I stared at that egg. I waited for meditation to take me into pure peace, soul consciousness and divine connection.

Unfortunately, a supremely hot BK girl was sitting right under the egg. And as I waited for my Damascene revelation to arrive, I couldn't help but wonder if this white-clad beauty was a fully paid-up follower or just a curious, maybe even single backpacker passing by and checking out the action. Perhaps I could ask her afterwards.

And that's when it hit me.

I was never going to make it as a Brahma Kumari.

Epilogue

The drive from our house in south-east London to Mum's flat in Oxford should have only taken an hour and a half, but a snow shower turned into a blizzard, the M40 froze into a vast slab of blackened ice, lorries jack-knifed across the lanes and our ancient, unheated Saab gave up trying to grip the road altogether. We were marooned.

It was the day before Christmas Eve. Our son Otto, eleven, and our daughter Pearl, nine, shivered in the back of the car while I called the AA and my wife NJ begged a coach driver to let her use his toilet. (He wouldn't.) We were visiting Mum before heading down to Cornwall to stay with NJ's parents, where we would enjoy a traditional Christmas in front of the telly. And I could picture Mum pacing her flat, straightening place mats, checking her phone every few minutes. She didn't like it when plans went awry.

Strangely, Mum had chosen to move to a place not far from her former husband. A decade earlier, Nev made his final act of surrender. He gave up his job, sold his flat in

Kensington, handed over the entire proceeds to the Brahma Kumaris and with twenty other Yogis moved in to the Global Retreat Centre, a grand stately home in Oxfordshire formerly owned by Rothmans, the cigarette company. On becoming a permanent resident of the Centre, Nev, no longer a groundbreaking and controversial science and medical correspondent, was assigned an official household appointment by the Brahma Kumaris. He was in charge of cleaning the men's toilets.

Mum's flat was a fifteen-minute drive from the Centre, although she certainly wasn't near it for the meditation. In the years after she and Nev split up, Mum forged on with her career. She followed up *Sex Is Not Compulsory* with an even more incendiary rant called *Unholy Matrimony: The Case Against Marriage*. She tried to make it a hat-trick of outrage with a proposed book called *Do You Really Want Children?*, which might make a son feel unwanted if he didn't realize he had a mother who would knock out any old stuff if someone was willing to pay for it. (In this case, they weren't.) She moved from her maisonette in Ladbroke Grove to a house in Shepherds Bush to a mansion block in Worthing before settling in Oxford, making money almost as quickly as Nev managed to shed it along the way.

After a breakdown truck ended our nine-hour motorway purgatory, we made it to Mum's flat, a spotless advertisement for single-woman living: its high-end kitchen featured every utility a person with absolutely no interest in cooking could wish for and its living room had a state-of-the-art 3-D and surround-sound television promising to enhance Mum's home entertainment experience, just as soon as she worked out how to use it. And for this pre-Christmas family get-together, she was allowing Nev to come over.

'I'll never forgive him for cutting you and Tom out of his will and leaving everything to the Yogis, but what's done is done,' she said, popping open a bottle of Prosecco as the children, changed into their pyjamas, clutched mugs of hot chocolate. 'You have to move on.'

Despairing of the oversized beige anorak, brown polyester trousers and Cornish-pasty-like shoes he wore on a daily basis, Mum had also taken Nev shopping.

'There's no reason why he has to look like he's just escaped from a lunatic asylum,' she said, shaking pizzas off a baking tray and onto the children's plates. 'So when I went to John Lewis to get Otto and Pearl's Christmas presents I took him with me. I bought him a nice cotton shirt, a smart tweed jacket, a pair of brogues and some jeans to replace those shapeless brown monstrosities he insists on wearing. And do you know what? He doesn't look half bad. Because he hasn't had a drink in 25 years and he spends most of his life meditating, he's actually quite handsome . . . for an old man.'

'Are you spending Christmas Day with Grandpa Nev, Granny Liz?' asked Otto, through a mouthful of pizza.

'No, I am not,' she told him as she slammed the oven door shut. 'I did last year, at the Global Retreat Centre, and it was the most miserable Christmas ever. The BKs may be good at penetrating the inner core of their beings, but they don't know how to throw a party. There was a lecture on the importance of peace in the world and not a glass of wine to be found.'

'Where *is* Grandpa Nev?' asked Pearl. 'Shouldn't he be here already?'

As if by Yogi magic, the bell went. The children ran to open the door and there he was, covered in snow, a plastic bag filled with presents in his hand, a Nevvy grin awaiting his grandchildren – and he was wearing his beige anorak, baggy brown trousers and Cornish pasty shoes. Mum screamed.

'What have you done to the lovely new jacket and shirt and trousers and shoes I bought you?'

'It's the strangest thing,' he said gently, taking off his shoes and anorak outside the flat so he didn't get any snow on Mum's new cream carpet. 'Karma decreed that I was not to possess such beautiful clothes, but merely to have them on loan for a week and a half.'

I looked at Mum. Odin, God of War came to mind.

Nev sat down by the table in the kitchen and cheerfully announced, 'I lost them.'

Once Mum calmed down enough to let Nev say he thought he might have left his jacket in Birmingham, at a conference on spiritual empowerment, he then told us he had ended up walking eight miles through the snow to join us after his car wouldn't start and a bus was nowhere to be found. 'Actually, it was quite delightful,' he said brightly, as the children darted off into the living room and worked out how to use the 3-D and surround-sound television in the time it took to find the remote control. 'The country lanes of Oxfordshire were transformed into a winter wonderland.'

'I'm glad they were so wonderful,' said Mum, 'because you'll be having a winter wander back along them soon.'

'Can't I stay the night?'

'Absolutely not. There's nowhere for you to go and besides, I don't want you using up my milk with your endless demands for cups of tea. Who knows when this snowstorm will end and I'll be able to drive down to the shops again? You'll just have to trudge back from whence you came.'

Mum did indeed boot Nev out into the cold that night, but he accepted his fate with equanimity, zipping up the beige anorak and pulling a woolly hat down until it met his metal-framed glasses before disappearing into the black.

The following morning, we drove to the centre, slowly, quietly, over the gritted roads cutting through woods and fields hidden by snow. Our car pulled up in front of the grand house and Nev appeared, rushing out to meet us.

'Quickly,' he said in an urgent whisper. 'Follow me.'

He took us to a side door and darted down a long corridor, which ended with steps going into a basement. 'We've got a retreat on and most people will be going to the canteen from the main entrance,' he said, puffing through the labyrinthine twists and turns of the basement as the children struggled to keep up with him. 'This way, we'll jump the queue.'

A smiling Indian woman in a white sari served us rice, dhal and chapattis, and we took our trays to a room in the basement filled with fellow Global Retreat Centre residents, who kept bringing Otto and Pearl gifts: chocolate biscuits, Christmas crackers, BK souvenirs. Few of the Indian sisters had children of their own. They couldn't help themselves.

Just as Nev was imploring Otto to at least *try* the dhal, new age music filtered through speakers on the walls. This was for a routine called Traffic Control: for a minute on the hour, everyone stopped what they were doing for a quick reflection on the eternity of the soul. We sat in silence, the children familiar with the drill. When it finished, Otto said, 'Were you OK last night, Grandpa Nev?'

'It was a bit mean of Granny Liz to chuck you out,' added Pearl, 'but you shouldn't have lost the new clothes she bought you.'

'Oh, I had an amazing journey,' he replied. 'There were no buses, so I just walked ever so slowly back home. I did get lost for a while, and it did take me longer than I expected, but every time I felt tired I just rested underneath a tree and looked out onto the fields of pure virgin snow under the twinkling stars of the night sky, and I was fine again.'

'When did you get back?' asked NJ.

'Four in the morning. Just in time for the first meditation of the day.'

After lunch, despite his seven-hour hike through the cold and the wet, Nev found the energy to take the children for a ride in the golf buggy the elderly sisters used to get around the grounds. 'We probably shouldn't drive it in the heavy snow,' said Nev, before doing exactly that. We zig-zagged through silver birches and hemlocks garlanded with icicles, past a hawthorn bush where a robin watched us with twitching curiosity, down the long, wide lawn leading to the River Thames, silent witness to our disastrous family boat holiday almost three decades previously. And when Otto and Pearl asked if they could ride the buggy by themselves, Nev let them. Otto promptly pressed down the accelerator and shot off towards a large oak. The buggy careered out of control and slid down the hill before coming to an abrupt halt against the tree, causing a mini-avalanche to thud down onto the buggy and the children inside it.

Nev bounded towards them. 'Kids! Are you all right?'

Otto and Pearl crawled out of the buggy, knocking off clumps of snow from their heads, and shouted in unison: 'All right? That was the best Yogi golf buggy ride ever!'

'I hope none of the sisters saw us,' said Nev, pulling the buggy out of the snowdrift into which it had sunk as he looked around for witnesses. 'I'll get into terrible trouble if they find out.'

While NJ took Otto and Pearl back to the house to dry off and warm up, I told Nev about meeting a man who, without knowing it, had a part to play in the story of our family. For the last decade or so I had been making a living as a music journalist, and I had recently interviewed Cat Stevens, the soulful, introspective Seventies songwriter whose album *Teaser and the Firecat* formed a soundtrack to Tom's and my pre-Brahma-Kumari childhood. In 1977, four years before Nev met the BKs, Cat Stevens became a devout Muslim. He changed his name to Yusuf Islam and gave up music entirely, but shortly before my interview he had started to perform concerts again. It felt like a thawing-out; a reconciliation between his religious beliefs and his past reality as a gifted songwriter with something to offer the world.

'He was my hero,' said Nev, puffing behind the golf buggy as we pushed it up the hill. 'I must have felt that his music revealed him to be a kindred spirit, because on those records he was searching for something and so was I. And although he might have made some silly mistakes, and he became a bit of a zealot, at least he really did it. He didn't compromise. He knew there had to be sacrifices.'

We reached the top of the hill, where it was safe to switch the buggy on again and drive it back to its garage around the side of the house without incurring the spiritually pure indignation of the sisters. Nev asked how family life was treating us. I told him I was worried about the usual things: money, the future, where it was all going to end.

'Really, Will,' said Nev, putting his hands on my shoulders and looking at me with a calm smile, a hint of sadness dulling the edges of his eyes, 'don't. Don't worry about anything. It's such a trap. Look at how wonderful Otto and Pearl are. Look at what you've got with NJ. You have everything you need. If you can find the strength to live in the present, you'll find that nothing else matters.'

On Christmas Day, as the children sat immersed in the aftermath of the present-opening orgy, NJ helped her mother get the turkey out of the oven, and her father dozed off with a glass of sherry in his favourite armchair, I called Mum.

'Oh yes, I'm fine,' she replied, when I asked her if she was happy spending Christmas on her own. 'I've got a glass of wine and a book. By the way, Tom called from Devon. They're *completely* snowed in. Trapped. Trapped in that house of horror.'

Tom lived in a tumbledown farmhouse on the wilds of Exmoor with his wife, three children and an ever-changing array of animals, in which he barricaded himself with crates of Barn Owl ale and reams of books, and published *The Idler*, his magazine extolling the virtues of whatever he happened to be interested in at the time. Mum hated the farmhouse, taking personally Tom's decision to live in close proximity to so much mud, but our children loved going down there, even if Tom did once call Pearl a silly girl for leaving the gate open and letting his old horse Moona wander out into the farmer's fields before realizing who the real culprit was: himself. Nev described life in the farmhouse as 'a wonderfully liberating environment . . . even if watching a chicken getting served up on the very table it was hopping about on earlier that day takes some getting used to.'

'You're not lonely, are you?' I asked Mum, thinking of how, after a lifetime of telling us that Christmas is just an excuse for people to be silly and sentimental and waste a load of money on each other, she had written an article for the *Daily Mail* about how miserable she was spending Christmas on her own now that her horrible sons had forgotten their poor old mum and preferred to enjoy the season roasting chestnuts, carving turkey and singing hearty carols in the yielding bosoms of their wives' families.

'Actually,' Mum replied, 'Nev's here. He's got that awful car of his working again so he drove over this morning. We're going to go for a walk along the river.'

'I thought you said you couldn't bear to spend another Christmas with Nev.'

'Did the children like their presents?'

Mum's power of selective hearing was definitely improving with age.

This was how the Hodgkinsons saw in Christmas, long-divorced parents spending it together and their sons off with their young families. I wanted to tell Mum and Nev that I loved them, that I appreciated everything they had done for us, but we've never been an emotional family and for four people who never stop talking, we don't actually like to say too much. So I put the children on the phone instead, and I thought of Nev, bumbling along the river bank and saying how everything was beautiful, and Mum, snapping at him for losing all his nice new clothes, and Tom, holed up in his country farmhouse with a jug of Barn Owl ale, holding forth on some theory or other, and I decided that, all things considered, we hadn't turned out too badly.

Glossary

Baksheesh: Tipping or charitable giving. Requested by beggars on the streets of India

Bhagavad Gita: A 700-verse epic, part of the *Mahabharata* and a cornerstone of Hinduism, which takes the form of a conversation between Lord Krishna and Prince Arjuna

Bhelpuri: A savoury snack associated with South India, Bombay in particular

Brahma Baba: Lekhraj Kripalani (1884-1969), a former jewellery trader from Hyderabad who formed the Brahma Kumaris after receiving a series of visions

Brahma Kumaris: A new religious movement, of Indian origin but now worldwide, which preaches peace and soul consciousness through meditation, vegetarianism and celibacy

321

Darshan: A Sanskrit term for seeing with reverence and devotion, used by the Brahma Kumaris to define open-eyed meditation with a senior BK or the Supreme Soul

Drishti: 'The focused gaze'; a technique used to aid concentration in meditation

Golden Age: Heaven on earth, which, according to Brahma Kumari faith, is the first stage in the 5,000-Year Cycle. It lasts for around 1,250 years

Hijras: Indian eunuchs with sacred purpose

Karma: The natural, spiritual law of cause and effect in which our actions denote our fate for this and future incarnations

Kalpa: The 5,000 Year Cycle, which is central to the Brahma Kumaris' cosmological worldview. Time is cyclical and passes through a series of stages, beginning with the Golden Age and ending with the current Confluence Age. An apocalyptic event makes way for the beginning of the cycle again, leading to a new Golden Age

Madhuban: 'Forest Of Honey'; the Brahma Kumaris' World Spiritual University in Mount Abu, India

Murlis: Scriptures delivered from God to Brahma Baba and, following his death, to senior female Brahma Kumari spirit mediums

Om Shanti: The Brahma Kumari greeting, meaning 'I am a peaceful being'

Raja yoga: The classical Hindu yoga form practised by the Brahma Kumaris, which recommends meditation, contemplation, restraint, abstinence and mindfulness of one's actions in order to focus on the soul

Rakhi: In Hinduism, this is the term for the sacred thread tied by a sister onto a brother to denote sisterly love. The Brahma Kumaris extend it into a ritual of communion

Sanskars: The traits and characteristics of a soul, developed over successive rebirths

Shanti Bhavan: Hindi for 'House Of Peace' and the name used during the author's childhood for a Brahma Kumari centre in North London

Soul: The point of consciousness, the eternal source of life, the spiritual being interacting through the body

Supreme Soul: The Brahma Kumari term for God

Toli: Indian sweets, filled with Yogi goodness

Tree Of Life: An analogy for the beginning, growth and decay of civilization, with God's wisdom, as received by the Brahma Kumaris, at the root

Yogi: A practitioner of the ancient Indian spiritual discipline of yoga; a person dedicated to the attainment of peace

Acknowledgements

I am grateful to my father Nev, my mother Liz and my brother Tom for being good-humoured and under-standing about *The House Is Full Of Yogis*, even if they may not agree entirely with my version of events and are forever claiming I have an overactive imagination. They were helpful and accommodating when it came to sharing their memories and reflections of our unconventional but not unhappy family life. All errors are my own. Thanks also to Tom for agreeing to the cover photograph.

Two people made the book happen: Simon Benham and Patrick Janson-Smith. Simon has read versions of this story in countless drafts over the years. He has been endlessly supportive, encouraging me to push on until I got it right. Patrick took a chance on the idea and then shaped and improved the manuscript beyond all measure. Thanks also to Laura Deacon at Blue Door for her editorial input and enthusiasm, to Luke Brown for the copy edit, to Stuart Bache for the cover and Terence Caven for the picture designs.

Thanks to Hanif Kureishi for providing the inspiration in the first place with *The Buddha Of Suburbia* and for suggesting I try something similar. Thanks to Sathnam Sanghera for his advice on the moral dilemmas and diplomatic considerations of writing a memoir and to Alex O'Connell for her encouragement.

I am grateful to the Brahma Kumaris for their wisdom and spirituality. There would have been nothing to write about had not they come into our lives. I'm also grateful to Will Lee, Polly Russell, Penny Lee and Clare Malcomson for helping with the photographs and the memories. Both Wills (Lee and MacCormac) were understanding about being included, as were Polly and Steve Rose. Thanks to Sandy and John Chubb, Pete Harris, Gael Mosesson, Adae Whitcombe, Richard Ball, Ben, Eleanor, Polly, Lara, Melanie, Malcolm, Jonathan Hughes, John A and all at Frensham, class of '88.

Special thanks — and all my love — to NJ, Otto and Pearl.